Fundamentals of Human Memory and Cognition

Fundamentals of Human Memory and Cognition

Third Edition

Henry C. Ellis
University of New Mexico

R. Reed Hunt
University of North Carolina, Greensboro

ɯɛb

Wm. C. Brown Company Publishers
Dubuque, Iowa

wcb group **Wm. C. Brown** Chairman of the Board
Mark C. Falb Executive Vice President

wcb Wm. C. Brown Company Publishers, College Division

Lawrence E. Cremer President
David Wm. Smith Vice President, Marketing
E. F. Jogerst Vice President, Cost Analysis
David A. Corona Assistant Vice President, Production Development and Design
James L. Romig Executive Editor
Marcia H. Stout Marketing Manager
Janis M. Machala Director of Marketing Research
William A. Moss Production Editorial Manager
Marilyn A. Phelps Manager of Design
Mary M. Heller Visual Research Manager

Book Team
Susan J. Soley Associate Developmental Editor
Lynne M. Meyers Production Editor
Kevin J. Pruessner Designer

This book is dedicated to my wife, Florence, and to our children, Joan, Diane, and John Ellis

and to my wife, Beth, and to our children, Reed, Jr., and Brandon Hunt

Contents

3 Attention 40

4 Short-Term Memory 61

9 Language 174

10 Concepts and Categories 197

11 Problem Solving   221

12 Final Thoughts   245

Preface

The purpose of this book is to introduce the substantive fundamental issues in human memory and cognition. It is written with the conviction that students can be introduced to cognitive psychology so that its fundamental principles are revealed in bold relief. We want to portray cognitive psychology as an exciting, problem-solving enterprise which will engage and stimulate students. To accomplish these objectives, we have chosen to discuss basic conceptual issues in detail, believing that the reporting of data makes little sense unless the problems and issues are clear. We think this approach is very important in introductory cognitive psychology where, in many cases, the conceptual issues tend to be very abstract. Empirical work, however, is not ignored in this book. Our approach is to discuss in depth selected experiments and their implications for the conceptual issues rather than attempt an exhaustive survey of the empirical literature. Again, we have found this approach to be effective when introducing students to cognitive psychology. Detailed discussion of selected experiments allows students to appreciate the intricacies of problem-solving activity in cognitive psychology. We also think students can more readily grasp the relationship between theory and data if given extensive discussion of a few experiments rather than if overwhelmed with a large amount of data. Following such an introduction, students should have a firm foundation on which to build additional complexity and subtlety in advanced courses.

The book is written with the conviction that the principles of human memory and cognition should be introduced in such a way that students see their direct pertinence to and potential impact upon human affairs. Illustrations of practical applications are liberally provided, with the hope that students will gain a fuller and richer understanding of the principles as they relate them to their personal experiences. These illustrations cannot, of course, perfectly reflect principles derived from laboratory settings, but they can approximate them, and thus, we hope, will lead students to think of other illustrations as well as of potential exceptions.

This book is generally organized around the information-processing framework of human cognition. Chapter 1 provides an orientation to this framework and generally describes the information-processing model. Chapters 2 and 3 then discuss the input processes of sensory storage, pattern recognition, and attention. Memory structures and processes are described in chapters 4 through 7. Short-term memory is the subject of chapter 4, and a discussion of encoding processes in long-term memory follows in chapter 5. Retrieval from long-term memory is the topic of chapter 6. Chapter 7 describes work on the structure and processes of semantic memory. In chapter 8, we bring the preceding discussion of memory to bear on the process of comprehension and discuss the encoding and memory of higher-order material. In chapter 9, we describe current developments in the psychology of language and in chapter 10 discuss issues associated with concepts. Finally, in chapter 11, we address current issues in problem solving.

Each major chapter ends with a set of examination items and explanatory answers. Students may use these items not only for review, but also for feedback in gauging their comprehension of the material. This, however, is not their only purpose, for we hope that the test items will stimulate students to raise new questions and to engage in additional thinking about the issues. Some of the questions are relatively straightforward, whereas others present issues from a somewhat different perspective to encourage students to stretch the imagination.

At the end of the book the Glossary describes the major technical terms defined in this book. The definitions are brief and do not, of course, provide all of the potential meaning of the terms. The Glossary provides a convenient refresher for students, but should not be relied upon exclusively. The understanding of technical terms and concepts comes when students can *use* the terms in the appropriate context.

Henry C. Ellis
R. Reed Hunt

Acknowledgments

We are indebted to many persons in the preparation of the third edition of *Fundamentals of Human Memory and Cognition*. We again thank Frank A. Logan, general editor of this series. We also thank the following people who have provided useful feedback regarding either the second or third editions, or who have reviewed the entire third edition or one or more of its chapters: Bernard J. Baars, State University of New York, Stony Brook; Brian Babbitt, Missouri Southern College; Charles Brewer, Furman University; Bruce Britton, University of Georgia; Fergus Craik, University of Toronto; Robert Crowder, Yale University; Tony DeCasper, University of North Carolina, Greensboro; Harold Delaney, University of New Mexico; William Gordon, University of New Mexico; Paula Hertel, Trinity University; Marcia Johnson, State University of New York, Stony Brook; Peder Johnson, University of New Mexico; William Johnston, University of Utah; Leah Light, Pitzer College; Cheryl Logan, University of North Carolina, Greensboro; Ernie Lumsden, University of North Carolina, Greensboro; Ruth Maki, North Dakota State University; Mark Marschark, University of North Carolina, Greensboro; John Mueller, University of Missouri; Jean Newman-Charlton, University of New Mexico; Marcia Ozier, Dalhousie University; Frederick Parente, Towson State University; Stan Parkinson, Arizona State University; Gary Ritchey, University of New Mexico; Michael Scavio, California State University, Fullerton; Ronald Shaffer, Western Washington University; Blair Stone, University of Utah; Sherman Tyler, University of Pittsburgh; and Eugene Winograd, Emory University.

The people at William C. Brown provided superb support and assistance throughout this project. We were fortunate in having the support and cooperation of a first-rate staff who were also encouraging. We especially thank Susan Soley, our editor, who has done everything possible to make our association with the William C. Brown Company an enjoyable experience. We also thank Lynne Meyers, senior production editor, who oversaw the complex job of getting the book through production and handled all of the numerous details that arose in this job. We thank Marcia Stout, marketing manager, who did a superior job in preparing materials, and Jim Romig, executive editor, whose help was always available.

The secretarial staffs at the University of New Mexico and the University of North Carolina not only contributed their typing expertise but also gave us frequent words of encouragement. We are especially grateful to Jan Claus, office manager at New Mexico, and Kathy Martin, secretary at North Carolina, for their help. Their skill and patience are most appreciated. Finally, we thank the students in our 1982 cognitive psychology classes who read and commented on earlier drafts of the manuscript.

Henry C. Ellis
R. Reed Hunt

Acknowledgments

Fundamentals of Human Memory and Cognition

Introduction to Cognitive Psychology

1

The book that you are about to read describes some of the major issues and problems currently addressed in contemporary psychology. More specifically, the topics described in this book have arisen from a particular perspective on psychology which is known as *cognitive psychology*. The sole function of chapter 1 is to give you an orientation to this topic.

What is cognitive psychology? In part, this is a question we hope to answer throughout the book, but a preliminary discussion of the question will be helpful in gaining a perspective on what you are about to read. Perhaps the simplest and most direct way to define anything, including cognitive psychology, is to consult a dictionary. If you do, you will notice that "cognitive psychology" is not listed. Rather *cognitive* is used here as an adjective to modify the noun *psychology*. Our dictionary search must then proceed to separate definitions of the two terms.

If, for example, we consider a dictionary definition, we might see that *cognition* is defined as "the action or faculty of knowing." *Psychology* might be defined as "the science of the nature, functions, and phenomena of the human mind." If these two definitions are now combined, *cognitive psychology* might be defined as "the scientific study of the intellectual functions of the mind, including sensation, perception, and conception." But as is usually the case with unfamiliar concepts, this type of dictionary definition, while providing some information, does not also provide any real sense of understanding.

Your appreciation for the activity of cognitive psychology can be increased by consideration of a few examples of everyday experiences that are also of theoretical interest to cognitive psychologists. Have you noticed the difficulty of simultaneously taking notes in class and understanding a lecture? How many times have you carefully proofread written work only to be embarrassed later by an obvious error you overlooked? When you dial Directory Assistance for a telephone number and do not have a pencil to record the number, why do you have to repeat the number until you have dialed it? And why do you have to repeat your call to Directory Assistance if someone talks to you before you dial the number? You may have heard a television commercial for aspirin claim, "You cannot buy a more effective pain reliever than our brand." Later you remember that this brand is the most effective pain reliever you can buy. Your memory of what was claimed is actually quite different from the assertion made by the commercial, a point we will address later in the book. Do you remember the experience of working on a problem or a puzzle which you were unable to solve, but after taking a break from the problem, you subsequently obtained a solution? These are just a few of the many examples of everyday experiences which are discussed throughout this book and which are directly relevant to the experiments and theory of cognitive psychology.

Two points about these examples should be considered as we attempt to gain an overview of cognitive psychology. First, all represent instances of difficulty or failure of mental processes. Interestingly, we tend to treat our mental functions or processes the same way we treat our automobile: We rarely think of them unless they fail to work. Failures of mental processes are immediately noticed because they can be frustrating, embarrassing, and sometimes even dangerous, and consequently, such failures become useful tools for the psychological analysis of mental phenomena. You should be alerted however to the fact that most of the analysis focuses upon the *successful* operation of the mental processes. Probably we tend to appreciate the successes less than we notice a failure, but adaptive success of the human intellectual machinery far exceeds its failure.

The second point is that cognitive psychology is interested in what is generally called *mental phenomena*. In this sense, the examples just discussed are consistent with the dictionary definition of cognitive psychology: "the scientific study of the mind." While it is hoped that the examples help clarify the definition, questions undoubtedly remain concerning how one goes about this "scientific study of mind." Such questions can be addressed by closely examining what is meant by *mind* and *scientific study*. Perhaps the best way to approach these issues is by briefly describing the historical origins of cognitive psychology.

A Brief History of Cognitive Psychology

Psychology began as a scientific study of human knowledge and experience. The problem of what knowledge is has intrigued philosophers for centuries, and the formation of a separate discipline of psychology was marked by the application of experimental methods to the problem of knowledge. This "problem of knowledge" is an involved issue, but here is one example. As strange as it may seem, the certainty of your sensory "knowledge" is not at all clear. For example, can you be sure that the book you are reading is really there? What a stupid question, you may think, but consider the problem. The information you have about the book arises from the reaction of your receptors to the physical energy from the environment. The receptors then begin a process of nervous transmission to the brain where the interpretation of the physical energy culminates. So what you really "know" is that a certain pattern of activity occurred in the brain, not that a book is really there. Sometimes the interpretive processes are "fooled" as in the case of perceptual illusions, in which case what you see is not what is "really" there. The general point here is that what we "know" consists of our own perceptual or mental process.

The first psychologists believed, just as you and I believe, that the physical energy from the environment is related to mental processes, or what we know. Consequently, psychology began as the experimental study of relationships between the environmental energy or stimuli and mental processes. Experiments generally involved manipulating some aspect of the environment in the form of a simple stimulus event followed by the subjects' report of their mental or psychological experience. The goal of psychology was to provide a theoretical description of the mind. In some cases, this took the form of trying to decide what elements make up the *structure* of the mind. In other words, what are the elements of psychological experience? Another important question focused on the operation of the mental processes. What can we learn about the processes of perceiving, attending, remembering, and thinking?

These early psychologists were then trying to provide a theory of mental elements and processes in much the same way that early physicists and chemists were developing theories of the elements of matter and the processes which affect matter. However, in the history of psychology, some theorists very quickly became impatient with this approach and set about to redirect the course of psychology. Rather than view psychology as the study of *mental experience,* these researchers shifted the subject matter to *overt behavior.* The champions of this new approach called themselves *behavioristic psychologists* and emphasized the idea that the proper study of psychology deals with directly observable behavior. Their primary concern was that mental processes cannot be reliably observed, and consequently the results of experiments are not always consistent. Since the cornerstone of the new science of psychology was the experimental approach, the lack of consistency in experimental outcomes was a serious problem. The proposed solution to this dilemma was to abandon the study of mental processes and to direct the effort toward something that can be measured reliably. That something was overt behavior, and by studying the relationship between environmental events and behavior, the behavioristic psychologists hoped to understand why human beings do what they do, without reference to mental processes. All of these fundamental conflicts arose between 1879 and 1920.

By 1930, however, some psychologists had begun to argue that even simple overt behavior cannot be understood without some reference to mental processes. In other words, the door was opened, at least partly, for the mental processes to become again the focus of interest in psychology. For example, consider the phenomenon known as the *goal gradient*. One instance of this phenomenon can be observed when a hungry rat learns to run down an alley to obtain food. The *goal gradient* refers to the observation that the rat runs faster the closer it gets to the goal. Why is this true? One straightforward explanation is that the animal "expects" to receive food, and the expectation becomes stronger the closer the rat gets to the goal. But *expectation* is a psychological concept, not an overt behavior. If expectation is necessary to the understanding of the behavior, we are then back to the study of psychological processes. At this point we are talking about a simple observation, even for rat behavior. Imagine how much more complex is the understanding of human behavior such as memory or language.

Beginning in the 1950s, a variety of events occurred which led to a renewed and vitalized cognitive psychology. It is beyond the scope of this book to capture all this history, and interested persons are referred to an excellent treatment of the history by Lachman, Lachman, and Butterfield (1979). A few highlights can be noted here. First, British psychologists interested in applied problems began to develop theories of human performance and attention. A leader in this movement was Broadbent (1958) who developed an early model of how human attention works. Other psychologists such as Miller, Galanter, and Pribram (1960) sounded a clarion call for "a new theoretical approach" to psychology which would allow for the study of plans, images, and other mental processes. In the same year in his presidential address to the American Psychological Association, Hebb (1960), described what he called "the American Revolution," a resurgence of interest in mental processes and cognitive psychology. Renewed interest in mental processes such as imagery (Paivio, 1969), search and scan processes in short-term memory (Sternberg, 1966), and organizational processes in memory (Mandler, 1967; Bower, 1970) served to bring cognitive psychology to the forefront. Developments in other areas of science also accelerated this trend. Rapid changes in linguistics, computer science, ethology, and other areas complemented developments in cognitive psychology. These changes can be but briefly sketched here. The important point to note is that the ferment and excitement during the period from roughly 1957 through 1970 led to renewed interest in cognitive psychology.

For the foregoing reasons psychology has again shifted course and returned to some of the earlier questions regarding the nature of *mental structures and processes*. Although the basic questions are quite similar to those of the early psychologists, the approach has changed in many respects. Among the more important changes are the conceptualization of mental processes and the techniques used to study these processes.

Mind and Mental Processes

With minor exception, psychology has consisted of the scientific investigation of mental processes, as our brief review of the history indicates. To this point, however, all discussion of what psychologists mean by *mind* has been avoided. The current view of most cognitive psychologists is that *mind* and *mental processes* are ways of describing brain activity. That is, human mental functioning is not a mysterious, nonphysical event, but rather is the activity of the brain. Of course, brain activity can be studied physiologically, but cognitive psychologists use a different approach. Since the brain activity of interest cannot be directly observed (for example, we have no idea what happens in the brain when a person remembers a grandmother), we must infer the existence of these processes and then describe the processes in abstract language. Let us look more closely at these two aspects of the method cognitive psychologists use.

Approach of Cognitive Psychology

Cognitive psychology proceeds with its study of mental functioning through the scientific method, which is just a way of trying to solve problems through a combination of thinking and data gathering. Thinking is typically known as a theoretical enterprise and data gathering is accomplished by experiments. The exercise begins with an idea or theory about how a particular mental process works. The idea or theory contains certain implications; so that if the idea or theory is reasonable, then certain other events should follow. An experiment can then be set up to see whether these events actually do happen.

For example, consider one of the problems mentioned earlier: Why is it so hard to simultaneously take notes and understand a lecture? One theory suggests it is because we can only attend to one thing at a time, and when we are attending to one event, the information about other events is completely ignored. One implication of this theory is that when attending to one event a person should have no memory of other events. As we shall see, experiments can be set up to approximate this situation and allow us to determine the validity of this particular theoretical idea.

An important aspect of the scientific process is inference; in this context inference is perhaps best seen as educated guessing. A situation in which we know the surrounding circumstances is established, and then the behavior of the person in this situation is observed. Based on our knowledge of the circumstances plus our observations of the behavior, we infer or guess what types of processes the person must use in order to respond in that fashion. The method is not unlike the problem-solving activity of everyday life. Suppose you try to start your car and it refuses to start. Those of us who are not mechanics usually try to isolate the problem through a series of observations allowing us to infer the nature of the problem. Is there gas in the tank? If the answer is yes, are the lights and radio functioning? If they are not, perhaps the problem is electrical. This sort of activity is continued until all possibilities are exhausted. Note that we often learn a great deal about the problem even though we may not have the vaguest notion of precise automobile mechanics. The work of inferring the nature of mental processes based on observations of overt behavior proceeds in much the same way.

An important aspect of this analogy is the knowledge we have about the system before we try to solve a particular problem. In the case of automobiles, most of us do know a little something about operating an automobile, like the necessity of fuel and electricity. But in the case of the human brain, so little is known that our ideas about what might be going on are based on *models*. A *model* is something we understand which seems to function similarly to the object we are trying to understand. In other words, we take what we know about the model and ask: Does the brain work in a similar fashion? One type of model is borrowed from the computer.

The Computer Model and Information Processing

Psychology has always used models as a means for understanding its subject matter. Freud proposed a hydraulic model of mental processes, and the behaviorists have long used a model of stimulus and response (adapted from physiology), just to name two. For the last twenty-five years, however, the computer has emerged as a prominent model for psychological processes. The computer is an appealing model for human cognitive processes because the computer accomplishes many of the intellectual tasks ascribed to cognitive functioning. The computer accepts incoming information, stores that information for further use, and uses it later for computation in solving problems.

The analogy between the general framework of computer functioning and human cognitive functioning is reasonably obvious. People take information in the form of environmental energy and store it for later use. Just like input is transformed into machine language, it is reasonable to assume important transformations of incoming information from the environment. We know that the brain cannot use electromagnetic energy, which is the physical energy involved in light. Electromagnetic energy is transformed into chemical energy and then into electrical energy in the course of transmission from the eye to the brain. The storage function of the computer is analogous to the process we normally think of as memory. The stored information can later be retrieved, used to solve a problem, and then expressed as output from the computer. Again, the analogy with a search process and problem-solving activities in human beings is striking.

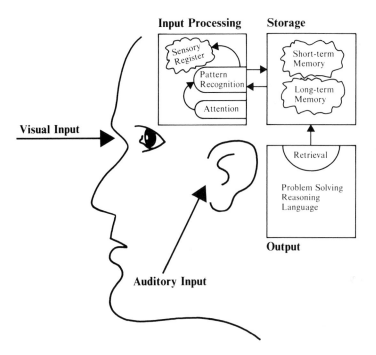

Figure 1.1 Sequence of information processing.

Use of the computer as a model is far from suggesting that the human brain works like a computer. The brain processes which correspond to such activities as perception, memory, thinking, and language are much more complex than any existing computer. Rather, the computer model provides a general way of thinking about human cognitive functioning. This general framework is known as information processing. The basic model is depicted in figure 1.1. As you can see, in figure 1.1 cognition can be divided into three components: input processing, storage, and output. Although it is convenient to think of these components as sequential stages, this need not always be the case. For example, in figure 1.1 feedback from long-term memory to the perceptual processes is indicated. The three components may all contribute to ongoing activity at any point in time. Regardless, the information-processing approach is a very useful tool in the analysis of human cognitive functioning.

Overview of the Book

The information-processing approach provides a logical organization for this book. At the heart of human information processing is the concept of *long-term memory*. Commonly we tend to think of memory as a static storage system from which we dredge up such rote facts as this: George Washington had wooden teeth. While the storage function of long-term memory is certainly important, long-term memory plays a dynamic role within the information-processing framework, a role which includes the interpretation of incoming information. Refer again to figure 1.1. Note the arrow going from long-term memory to the input stage, particularly to pattern recognition, which represents the assumption that what a person knows about the world, as represented by long-term memory, influences perception of incoming information. Furthermore, to say that we recognize something is to say that its representation has been activated in long-term memory. Thus, although we begin with the input sequence, we shall see that long-term memory has a pervasive influence throughout the system.

This book begins with the origin of the processing sequence, at that point of contact between the physical energy from the environment and the organism's receptors. The *sensory register,* the first concept discussed, stores the information received by the receptors. The sensory register is a memory system, but one whose properties are very different from those of long-term memory; the information lasts for a very brief period, and more important, the information has not been processed for meaning at this early stage. Consequently, the next step in the flow of information is meaningful processing. This processing is represented by the concept of *pattern recognition,* which extracts the information from the sensory store and matches that information with a representation in long-term memory. When this process is completed, the information has been recognized; that is, we know what it is. In this sense, the incoming information attains meaning.

It is important to realize, however, that not all of the information reaching the sensory register can be processed in pattern recognition. One consequence is that some process must guide or focus pattern recognition in selecting information. This function is served by the concept of *attention,* the process which determines which information will be processed in situations where all of the available information cannot be processed. As we shall see, a number of such situations arise involving processes in addition to pattern recognition. This discussion implies that human beings can only do one thing at a time, but we shall also see that this is an important and controversial assumption. How limited is the information-processing system?

The primary storage mechanisms in human information processing are the *short-term memory* and *long-term memory* systems. Some people think that memory for recent events operates differently than does long-term memory. Research thought to show structural differences between short- and long-term memory is discussed, and an argument that such distinctions may not be useful is presented. However, the need for a concept like short-term memory, in large part to understand the limitations of conscious thought, is also emphasized.

Included in the discussion of long-term memory are a number of important general issues, all of which focus upon the factors producing good memory. For example, what are the best circumstances for experiencing or studying something? This is a question of input processing, as are all of the concepts discussed to this point. Additional points are raised, however, including organization and distinctiveness.

Information in long-term memory is useful only if it is accessed, or retrieved. Thus, chapter 6 is devoted to understanding the process of getting to information in long-term memory.

The structure of long-term memory is also an important issue, and chapter 7 on semantic memory describes current research and thinking on the organization of knowledge stored in long-term memory.

Once information is accessed in memory, it may be used in a variety of ways. Chapters 8 through 11 discuss some of these situations. In particular, the processes of comprehension, language, concept formation and categorization, and problem solving are considered. Thus, this book is designed to introduce you to the theory and research of cognitive psychology from the initial reception of information to the complex utilization of that information.

Summary

Cognitive psychology is the scientific study of mental processes. Although psychology historically was established as a discipline devoted to such study, confusion concerning the meaning of *mental processes* diverted attention from the original goal. With the contemporary view that mental processes are synonymous with brain processes, psychology has returned to its original mission. Cognitive psychology proceeds through a combination of theory and experiment, as does all of science. Observations of performance are used to infer the psychological processes which must be necessary to produce the performance. With the help of the computer model, the cognitive psychologist develops ideas about the most important and interesting questions facing science: the structure and function of mental processes which account for human behavior.

Sensory Register and Pattern Recognition

2

In chapter 2 the initial stages of information processing, beginning with the activation of sense organs by physical energy from the environment, are discussed. The goal is to understand how physical energy is translated to psychological experience. For example, visual recognition of an object is based upon the physical energy of light. Yet, the physical description of light waves bears little resemblance to the psychological experience of the object we see. The light waves are precategorical, which means that the physical energy has not been categorized or has no meaning. Psychological processes must interact with this physical energy in order to add meaning to sensory experiences. The following example helps clarify this point.

Imagine that you are playing a variation of the old game twenty questions. The game is very simple: one player describes an object to another player who must guess the object from the description. In our special version of the game, however, your description must be limited to the way the object looks. You can provide as cues only the visual attributes of the object. Does this sound simple? Try to describe an apple using only the properties which are available to vision so that another person will be able to guess that you are describing an apple. Do not use attributes which cannot be seen such as *tart, juicy, crunchy,* or *fruit.* This exercise will probably demonstrate that just providing the visual description of a common object is difficult enough, and that a person attempting to guess what the object is will probably require several tries. When we recognize an object in the environment, the information-processing sequence begins with the same type of raw sensory information. Nonetheless, we rarely experience difficulty in moving from sensory information to full identification of a familiar object. How does this commonplace but remarkable event occur? This example illustrates the central issue of *pattern recognition,* translating patterns of sensory signals into psychological experiences of recognizable objects. Before pattern recognition is considered, however, we must discuss the first step in information processing, the *sensory register.*

Let us return to the example of the modified twenty questions game. Why is it so difficult to identify an object when cues are based solely on visual description of that object? The difficulty is due, at least in part, to the fact that visual properties do not exhaust the *meaning* of an object. Indeed, the visual properties alone have very little meaning in the sense of precisely specifying an object for someone else. When we extract meaning from visual experience, we actually add information to that experience. For example, the visual properties of an apple somehow activate other knowledge of apples, such as their taste and smell and abstract information such as apples are fruit. This constellation of information then constitutes the meaning of apple, and activation of this information allows us to identify the visual experience as apple. Notice that we have now moved far beyond the visual information initially provided to the retina of the eye.

Critical for our present purpose is the realization that the enrichment of sensory information takes time. In the twenty questions game, some amount of time is obviously required to guess the object being described. During this time, the guesser is searching for objects which meet the description. Although visual information processing rarely requires such a lengthy period of deliberation, some real time elapses between reception of visual information and recognition of the object represented by that information. If this point is understood, the function of the sensory register is easily grasped.

The Sensory Register

The sensory register is a memory system designed to store a record of the information received by receptor cells. Receptor cells are the specialized sense organs of the eye, ear, nose, tongue, and skin which respond to physical energy from the environment. Firing of the receptor cells begins the psychological processes of sight, hearing, smell, taste, and feeling. Once these receptor cells have been activated, the record of this activation is preserved or stored on the sensory registers. The stored record is known as the *sensory trace.*

Unlike the short-term and long-term memory traces, the contents of the sensory register are not open to introspection. That is, we cannot reflect upon and, indeed, are unaware of the sensory trace. You can gain, however, an appreciation for the existence of the sensory trace with the following exercise. Ball up your fist and then extend and contract your fingers as rapidly as possible. As you do this, watch your fingertips. If you observe carefully, you will see your fingers extended while they are already on the way back to making a fist again. You must observe carefully, because you will be able to see this for only a very brief period. You are seeing a record of what happened previously. Your fingers are no longer extended, but you still see them in that position. The visual system is responding to the memory or sensory trace of a previous event.

Information processing thus begins with the activation of sensory receptors, and this pattern of activity is stored in a memory system, the sensory register. Some persons think it is strange that the initial stages of information processing includes a memory system. Why do we need to store or maintain the sensory trace? Why not assume that the processing of receptor activity begins immediately, without the necessity for storage? Actually, the concept of the sensory register serves a very specific function.

Function of the Sensory Register

To understand why the sensory register is assumed to be important, let us again return to the example of the twenty questions game. Guessing the identity of an object from its visual description takes time. We now assume that "guessing" an object from the receptor activity also takes time. That is, processing the sensory information for meaning, adding information to the sensory pattern, is not accomplished instantaneously. Furthermore, we assume that we are limited in our ability to process multiple patterns of sensory information. In other words, we can only determine the meaning of one sensory pattern at a time. Imagine the impossibility of *simultaneously* guessing the identity of two objects from two different visual descriptions in the twenty questions game. These two assumptions now demand that we have a sensory register.

To understand this point, suppose that you are actually looking at an apple. While you are interpreting the information corresponding to "apple," a worm pokes its head out of the apple for a fraction of a second. The physical energy corresponding to the worm activates the sensory receptors, but the processing system is occupied interpreting the previous information corresponding to apple. What happens to the information about the worm? Does it simply fade away without being interpreted? Obviously such a situation would be very maladaptive; in this example, we would never know that the worm is in the apple. Of course, other more catastrophic events than eating a worm would result if we were unable to process much of the sensory information impinging upon the receptors. What is needed is a buffer or holding bin for the sensory information until the interpretive processes are free. This, then, is the function of the sensory register.

The sensory register maintains sensory information until other cognitive processes are capable of interpreting or adding meaning to it. With this initial memory system, we avoid losing present information while we are processing information which has just occurred. Each sensory modality has a corresponding sensory register, but in human beings the most widely studied systems are vision and audition.

The need for a sensory memory may be more acute in audition. For example, when we comprehend conversation, the extraction of meaning lags behind the rate of speech. That is, we do not compute the meaning of each word as it is spoken, but rather speech continues while we are determining the meaning of what was just said. Unless some means for storing the ongoing speech were available, we would lose much of what is currently being said while we determine the meaning of what was just said. The auditory sensory register then serves the purpose of briefly holding information which cannot be immediately processed.

The sensory register thus functions to maintain sensory information until it can be processed, but as we shall now see, this function can be served only if the sensory register has certain characteristics.

Characteristics of the Sensory Register

Three important characteristics of the sensory register allow the system to serve its storage function optimally. First, the information is stored in a *veridical* form. This simply means that the information stored should accurately reflect what happened at the sensory receptor. The second important characteristic is that the sensory register needs to be *relatively large,* at least large enough to store all of the information impinging on the sensory receptor. Both of these characteristics are necessary because the sensory trace is precategorical. The information has no meaning at this stage, so it must *all* be preserved in its *veridical* form to allow subsequent interpretation. Otherwise, the primary function of the sensory register, holding information for processing, would be defeated. The third important characteristic is that the information remain on the sensory register for a *brief* time. Since the sensory register stores all information from the sensory receptors and the receptors are continually receiving information, the sensory register must be cleared quickly to avoid superimposing information from two exposures. For example, the information on the visual sensory register would be blurred if two scenes were registered in quick succession. The resulting image would be difficult to interpret, much as a photographic double exposure supplies blurred images. One conceivable means of avoiding this problem is a rapid decay time for sensory memory. A second way in which the superimposition of two discrete events can be avoided is for the second event to erase the first. Incoming information might displace the existing information on the sensory register. These two mechanisms, rapid decay time and erasure, could clear the sensory register of old information to allow vivid representation of information.

Experiments have provided evidence for each of the three characteristics listed here. Since these studies provide the primary evidence for the sensory register, it is important that these experiments be discussed.

Size and Duration of the Sensory Register

Sperling's (1960) research on the visual sensory register illustrates the technique and data used to argue for the large but brief memory system we call a sensory register. Sperling's work is important not only because it addresses the size and duration of the sensory register, but also because it provides clever solutions to several difficult methodological problems. Understanding these problems and Sperling's solutions to them will help you understand the sensory register.

The first problem was the presentation of the to-be-remembered material. Since the sensory register stores information directly from the sensory receptors, a pure test of the system would measure retention from a single activation of the receptors. But how can material be presented such that the receptors are activated only once? In vision, the eyeball tremors or moves every one-fourth of a second to prevent a single receptor from receiving constant stimulation. The answer to this question is to present the to-be-remembered material at a rate more rapid than that of eye movement. Sperling presented the materials for 50 milliseconds (1 millisecond $= 1/1,000$ seconds), a rate you can approximate by closing your eyes and then opening and closing them again as rapidly as possible. In order to have such rapid presentation, special equipment is necessary to provide precise timing and to ensure that the subject is fixating upon the point at which the materials will appear. The device typically used for this purpose is a tachistoscope. The stimulus materials were matrices of consonants, containing either nine or twelve letters. As you can see in figure 2.1, the matrices were arranged in three rows of three or four letters each.

With the issue of how to present the material resolved, Sperling could measure what a person remembers from a single glance at a letter matrix. Now, however, a second serious problem arises which basically questions the need for such an experiment. Prior to Sperling's research, it was a well-known fact that people could remember only about four letters from a set of nine or twelve letters. These data are inconsistent with expectations based on the sensory register. If all of the information from the receptors is stored on the sensory register, memory should be virtually perfect. Sperling argued, however, that the temporal characteristics of the sensory register prevent human beings from demonstrating how much information is actually available.

The sensory trace is assumed to fade from memory very rapidly, and consequently the time required to report a few items is sufficient to allow decay of the remainder of the sensory register. The problem now becomes one of demonstrating that subjects have perfect memory for the letter matrix without asking them to recall all of the letters.

The ingenious answer Sperling provided to this problem is based on a technique used by most teachers in assessing what students have learned.

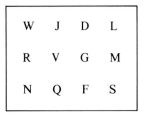

Figure 2.1 Example of a letter matrix used in a partial report experiment.

Rather than to ask for recall of all of the material, a procedure known as *whole report,* a person can be asked to report only part of the material. If the person does not know which part of the material will be tested, the only sure way to do well on the tested material is to know all of the material. Thus, the teacher can assume that the student's performance on the tested part of the material reflects knowledge of all the material.

The procedure just described is known as the *partial report technique* because the subject has to report only part of the information. Sperling used the partial report technique in the following manner. The letter matrix was shown for 50 milliseconds, and immediately upon termination of the matrix, a tone sounded. The tone was either high, medium, or low frequency and served as a signal for which row to report. The high tone indicated that the top row of letters was to be reported, the middle tone signaled the middle row, and the low tone signaled the bottom row. Thus, only one row of letters was reported on any trial, but the subject didn't know which row to report until the matrix disappeared. Thus, the responses had to be based on memory for the matrix.

With this procedure, Sperling found that the subjects were quite accurate, remembering almost 100 percent of a nine-letter matrix and about 75 percent of a twelve-letter matrix. With both nine- and twelve-letter matrices, the partial report technique suggests that the subjects have approximately nine letters available on the sensory register. This is a marked contrast to the whole report procedure where subjects are asked to recall the entire matrix, and they remember only three or four letters. The higher level of memory in the partial report condition suggests that all of the information in the matrix was available immediately on cessation of the stimulus, just as the reasoning about the sensory register suggests that it should be. Moreover, the difference in performance between partial and whole report performances suggests that the information in visual sensory memory decays very rapidly.

This latter point concerning the duration of visual sensory memory was examined more thoroughly by Sperling in the same experiment. On

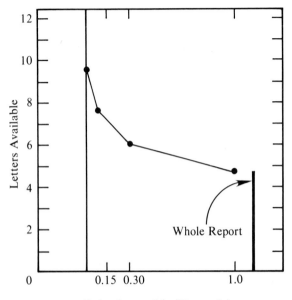

Delay Interval (milliseconds)

Figure 2.2 Number of letters recalled in Sperling's experiment as a function of delay between offset matrix and onset of partial report cue. (From "The Information Available in Brief Visual Presentations" by G. Sperling, *Psychological Monographs*, 1960, *74*, Whole No. 948. Copyright 1960 by the American Psychological Association. Reprinted by permission of the publisher and author.)

some trials the indicator tone was delayed following offset of the letter matrix. The delays ranged between 0 and 1 second. The delay conditions were added to see what happens to performance under partial report conditions when the report is not immediate. The results of the delay conditions, as well as the immediate partial report and whole report results, are shown in figure 2.2. Notice the high performance at 0 delay of the tone (immediate partial report). As the tone is delayed further, performance steadily declines to about 1 second. At this point, partial report performance is equivalent to that of whole report. The rapid drop in performance across these short intervals is indicative of a very transient *trace*. Indeed, significant trace decay seems to have occurred following a 300-millisecond delay, which suggests that visual sensory memory has an effective life of about one-third of a second.

Supporting evidence for this conclusion has come from studies of *backward masking*, a phenomenon discovered by Averbach and Coriell (1961). Masking refers to the technique designed to erase the information

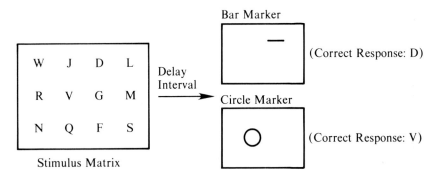

Figure 2.3 Example of the use of bar and circle markers showing the input (stimulus) matrix followed by the marker.

on the memory register. For example, suppose a letter matrix is presented and immediately upon offset of the matrix a cue is given for the partial report. Rather than a tone, however, suppose the cue is either a bar appearing under the position formerly occupied by a letter or a circle surrounding the position formerly occupied by a letter. The subject's task is to report the letter indicated by the marker, a partial report task requiring the subject to report one letter. An example of the use of bar and circle markers is given in figure 2.3. Keep in mind that the markers occur following offset of the matrix. The bar marker produces partial report performance similar to that found by Sperling. With the circle as a cue, however, performance is very poor. Why does a circle disrupt performance in the partial report situation?

The answer to this question appeals to the erasure of information from the sensory register. The circle appears in the same location as the letter and consequently may displace the letter on the sensory register. Since the bar marker is slightly removed from the location of the letter, it would not interfere with the letter's representation. The disruption produced by the circle is due to the masking or erasure of the letter. Since the circle occurs after the letter and its effect must operate backward in time, the technique is known as backward masking.

Estimates of the duration of visual sensory memory have been obtained using the technique of backward masking. Since the masking stimulus has its deleterious effect by erasing the sensory representation, the mask should be effective only as long as the information is on sensory memory. Once the information has left sensory memory, either through decay or selection for higher-order processing, performance following a masking stimulus should be no worse than following a nonmasking partial report cue. Thus, the duration of sensory memory can be estimated by systematically delaying the mask following the offset of the target stimulus. Studies using this method show that the mask disrupts performance if it is imposed between 0 to 300 milliseconds after offset of the target. Delays greater than 300 milliseconds seem to eliminate the negative effect of the mask. During the first 300 milliseconds following the offset of the target, an active representation is available, and the mask interferes with this representation. After 300 milliseconds, the mask is ineffective because the sensory representation has decayed. Thus, the estimates of visual sensory memory duration using backward masking have been very similar to those proposed by Sperling, on the order of one-third of a second.

Veridical Representation

The final characteristic of the sensory register is that the representation be veridical to the activation of the sensory receptors. The information on the sensory register reflects the pattern of receptor activity. Now recall the earlier discussion of the precategorical nature of receptor activity which described physical energy as precategorical. *Precategorical* means that the physical energy and corresponding receptor activity have not been categorized with respect to the object they represent. These patterns do not yet specify any particular object; further processing is necessary for object identification. The primary implication of the assumption of veridical representation is then that information on the sensory register will be precategorical. Can we demonstrate that the sensory information requires further processing to attain meaning?

Several studies have addressed this issue by using Sperling's partial report technique in a special way (e.g., von Wright, 1968). Suppose the stimulus matrix presented the subject consists half of letters and half of numbers. For a partial report cue, you use letters or numbers; notice that this procedure conforms to partial report in that only part of the information must be reported. But an important difference exists between this partial report cue and the spatial cue used by Sperling. To label a visual pattern a letter or number requires categorization of the visual pattern. In other words, each symbol has to be processed to decide whether it is a letter or a number before that symbol is reported. If every symbol must be processed to use the partial report cue, the advantage of partial report is lost. Notice that sensory cues, such as spatial location, do not impose similar requirements. If the cue signals a single row to be reported, no other symbols in the matrix need be processed.

According to the previous discussion, the additional processing for categorization will take time and the sensory memory will decay. Thus, if the information in the sensory register is precategorical, any partial report cue which requires that the meaning of the information be processed to determine what is to be reported will produce very poor performance. On the other hand, if the sensory register contains meaningful information, a categorical cue, such as letters or numbers, should give the standard advantage of partial report over whole report.

The data from these studies are clear. A subject given a categorical partial report cue, such as "Report all the letters," does no better than a subject given whole report instructions. Apparently the processing time required to determine if information in the sensory register is a letter or number is great enough to allow remaining information to decay. The results of these studies strongly suggest a precategorical memory system.

So the picture which emerges from research on visual sensory memory is of a brief storage system which holds all of the information received by the receptors. The information is in precategorical form, awaiting further processing to allow interpretation of the information and to bring it to our awareness. In the absence of this further processing, the information will be totally lost, particularly if the external source of stimulation has ceased. But that portion of the information selected for further processing represents what we come to know about our world.

Auditory Sensory Register

The reasons for assuming that a sensory register would be useful are persuasive, and the research on visual sensory memory substantially coincides with expectations. On the other hand, experiments on the auditory sensory register have less clear implications. As in studies of visual sensory memory, the basic technique is to present more information than can be processed and then test the subjects with partial report or whole report cues. For example, Darwin, Turvey, and Crowder (1972) asked subjects to listen to three different messages, played simultaneously over three different speakers. In the whole report condition, the subjects simply tried to recall as much as possible. Partial report involved recall of information from only one speaker. As with visual sensory memory, partial report performance was superior to that in the whole report condition.

Remember that the partial report superiority is attributed to the additional processing time required in the whole report condition. The additional time is required because the whole report procedure requires that more items be processed than for the partial report. Although several studies have reported the partial report advantage in auditory sensory memory, the interpretation is complicated by difficulty in demonstrating that the auditory sensory trace is precategorical. The precategorical status of visual sensory memory was established by experiments such as the one discussed which compared partial report using letters and numbers versus spatial location as cues. Letters and numbers are categorical, and hence the additional processing required to use these cues should offset the partial report advantage. Unlike studies of visual sensory memory, categorical cues provide performance equivalent to spatial cues in auditory sensory memory (Darwin, Turvey, & Crowder, 1972; Massaro, 1975).

For example, suppose we present a list of twenty symbols, half letters and half numbers, over two different speakers. The symbols are presented simultaneously over the two speakers, and following presentation of all twenty symbols, some subjects are asked to report all letters, a categorical partial report cue, and some subjects are asked to report all symbols from one of the speakers, a spatial partial report cue. In several such studies, the two types of cues do not differ in effectiveness. This result raises confusing questions about the precategorical nature of the auditory sensory register.

Another difference between visual sensory memory and auditory sensory memory is the estimate of the duration of the memory. We have seen general agreement that visual sensory memory persists for approximately 300 milliseconds. Estimates of auditory sensory memory, however, have ranged all the way from 250 milliseconds to 15 minutes. To the extent that there is any consensus, a value of about 2 seconds seems reasonable. This duration is considerably longer than that of visual memory, but the nature of auditory processing might require this additional storage time. Unlike vision where the information is related spatially and a great deal of information may be taken in at once, audition generally requires the temporal integration of discrete events. In order to understand a sentence, the subject must be related to the predicate, but some amount of time separates the two parts of the sentence. The auditory memory system thus may need a longer duration than visual memory by virtue of the different demands placed on the two senses. Nonetheless, greater consistency in estimates of the auditory sensory trace duration is important to gain clear interpretations of an auditory sensory register.

Visual Sensory Memory and Reading Disability

The sensory register operates at a preattentive level, which means we have no conscious control over its functioning, nor are we aware of its contents. Partially for this reason, the concept may appear esoteric and of little use in understanding real-world behavior. To the contrary, the sensory register has been applied to several problems of considerable importance.

A particularly interesting example is the use of visual sensory memory to study specific reading disability. *Specific reading disability* is a syndrome which has long been of interest to educators and psychologists because of its unique characteristics. Initially, the only obvious difficulty the person presents is in reading; no organic damage is present; the IQ score is in the normal range; and no intellectual deficits are apparent beyond the reading problem. The pattern then is of an otherwise perfectly normal individual who has great difficulty reading. Actually, only young children show this pattern, because beyond a certain level of formal schooling, roughly the sixth grade, the reading deficit begins to pose a serious obstacle to performance in other disciplines, including mathematics. Thus, if it is undetected early, specific reading disability eventually is disastrous to the academic achievement and maturation of an otherwise capable person.

For many years, the primary hypothesis concerning specific reading disability was the *perceptual deficit hypothesis.* In its simple form, the idea suggested that reading-disabled children did not see the same images as do normal readers. For whatever reason, the visual system of disabled readers was assumed dysfunctional such that the information available was distorted. This general hypothesis was rather disheartening in that it suggested some critical but unspecified organic difference between the good and poor readers which could not be remediated in the classroom.

The data supporting the perceptual deficit hypothesis were based, by and large, upon simple perceptual tasks. For example, a child might be shown a single letter or a small set of letters and then asked to say or write the letters after they were removed. The reading-disabled child was likely to perform more poorly than the normal reader and to make mistakes such as letter reversal (mistake *b* for *d*) in these simple tasks. Since the test was administered very soon after termination of the stimuli, the task was assumed to measure the sensory information available to the child, not memory. With the advent of the information-processing framework, a new perspective on the simple perceptual task was available. Perhaps the reading-disabled children did see exactly the same images as the normal readers, but memory performance between the two groups differed. In other words, the good and poor readers may register the same information on visual sensory memory, but then differ in their *ability to process the information* off of the sensory register.

This idea was tested by Morrison and colleagues (Morrison, Giordani, and Nagy, 1977), using groups of good and poor readers from the sixth grade. The procedure used was a variation of Sperling's partial report in which the subjects were shown a circular array of eight symbols. Three types of stimuli were used: letters, geometrical shapes, and random shapes. The stimulus array was shown for 100 milliseconds and was replaced by a marker at the position of one of the eight symbols. The marker was presented at delays following offset of the array varying from 0 to 2 seconds. After the marker appeared, the child was shown a card containing several symbols. The child's task was to indicate which of the symbols on the card had appeared at the position of the marker on the original array. The test was thus recognition rather than recall. The primary questions addressed in this study are: Do poor readers differ from good readers? and if they do, is this difference a function of the delay interval? The perceptual deficit hypothesis would predict superior performance by good readers at all delay intervals.

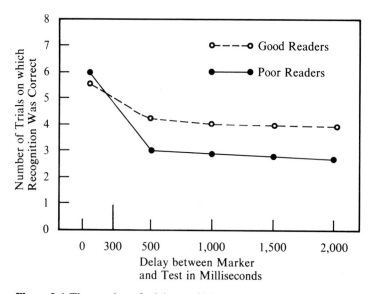

Figure 2.4 The number of trials on which correct recognition responses were given by good and poor readers following various delay intervals. Notice that both good and poor readers begin to differ only after a delay of 300 milliseconds. (From "Reading Disability: An Information Processing Analysis" by F. J. Morrison, B. Giordani, and J. Nagy, *Science,* 1977, *199,* 77–79, Fig. 2, 1 April 1977. Copyright 1977 by the American Association for the Advancement of Science.)

The results, which are presented in figure 2.4, were quite striking. As you can see in figure 2.4, no difference in the number of trials on which correct recognition occurred until the indicator was delayed by about 300 milliseconds. Beyond this point, the good readers recognized more items than did poor readers. This outcome was consistent across all types of stimuli.

Using the previous estimates of the duration of visual sensory memory, Morrison's data clearly indicate that poor readers perform as well as good readers when the information is in sensory memory. It is at the point of *higher-order processing* that the poor reader is disadvantaged. The deficit may be a problem of translating visual information to phonetic information, or it may be some confusion of the visual information, but regardless, Morrison's study shows that good and poor readers do register the same sensory information, contrary to the perceptual deficit hypothesis. This is important information in both the understanding and treatment of specific reading disability.

Pattern Recognition

Among the oldest and most fascinating questions facing psychology is the relationship between physical energy in the environment and psychological experience. What are the processes which govern the transformation of physical energy, such as light, into a meaningful psychological experience? Our ability to recognize patterns of physical energy is obviously an absolute necessity for survival. Perhaps not so obvious, however, is the flexibility and complexity of the pattern-recognition process. Consider first the enormous range of patterns which a person can recognize. The number of people, objects, and events which are immediately and effortlessly recognized by adults are virtually uncountable. You may have difficulty recalling the name of a particular person or object, but rarely do you have trouble recognizing the pattern as a person, or a tree, or an airplane. In fact, pattern recognition at this level is accomplished with such ease that the entire issue may appear trivial.

But the ability to recognize patterns of sensory information is neither simple nor trivial. The complexity of pattern recognition can be illustrated by considering some very common situations. You and a friend are standing by the ocean, and you see an object in the distance. You point out the object to your friend and remark on the danger of a swimmer being that far from shore. Your friend laughs and says that the object is not a person but is a sea turtle. You look again, and still see a person. A mild argument ensues. Cases of two people disagreeing about a pattern when both are receiving approximately the same physical information are notoriously common. Indeed, you may be surprised to learn that you will frequently respond differently to exactly the same pattern of physical energy. For instance, examine the top row of figure 2.5, which is taken from an experiment of Bugelski and Alampay (1961). What is the fifth symbol in that row? Now examine the second row of figure 2.5. What is the fifth symbol? In the top row, the fifth symbol is easily recognized as a rat, but in the second row the same pattern is just as easily recognized as a face. The same auditory patterns can also give rise to different recognition responses. In normal conversation, the physical pattern of the utterance "new display" is the same as that of "nudist play." Rarely, however, would we fail to recognize the appropriate pattern in normal conversation. Our attempts to understand the apparently simple process of pattern recognition are then complicated by the ability to recognize appropriately the same physical energy as different patterns.

The other side of this coin also must be considered. Different patterns of physical energy are frequently recognized as the same pattern. Think, for a simple example, of the enormous variety of ways in which the letter *A* may be written: not only is everyone's handwriting different, but also

Figure 2.5 Example of the same pattern recognized as two different objects. (From "The Role of Frequency in Developing Perceptual Sets" by B. R. Bugelski and D. A. Alampay, *Canadian Journal of Psychology*, 1961, *15*, 205–211. Copyright 1961 by the Canadian Psychological Association. Used by permission.)

infinite variations in size and shape are possible. In spite of the incredible variability presented by physical information, the psychological mechanisms respond consistently and accurately. This flexibility in the pattern recognition process is highly adaptive and again illustrates the complexity of the interface between physical energy and psychological experience. The flexibility of human pattern recognition has been extraordinarily difficult to simulate in machines. Computers can recognize patterns, but the input must be unambiguous. The bizarre numbers on credit cards are necessary for computer recognition because normal Arabic numerals are too similar for consistently accurate recognition by a computer.

Thus, the study of pattern recognition addresses a number of complex issues related to the process of extracting meaning from sensory experience. First, how are we to conceptualize the extraction of meaning from sensory information, capturing both the speed and accuracy of pattern recognition? Moreover, the conceptualization must account for the enormous flexibility of the pattern recognition process, including the influence of contextual information. The complexity of some of these issues is so great as to allow only a general understanding at the moment, but the discussion of the general conceptualization will lead to more specific ideas and research.

Pattern Recognition and Memory

Within the framework of information processing, pattern recognition is a process which interacts with the information on the sensory register. In a sense, information is read off of the sensory register through the process of pattern recognition. Remember that information on the sensory register is assumed to be *precategorical* or without meaning. Pattern recognition is the process by which meaning is derived. In general, pattern recognition is assumed to involve the match between sensory information and the corresponding representation stored in long-term memory. The sensory pattern is recognized as one of the patterns stored in the long-term system. Once this recognition occurs, the information associated with the pattern in long-term memory is available, and in this sense the sensory pattern acquires meaning. Pattern recognition, then, is a process which interprets sensory information by matching that information to previous experiences stored in long-term memory.

Within this general framework, more specific questions can be asked of the pattern-recognition process. For example, pattern recognition requires the interaction of two separate memory systems, sensory register and long-term memory. What is the nature of the memory codes which are to be matched between these systems? Moreover, how is the decision concerning the "goodness" of the match reached? In other words, the description must consider not only the nature of the codes to be matched, but also the processes which are responsible for the matching. In order to give a feeling for the necessary complexity of an adequate description, we shall begin with a very simple theory of pattern recognition.

Template Theory

Perhaps the most intuitive hypothesis of pattern recognition involves a direct match between the sensory experience and the literal copy of that experience. The literal copy, known as the *template,* is stored in long-term memory. The pattern presented by the sensory experience is compared to templates stored in long-term memory until a direct match is found. The matching or decision process is made on the basis of perfect overlap between the sensory pattern and the template, and once overlap is achieved, the pattern is recognized as the template. Template theory in this simple form is essentially a lock-and-key type of hypothesis. The match process continues until a template is found that fits the sensory experience.

The difficulties with the simple template hypothesis concern an understanding of the speed, accuracy, and flexibility of pattern recognition. For example, in day-to-day activities, most familiar patterns are recognized rapidly. Identification of familiar objects in the environment, such as a face, a type of car, and so forth, seems to occur instantaneously and with no effort. Although we now know from laboratory studies that pattern recognition does require measurable amounts of time, the brief period of time required does not seem perfectly consistent with description of pattern recognition of the template theory. A potential solution to this problem is to assume that the sensory experience is matched against all templates simultaneously, a process known as parallel processing.

Serial and Parallel Processing

According to template theory, the number of templates stored in long-term memory have to equal the number of patterns a person can recognize. This would be a very large number indeed if you consider all of the possible variations of all of the possible patterns you can recognize. If each sensory pattern is matched against each template, the process could be quite time-consuming. One solution to this dilemma is to make an assumption about the comparison process. Rather than match the sensory patterns to each template one at a time, which is known as *serial processing,* perhaps the match is made against all templates simultaneously. Matching the sensory experience against a number of templates simultaneously, known as *parallel processing,* would greatly enhance the speed of the matching process.

Although parallel processing is not intuitively plausible, probably because of the difficulty of doing two complex things simultaneously, Neisser (1964) provided some evidence in favor of parallel processing in pattern recognition. Neisser's experiment required that subjects scan a sheet of paper containing fifty lines of four letters each and press a button as soon as they detected a particular target letter. The target letter was randomly positioned among the letters on the sheet. In the first condition, the subjects were given only one target letter, but in the second condition, the subjects were told to respond to any of ten different letters. If we assume that the instructions concerning the target letter activate the template for that letter, the sensory patterns are then compared to the activated template. The critical aspect of the experiment for evaluation of serial processing and parallel processing is the number of templates against which the sensory pattern must be matched. If pattern matching is serial in nature, specifying one letter should produce faster recognition than specifying ten letters. With ten letters, each sensory experience, that is, each letter on the sheet, would have to be matched against ten templates one at a time, whereas the other condition requires only one match for each letter. Parallel processing, however, should produce no difference in match time as a function of the number of potential targets. All activated templates would be matched simultaneously against the sensory pattern such that the number of activated templates would be irrelevant to the decision time. The results of this experiment, and others since, have in fact shown no difference in the time to detect targets as a function of the number of targets. These data are consistent with ideas about parallel processing, and parallel processing offers a potential solution to one of the problems facing template theory. Unfortunately, other, more serious problems exist.

Preprocessing

Yet another and perhaps more serious difficulty arises for template theory when we try to explain the ability to recognize patterns in spite of wide variation in their physical form. The most obvious position for template theory is to argue that a template exists for every recognizable variation of every pattern. Considering again only the numerous variations in the pattern that can be recognized as *A*, the number of templates necessary is very large. If all of the potential variations of all of the patterns a person can recognize are imagined, the required number of templates is staggering. The large number of templates requires massive long-term memory capacity and the ability to resolve ambiguity concerning which of two or more possible patterns an ambiguous or unusual sensory pattern represents.

One solution to this difficulty is to assume some *preprocessing* of the sensory pattern prior to the matching decision. Preprocessing essentially functions "to clean up" the pattern, for example, to place it in proper orientation, to reduce or expand its size, to remove extraneous information, and the like. For example, the pattern V might be rotated 180 degrees to form the pattern A prior to being matched with a template. The advantage of preprocessing is that it reduces the number of templates needed in long-term memory. A further logical problem now arises, however. In order for preprocessing to function efficiently, it seems that the pattern must already have been recognized. That is, to reorient or clean up the pattern, you may need to know what the pattern is; yet, this is the very process that preprocessing serves. In other words, how does preprocessing decide to reorient V to A as opposed to removing the extraneous horizontal line to form V?

A possible solution lies in the influence of contextual information; the context in which a pattern appears delineates the possibilities. For example, the context of V might be such that an upside-down A is more probable than a V, and hence preprocessing reorients the pattern rather than removes the horizontal line. Indeed, some evidence is available to indicate that reorientation does occur in contextually constrained situations.

If the task is to decide whether you are seeing the pattern R or its mirror image Я, and the pattern is presented in other than its normal orientation, for example, R, the amount of time to make the decision systematically increases as the stimulus departs from its normal orientation (Cooper and Shepard, 1973). One interpretation of this finding is that the pattern is being *mentally rotated* prior to the match decision. Notice, however, that the alternative patterns have been specified in advance; the subjects *expect* particular patterns. This expectation or prior knowledge can be described theoretically as the activation of the long-term memory representation of the patterns prior to the presentation of the actual stimulus. Activation of the memory representation prior to presentation of the stimulus is under control of the instructions in this task, and these instructions serve as the contextual constraint. Preprocessing becomes possible under these circumstances because the sensory pattern, once it is presented, can be rotated or refined in other ways until it matches the activated template.

This situation is analogous to the rather common experience of looking for a particular person in a crowd, searching for a friend at a football game or large party. You know for whom you are looking; that is, the template for that face is activated. If the person for whom you are searching has changed in physical appearance (grown a beard, for example), it is still possible to clean up the pattern to match your memory of the person. Remember, however, the previous criticism of preprocessing. Preprocessing requires that the pattern to be recognized already be activated in long-term memory; while contextual constraints may serve this function, we certainly are capable of recognizing patterns in the absence of knowledge of which pattern is to be recognized. We recognize a face even when a person is unexpected.

Simple template theory has proved inadequate in describing the richness and flexibility of pattern recognition. Even when supplemented with concepts such as preprocessing, template theory leaves many questions unanswered. As is often the case in science, however, the inadequate theory is invaluable in raising questions for other theories to answer. It is to one of these other theories that we now turn.

Analysis-by-Synthesis

The general class of theories now discussed were initially proposed by computer scientists (e.g., Selfridge, 1959) interested in machine pattern recognition and subsequently were brought to the attention of psychologists by Neisser (1967). Although several versions of this approach are available, certain basic ideas are common to all, and we shall discuss these ideas under the general rubric of analysis-by-synthesis. The term *analysis-by-synthesis* describes the process by which pattern recognition is assumed to occur. The initial step in the process is analysis or breakdown of the pattern of sensory information on the sensory register. Recognition ultimately occurs through synthesis or reconstruction of the pattern from its component parts. The synthesis process involves the comparison of the sensory information with corresponding representations in long-term memory and a decision concerning the sufficiency of the match between the two. For example, the letter *A* might be analyzed into two oblique lines and one horizontal line, /, \, −. The list of components are then *compared* to lists stored in long-term memory which represent patterns. During the comparison stage, several patterns having some of the features provided by the analysis are uncovered. For example, *M, N, R, V, W, X,* and *Y,* in addition to A, all have oblique lines. Horizontal lines are present in *A, E, F, H, I, J,* and

Z. Thus, the comparison stage might generate several candidates from long-term memory, necessitating a *decision* concerning which is the best match for the sensory pattern. The decision stage determines the amount of evidence for a particular recognition response.

As can be seen from this overview, analysis-by-synthesis involves more complicated *processes* than the simple pattern match proposed by template theory. As will be discussed, the additional complexity adds explanatory power to the analysis-by-synthesis approach. It also should be clear from the outset that analysis-by-synthesis requires a different kind of long-term memory representation. Rather than holistic templates, analysis-by-synthesis assumes patterns are represented by component *features.*

Features

All patterns consist of a configuration of elements, and theoretically any pattern can be broken down into these basic elements. Tł ɔ basic elements or parts of a pattern are known as *features* of the pattern. For example, the letter *A* consists of the three features /, \, and −. Angles might also be included as features, in which case *A* also has the feature obtuse angle. Any visual pattern thus can be described by listing its features. Likewise, acoustic patterns, the sensory information in speech perception, can also be analyzed as combinations of features. As lines and angles seem to be important visual features, speech contains basic units of sounds, called *phonemes,* which determine meaning. The sounds of *b, c,* and *h* in the words *bat, cat,* and *hat* are phonemes in that each of the distinct sound patterns changes the meaning of the word. Much of the exciting research in speech perception is currently devoted to identifying acoustic features.

If physical patterns of light and sound can be described in terms of their components, it then seems reasonable that long-term memory be composed of lists of features describing patterns. Thus, some theorists suggest that patterns are represented in long-term memory as *feature lists.* To recognize a sensory pattern, it then becomes necessary to transform that pattern into the same code as that of long-term memory; specifically, the pattern would have to be analyzed into its component features. The features are then compared to the feature lists of long-term memory to reach a recognition decision.

The concept of features may appear to complicate unduly the process of pattern recognition, particularly compared to the rather straightforward template hypothesis. What advantage does the concept of featural representation offer which could possibly justify the complexity?

The feature hypothesis handles several problems which are difficult for the template theory. For example, template theory is forced to postulate an enormous number of templates in long-term memory corresponding to each pattern we recognize. Feature theory, on the other hand, can reduce this load on long-term memory by assuming that only the finite set of features are represented in long-term memory. That is, the number of possible lines and angles of visual stimuli is large but not as large as the total number of patterns we can recognize. By assuming that any pattern can be described as some combination of features, long-term memory need only contain one complete listing of features, and each pattern is represented by the activation of some unique subset of the features. Thus, feature theory enjoys a conceptual advantage over template theory in terms of the burden placed on long-term memory.

Further justification for a featural representation is derived from studies demonstrating the psychological reality of features. Research from both physiological and behavioral perspectives yield results highly consistent with feature theory. For example, a number of physiological studies on a variety of animals have shown that specific cells in the visual system respond differentially to simple stimuli such as line orientation or angles (Hubel & Wiesel, 1962; Lettvin, Maturana, McCulloch, & Pitts, 1959). These cells seem to be specialized in detecting the simple visual stimuli which correspond to what have been called features of a pattern. Cells have even been identified in the frog's visual system which respond only to small, dark, moving objects. Perhaps these cells function as a lunch detector for the frog. Equally impressive are data demonstrating cortical cells in monkeys which fire only to the visual stimulus of a monkey paw! The important point here is that neural mechanisms fire to specific patterns, a fact which corresponds well with feature theory.

Behavioral data also have been offered in support of feature theory, particularly in the form of confusion matrices. Confusion matrices summarize the patterns of errors a person makes in making judgments about rapidly presented letters. For example, when the letter *A* is presented very rapidly and a mistake in judgment is made, the letter reported is likely to share visual features with *A,* such as do *H, K,* or *N.* If the process of recognizing these patterns entails the use of basic features, confusion among patterns sharing features would be expected. Feature theory thus helps us understand data from both behavioral and physiological research and therefore gains credibility. Armed with both logical and empirical justification for a feature code in memory, the analysis-by-synthesis approach describes a series of steps by which the sensory features of a pattern are matched in long-term memory.

The Process of Analysis-by-Synthesis

Essentially three steps are involved in analysis-by-synthesis. The first step is extraction of information from the sensory register. Unlike template theory which assumes that the holistic sensory representation is lifted from the sensory register, analysis-by-synthesis assumes that the sensory representation is analyzed into component features. The first step is then to extract information from the sensory register through the featural analysis of the pattern. The identification of these features is the second step. Here, the features contained in the pattern are matched to features in long-term memory. As you can see, this stage of pattern recognition is very similar to template theory. Each sensory feature must be matched against what amounts to a template in long-term memory. In spite of this similarity, the advantage of feature theory is that the number of feature templates necessary to describe all patterns is assumed to be smaller than the total number of patterns. The third step is the decision process itself in which the set of features selected and identified in the first two stages are compared with feature lists in long-term memory. The best match in terms of the number of overlapping features is selected as the pattern represented by the sensory information. The pattern in long-term memory containing the most features in common with the sensory pattern is then selected as the recognition response. The process of analysis-by-synthesis thus proceeds from initial analysis of the sensory pattern into component features to identification of these features to the final decision concerning what pattern is represented by the features. The final step represents a synthesis in that the separate features are now put together in the pattern decision.

As described thus far, analysis-by-synthesis appears to be completely *data driven.* That is, the entire process seems to be guided by the features of the sensory pattern. As we have previously seen, however, certain recognition decisions cannot be determined solely by the sensory data; the same sensory pattern may be recognized as a different pattern in a different context. Refer again to figure 2.5. Since the sensory data from the specific pattern are the same in the two situations, some other information and process must account for the recognition decision. The additional information is derived from the context in which the pattern occurs, and the context is assumed to affect recognition by activating conceptual information or *presynthesizing* the pattern.

Let us illustrate the effects of context and the process of presynthesis through an experiment by Reicher (1969) on letter recognition. Suppose that the word *BOOK* is presented at a very fast exposure rate. Immediately at the offset of the word, the subject sees _ _ _ ?, and the task is to report the letter which had appeared in the space occupied by the question mark, in this example, *K*. In order to estimate the influence of the word context upon letter recognition, it is also necessary to measure recognition in a nonword context. For example, the stimulus *OBOK* could appear, followed by the same test query, _ _ _ ?. Note that in both cases *K* is the pattern to be reported, but in one instance, *K* occurs in the context of a word and in the second instance, it occurs in nonword context. The results of such comparisons show both more accurate and more rapid recognition when the letter occurs in the context of a word.

This result, however, is not perfectly straightforward because the probability of guessing the correct letter is higher in the word context. That is, the subject may not have seen *K,* but only *BOO_.* Knowing the response should be a letter which completes the word beginning in *BOO* makes *K* a fairly obvious guess. Alternately, guessing in the nonword context is much less likely. Thus, the advantage provided by word contexts may have little to do with true recognition, but may result simply from a higher probability of guessing. It is possible, however, to control for guessing by changing the test to recognition with alternative choices, either of which would make a word. For example, the test alternatives for *BOOK* might be *K* and *T,* and the subject must choose the correct response. The same test is given following the nonword context. The important point is that any differences between the two conditions can no longer be attributed to guessing from the word context. With the guessing probability thus controlled, recognition of the final letter is still more accurate when that letter was presented in the context of a word.

How does the analysis-by-synthesis approach describe this facilitating effect of context? First, it should be apparent that context serves to narrow the possible choices among the incoming patterns. Whether we are talking about a letter, an object in the environment, or a face, the context in which a pattern occurs limits the possible choices. Another way of saying this is that the context establishes expectations concerning incoming patterns. Analysis-by-synthesis tries to capture this expectation through the concept of presynthesis. Remember that the final stage of recognition involves synthesis of the sensory features, in that the previously analyzed sensory features are compared to feature lists in long-term memory. Contextual information, however, could serve to activate the patterns in long-term memory prior to the appearance of the actual sensory representation of the pattern. In other words, the context leads us to expect a particular pattern, which may be constructed with minimal reference to the sensory information.

A competent reader, for example, certainly does not analyze each letter in each word. Indeed, reading seems to involve much in way of presynthesis or anticipation of patterns. Adult readers rarely notice the omission of articles such as *the* and *a.* Did you notice that the sentence before last omitted *the* prior to *way?* We seem to fill in the blanks with patterns which fit with the prevalent context. This process is an example of conceptually driven pattern recognition in which the final recognition decision is guided by long-term memory rather than by sensory information. The startling implication is that persons may "recognize" patterns *without* any sensory experience with those patterns!

Since presynthesis amounts to constructing a pattern based on expectation of what the pattern should be rather than on sensory information, certain situations are likely to lead to embarrassing recognition failures. A prime example of such a situation involves proofreading a paper. People commonly fail to detect misspellings or typographical errors when proofreading their own written work. In terms of the analysis-by-synthesis model, you usually know what you have written or at least what you meant to write. Consequently, in proofreading, you are likely to construct patterns on the basis of your expectations, and it is sometimes difficult to force yourself to check carefully the sensory pattern, the actual writing itself. Errors may thus go undetected even after "careful" proofreading of the material. If you understand that pattern recognition in normal reading usually proceeds with a great deal of presynthesis, you may realize that extra effort is required to avoid presynthesis or at least to force yourself to check the presynthesized pattern against the sensory information. An effective means of doing this is to get someone to help you proofread important material. One person reads the material aloud to the other person who follows along, using another copy of the material. By reading aloud, you can slow the normally rapid pattern recognition in reading and perhaps reduce the tendency to rely heavily on presynthesized patterns. By having a person unfamiliar with the material read along with you, you further increase the chance of detecting errors. Although this may seem to be a rather extreme measure just to correct minor errors (it certainly requires a good friend to tolerate the tedious task), you should not underestimate the impact minor errors can have upon supervisors, clients, or colleagues in whatever career you choose. You probably already know of professors' reactions to "minor" errors. The point is that the normal operation of the pattern recognition system can work to your disadvantage, and sometimes it is worth extraordinary effort to ensure that what you think you saw is really there.

Summary

The emerging picture then is of a memory system in which the stimulus is available to the subject both during and immediately after cessation of the stimulus. This information decays very rapidly, however, and much of what is available will not reach meaningful processing. Since the information on the sensory register is assumed to be precategorical, it must undergo additional processing to attain meaning. During the brief time required for additional processing, the remaining information decays.

The implication of this situation is quite striking: the vast majority of the information that activates the senses goes totally unnoticed because of the time and effort required to process some minuscule portion of that information. Much of the information stimulating the receptors remains unknown. The ramifications of this conclusion are quite fascinating. What is *missed?* Even more important for cognitive psychology, how is information from the sensory register (which has no meaning) *selected* such that the information selected is consistent with the meaning of what has been processed? As we shall see, this has been a major question in the study of selective attention.

Pattern recognition is the process by which sensory information is extracted from the sensory register. Through contact with long-term memory, the meaning of the sensory information is then derived. Adequate descriptions of pattern recognition require considerable complexity, as illustrated by the analysis-by-synthesis model. Analysis-by-synthesis assumes a featural representation of patterns in long-term memory, which in turn requires the assumption that sensory patterns are analyzed into features to match long-term memory. Moreover, context affects pattern recognition such that a pattern may be recognized with minimal reference to the sensory information. In some sense, context allows us to make a highly educated guess about a pattern, avoiding the more time-consuming analysis and synthesis of the sensory pattern. Presynthesis of the pattern may increase the speed of pattern recognition, but the potential for error is also increased because the sensory data may contribute minimally to the recognition decision.

To the Student

Beginning with chapter 2, a set of multiple-choice, true-false, and discussion items are provided at the end of each chapter. The answer to each multiple-choice and true-false item is given along with a brief explanation. These items sample some of the chapter content and thus provide some index of your comprehension of the material. The items are not, however, exhaustive of the content of the chapter and hence should not be relied upon exclusively for study and review. Some questions tap the factual information of the chapter, whereas others attempt to apply concepts and principles to new situations not directly described in the text. Thus the questions sample the types on typical examinations.

Multiple-Choice Items

1. The sensory register is an initial memory system which has the following characteristics
   a. large capacity and short duration
   b. small capacity and short duration
   c. large capacity and long duration
   d. small capacity and long duration

2. The primary function of pattern recognition is
   a. totally independent of the sensory register
   b. to add meaning to the sensory information
   c. easily described as a simple template matching
   d. to increase the duration of information on the sensory register

3. The property of the sensory register which makes pattern recognition absolutely necessary is
   a. its large capacity
   b. its short duration
   c. precategorical code

4. The sensory register functions
   a. to recognize information
   b. to supplement the other memory systems
   c. to hold information until it can be processed
   d. to process information for meaning

5. Backward masking studies have been very helpful in establishing
   a. the duration of the sensory register
   b. the size of the sensory register
   c. the type of code in the sensory register
   d. the relationship between pattern recognition and the sensory register

6. The primary problem for template theories of pattern recognition is
   a. the assumptions they make about the sensory register
   b. the requirements they impose on long-term memory
   c. preprocessing
   d. the results of physiological studies demonstrating the presence of features

True-False Items

1. The reason we need the concept of sensory register is because people remember so much after such a short period of time.

2. The major advantage of a feature theory of pattern recognition is the smaller amount of information needed to recognize large numbers of patterns.

3. Long-term memory is very important in pattern recognition.

4. Partial report of a briefly presented matrix produces better performance than whole report.

5. The auditory sensory register seems to be much shorter in duration than the visual sensory register.

6. Presynthesis implies that a pattern may be recognized without any sensory input.

Discussion Items

1. Discuss Sperling's experiment and describe how the results indicate a short-duration but large capacity memory system.

2. Why is template theory inadequate to describe the pattern recognition process? How does feature theory deal with these inadequacies?

Answers to Multiple-Choice Items

1. (a) The sensory register contains a large amount of information but only for a brief period.
2. (b) Pattern recognition is the concept which describes the process of determining the meaning of sensory information.
3. (c) Since the information on the sensory register is precategorical, an additional process is necessary to add meaning.
4. (c) The sensory register holds information until it can be processed for meaning.
5. (a) Backward masking studies have been used to confirm Sperlings estimate of the duration of the sensory register.
6. (b) The problem for template theory is that it requires a very rapid search through a large amount of information in long-term memory.

Answers to True-False Items

1. (False) The reason we need a sensory register is because the processing of sensory information requires some time and a memory system is necessary to hold sensory information until it can be processed.
2. (True) With a feature representation, an infinite number of patterns can be constructed from a finite number of features.
3. (True) Pattern recognition is assumed to involve a match between sensory information and long-term memory.

4. (True) Reporting only part of the matrix produces better performance than reporting all of it.

5. (False) The information on the auditory sensory register seems to last longer than information on the visual sensory register.

6. (True) Presynthesis is a concept describing the recognition of a pattern based on expectations rather than on sensory input.

Attention

3

As class begins, you and your friends stop talking and begin listening to the lecture. Today's class is on the topic of attention and the professor is describing something called a *switch model*. As usual, you are trying furiously to take accurate notes. Suddenly the professor asks the class to predict how much unattended information would be processed according to the switch model. Although you have heard everything said thus far, as attested by your detailed notes, neither you nor your friends can answer the professor's question. This is somewhat strange, because the material is actually easy to understand. Once again you realize how difficult it is to simultaneously take good notes and follow the meaning of a lecture. The lecture continues with the professor relating a story about the year she spent in England at Oxford University and her study with a researcher named Broadbent. Your mind begins to wander to your date of the previous evening and soon you are absorbed in thinking about an argument you and your date had. You are only vaguely aware of the professor's voice, and as you continue to be occupied with the disagreement of last night, you have little idea of what the professor is saying.

Common situations such as this illustrate phenomena central to the study of attention. At the heart of attention research is the issue of how many tasks can be done at the same time. Taking notes and understanding a lecture are two different activities. Why is it so difficult to do both simultaneously? Is it because one can only process one source of information at a time? If this is true, what happens to the unattended message? We know that the unattended material activates the sensory receptors and thus must appear on the sensory register. Does the unattended information simply decay from the sensory register because it was not selected for pattern recognition? The locus of attention, before or after pattern recognition, is a theoretical issue with important implications for the fate of unattended material. Thus, it is profitable to consider briefly the relationship among the concepts of sensory registration, pattern recognition, and attention.

Attention, Sensory Register, and Pattern Recognition

As discussed in chapter 2, all incoming information is stored on the sensory register. Some small proportion of that information is then processed through pattern recognition. We must now confront the difficult issue of how information is selected for processing. Our ability to behave consistently and rationally depends upon selecting information from the sensory register which maintains continuity in meaning with what has gone before. The pattern-recognition process must be directed to sensory information consistent in meaning with previous information. Thus, the decision to select particular information for pattern recognition is critical, and the decision to allocate processing resources, such as pattern recognition, is what we mean by attention.

A major focus of research in attention has been the localization of attention in the pattern recognition process. Does the decision to process or respond to sensory information occur prior to activating the meaning of that information? For example, while you are concentrating on your daydreams in a lecture, do you have any idea of the meaning of the lecture material or do you completely block out the unattended material? This question was thoroughly investigated within the framework of filter models of attention.

Filter Models of Attention

When we use the word *attention* in everyday language, as when we say, "Johnny, pay attention," we are referring to the selective aspect of the attentional process. A classic example of the ability to attend selectively is the well-known cocktail-party phenomenon. Suppose you are at a large party, with much good conversation and perhaps even music. The result is a noisy situation. Yet, you have little difficulty "paying attention" to the conversation in which you are involved. More impressively, if someone far across the room should mention your name, you hear it and may even switch your attention to that conversation. Most people have had this experience, which requires ignoring the adjacent conversation and focusing upon a discussion some distance away. How do we accomplish this rather remarkable feat?

Early-Selection Filter Models

Perhaps you can understand this ability by assuming that only one source of information is allowed to reach the stage of meaningful processing. Perhaps unattended information is actively filtered or blocked early in processing such that it never competes for the scarce resources of higher-order processing. Maybe we can attend to one conversation at a cocktail party because all others are successfully filtered or blocked at the sensory level. Such a position is at the heart of what are called early-selection filter theories of attention. *Early selection* means that attention operates early in the information-processing sequence.

Switch Model

According to the early-selection model, attention operates like a simple on-off switch, a light switch, for example. Broadbent (1958) first proposed this model, which subsequently generated a tremendous amount of important research. Operating as a switch, attention serves to direct processing to one input message or channel. This message will be fully analyzed for meaning. Since the switch operates in an all-or-none fashion, however, any additional messages are completely blocked or filtered. At any given time, only one channel is "on." This simple idea explains how we focus on one message and ignore all others, but it also raises an immediate question concerning how we select the appropriate message.

Since we are receiving continuous sensory input or messages, it is important to explain what cues are used to set the switch. In other words, what information determines which message receives attention and, equally important, allows us to continue to attend to this message in the face of other messages? Broadbent suggested that attention is attracted and maintained by sensory or physical attributes of the messages. For example, your attention to various conversations at a cocktail party is controlled by the voice qualities of the people conversing.

One good reason for assuming that physical cues control attention is the relationship between attention, sensory register, and pattern recognition. The relationship between these three concepts is depicted in figure 3.1. Notice that the attention switch occurs prior to pattern recognition. Thus this is an early-selection model because attention operates early in the information-processing sequence, guiding the pattern-recognition selection from the sensory register.

The early-selection idea of the switch model quickly became the focus of experimental tests. With a bit of reflection, we can see that the critical test concerns what is known about the unattended message. Since the switch is set at the level of physical analysis, human subjects should only be able to report physical features of the unattended message, not the meaning of that message. In order to perform such a test, however, some technique is necessary to ensure that the switch is set. Such a paradigm was available by combining dichotic input with a shadowing task.

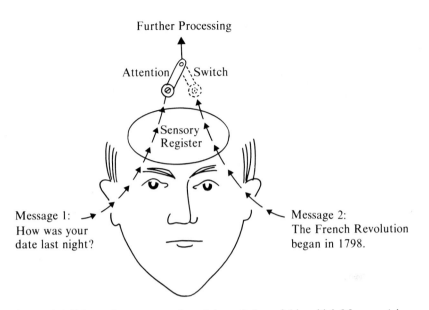

Figure 3.1 Schematic representation of the switch model in which Message 1 is attended and Message 2 is blocked.

Dichotic Listening and Shadowing

The experimental paradigm which proved quite influential in evaluating early-selection filter theories was introduced by Cherry (1953) and consisted of a combination of *dichotic listening and shadowing. Dichotic* means to present different messages to each of the ears at the same time. In the dichotic listening task, the subject is instructed to attend to one message presented to one ear and to ignore the other message simultaneously presented to the other ear, a situation similar to that of the cocktail-party phenomenon. What would Broadbent's switch model predict in the dichotic listening task? The most straightforward expectation concerns the unattended message; since the switch is set to the attended message, the only facts a subject can know about the message in the unattended ear are its physical characteristics. Suppose the two messages are prose passages, one read by a man and the other by a woman. After both messages have been presented, we would expect the subject to be able to report the contents of the message in the attended ear, and according to the switch model, knowledge of the information in the unattended ear should be restricted to the sex of the speaker, physical information. Nothing about the meaning of the unattended message should be available.

But suppose the subject can tell something about the meaning of the unattended message. Does this cause difficulty for the switch model? Not really. The dichotic listening task does not allow us to determine when attention is shifted, and because of the shifts between the attended ear and unattended ear, the subject may know something of the meaning of both messages. What we need is some means of determining on which message the switch is set. The shadowing task serves this function.

Shadowing is a procedure in which the listener is required to follow one of the dichotically presented messages by repeating that message as it occurs. The subject must repeat the shadowed message word by word immediately as each word occurs, a very difficult task, of which you will be convinced of by trying to shadow a friend's conversation. The very difficulty of shadowing provides its primary rationale; a subject effectively shadowing one message cannot possibly switch to the other message. Thus, shadowing switches the subject to one message. Furthermore, if the subject does switch attention to the unattended message, shadowing of the attended message is disrupted. Hence, shadowing not only forces the subject to attend to one message, but has the added advantage of allowing determination of when attention shifts. Shadowing in conjunction with dichotic listening provides an ideal technique to test the switch model. As long as shadowing is effective, the subject should only know about the shadowed message. If shadowing breaks down, the subject might know something about the unattended message at that point.

Experiments using the shadowing technique (e.g., Moray, 1970; Treisman, 1960) resulted in extensive revision of the switch model. The results were inconsistent with Broadbent's initial idea, in that subjects know too much about the unattended message. The content of the nonshadowed channel was shown to influence performance, an event which should not occur if the nonshadowed message is blocked. For example, consider Treisman's experiment in which subjects received dichotic presentation of sentences and were required to shadow the message in one ear. Furthermore, compound sentences were used: for example, *Swann caught the ball, and he ran for a touchdown,* or *Ronstadt sings marvelously, but her selection of music is strange.* The critical manipulation was that half of one sentence was presented to the shadowed ear and the other half presented to the nonshadowed ear. Simultaneously, the same thing happened to the other sentence. The result was as follows: *Swann caught the ball, but her selection of music is strange* occurred in one ear, while *Ronstadt sings marvelously, and he ran for a touchdown* occurred in the other ear.

According to Broadbent's all-or-none switch model, we should have no difficulty shadowing one of these messages and ignoring the other. In fact, people find it virtually impossible to shadow consistently the appropriate message. When the meaning of the shadowed sentence switches to the nonshadowed ear, shadowing is disrupted; the subject experiences confusion, and many times switches to the ear which is supposed to be nonshadowed. Instead of attending to the physical cue of location of the message, the subject follows the meaning of the message.

The critical point for Broadbent's model is that meaning of the nonshadowed message must be getting through to influence the subjects' performance. This is a very important conclusion, which is counter to subjective experience. Although you are attending to one conversation at the cocktail party or to your daydreams during a lecture, you probably are detecting some aspects of the meaning of a second conversation at the party or of the lecture in class. Usually we are completely unaware that this is happening. The question now becomes: How much of the unattended message is analyzed? One response is an alternative early-selection filter model, the attenuator model.

Attenuator Model

Treisman (1964) proposed a more flexible early selection theory, based on a different kind of mechanical switch. Rather than a simple off-on mechanism, Treisman suggested that attention operates more like an attenuator. An attenuator is a switch that allows gradations in the amount of energy passing through it; the volume control on a radio or television receiver is an attenuator which can be adjusted to allow more or less of a signal through. If attention operates as an attenuator, then different amounts of information can come through each channel.

Attention thus becomes a matter of degree in the attenuator model. A schematic diagram of the attenuator model is provided in figure 3.2. Notice in this diagram that most of the information from the attended message is allowed through the attenuator. Simultaneously, some of the unattended message may also reach the level of pattern recognition. The attenuator model is still an early-selection theory in that attention filters information prior to meaningful analysis or pattern recognition. Unlike Broadbent's all-or-none approach, however, the attenuator model allows for the processing of more than one input at a time.

As with the earlier switch model, the attenuator theory must specify what cues attract and hold attention. Consistent with the switch model, Treisman suggests that physical cues are used to tune the attenuator such that changes in the physical cues can serve as the basis for adjusting the attenuation on various inputs. Unlike the switch model, however, the attenuator may also be influenced by the meaning of previously analyzed material. When the attended message switches channels, two events happen: the new information becomes incongruent with the previous information on the attended channel, and the previously unattended channel now contains information congruent with the previously attended channel since some

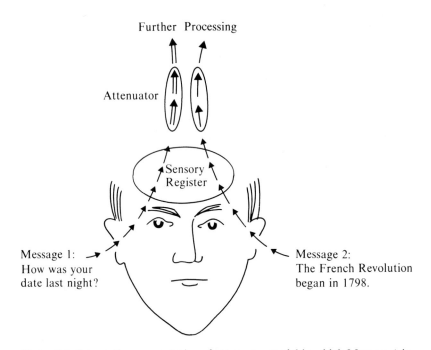

Figure 3.2 Schematic representation of attenuator model in which Message 1 is attended and in which some of Message 2 also gets through for further processing.

of the meaning of the unattended message has been processed. Thus, attenuator control is exerted by both sensory and semantic information. Notice that the attenuator model can now explain the difficulty subjects have shadowing sentences whose meaning alternates from ear to ear.

Let us illustrate the operation of the attenuator model with a common situation which we will call the mini-cocktail-party phenomenon. Suppose you are one of a group of five people. Three of you are involved in the same conversation, while the other two are engaged in a separate discussion close by. If you think about this situation, you will realize that the conversation in which you are directly involved can usually be processed with little difficulty. You can attend to each of the other participants in turn and follow the continuity of the conversation. Assuming the meaning or content of the conversation remains consistent, the switching between the two speakers is accomplished primarily on the basis of physical cues, in this case the voice qualities of the participants. But what of the separate conversation occurring close by? In many cases, you have some idea of what the other people are talking about, although you do not hear everything they say. In terms of the attenuator model, some of the information in the unattended conversation has filtered through, even though the attenuator is set fairly high on this channel. The information picked up from the unattended channel allows you to enter the second conversation if you wish, with some idea of the topic.

To summarize early-selection filter theories, the revision from the switch model to the attenuator model represents loosening of the strictures on how many activities can be done at the same time. As the example illustrates, the attenuator model allows for the processing of more than one message for meaning. The attenuator model, however, was viewed by many theorists as too cumbersome. Furthermore, early selection theories of attention pose a logical problem in that the selection of information based on sensory signals seems to require recognition of information before it is processed. The decision to allocate processing capacity to one message and deny capacity to another message serves the goal of maintaining continuity in meaning. But how can we sift through various sources of information for continuity in meaning without determining the meaning of all inputs? The attenuator model attempts to deal with this issue by suggesting that partial analysis of all signals occurs. Some theorists view this solution as a half-measure. Why not assume that all incoming sensory information activates a meaningful representation? Selective attention then becomes a matter of deciding to which input to respond, which is the fundamental premise of late-selection filter models.

Late-Selection Filter Models

Certain theories, most notably those of Deutsch and Deutsch (1963) and Norman (1968), are known as *late-selection* filter models because selective attention is assumed to operate on response output. In contrast to the assumption that information is filtered or blocked prior to recognition, all information is assumed to activate its long-term memory representation. Very simply, the late-selection model proposes that all information is recognized. The human system, however, is assumed to be limited in the ability to organize a response to all of the sensory input. That is, we are unable to focus or concentrate upon all of the information activated in long-term memory and must select some fraction of that activated information to which we shall respond.

The difference between early- and late-selection theories would appear easy to test. Suppose we have dichotic input with subjects shadowing one of two messages. Why not simply ask the subjects, after both messages have been completed, what they can tell us about the nonshadowed material? In fact, several experiments have done just this and report that subjects know little about the nonshadowed message. However, late-selection theorists do not see these experiments as critical for at least two reasons.

First, a test for nonshadowed material following presentation of both messages requires a considerable delay between presentation and test of the information. During the delay, the nonshadowed material may simply have been forgotten. Even though all sensory information activates long-term memory, the nonshadowed information, which does not require an overt response at presentation, may be rapidly forgotten before the test. If this were the case, a slight modification of the proposed experiment would be more appropriate. Suppose the nonshadowed material is tested immediately after it occurs. That is, the shadowing is stopped at any point and the subject is asked what just occurred on the nonshadowed message. Should the immediate test not reveal some knowledge of the nonshadowed message?

Surprisingly, the late-selection model need not predict that the subject will be aware of unattended material, even if tested immediately. Perhaps a better understanding of this argument, and of the second reason that shadowing experiments are inconclusive in regard to late-selection theories, can be gained by examining a specific experiment. Treisman and Geffen (1967) designed what appeared to be a straightforward test of the late-selection model. Subjects heard two prose passages presented dichotically and were required to shadow one of the messages. In addition, the subjects were given a second task involving both the shadowed and nonshadowed passages. Certain words were designated targets, and anytime a target word occurred in either the shadowed or the nonshadowed message, the subject was to tap on a table. Treisman and Geffen (1967) found that the target words were detected 87 percent of the time in the shadowed message, but only 8 percent of the time in the nonshadowed message. The detection task required a response immediately upon presentation of the target word. Therefore, if all information is recognized, as the late-selection model argues, why are so few targets detected in the nonshadowed message?

The late-selection theorists argue that such results are due to the extraordinary demands of the shadowing task. Shadowing was initially devised for attention research because its very difficulty ensured that a subject focused upon one message. But if we assume that all information is recognized and that the limitation in our processing ability is in organizing responses, the difficulty of the shadowing task makes it impossible to determine how much a subject knows about an unshadowed message. Since only one response can be pursued, the subject cannot shadow one message and simultaneously perform *any* other response to indicate recognition of a nonshadowed message. Indeed, the late-selection theorists argue that awareness itself is a response, and if an integrated response such as shadowing is required for one message, the subject's ability to organize a second response to a different message, even as simple a response as perceptual awareness, will be sorely limited.

You may now realize that we are in a quandary. Early-selection theories require a stringent response to the attended message to ensure that attention is not switched to the unattended message; late-selection theories argue that all messages activate meaning, but a response to two different messages is not possible. It thus appears impossible to design an experiment which would localize attention at the sensory level or at the level of response selection. This sort of dilemma in science typically produces attempts at compromise between the competing theories. In the study of attention, the compromise begins by assuming that perhaps both early and late selections contribute to the difficulty of doing two tasks simultaneously. Rather than view attention as a selective filter located at one point in the processing sequence, a new approach considers *limitation of the entire system* in relation to the particular task requirements.

Capacity Models of Attention

As we have seen, the primary question addressed by theories of attention concerns the limitation on our ability to deal with multiple input. Capacity models of attention (Kahneman, 1973) approach this issue by assuming that our psychological resources are finite; that is, we have a certain amount of *cognitive capacity* to devote to the various tasks confronting us. Different tasks require different amounts of this capacity, and the number of activities which can be done simultaneously is determined by the capacity each requires. If a single task demands intense concentration, no capacity will remain for an additional task. Within this approach, *attention is the process of allocating the resources or capacity to various inputs.* Attention then is important in determining which tasks are accomplished and how well the tasks are performed.

Resource-limited and Data-limited Tasks

Our performance in any situation is under two types of constraints. Norman and Bobrow (1975) have differentiated tasks as imposing either *data limitations* or *resource limitations*. Consideration of this distinction may help us understand how capacity models represent a compromise between early- and late-selection filter models.

Data-limited tasks are those which are difficult or impossible even if we devote all of our processing resources to the task. Suppose you were suddenly put in charge of landing a jet airliner. The entire flight crew contracted food poisoning, and you are selected to land the plane. Most of us know nothing about landing jet planes, but in this situation most of us would be intensely absorbed in the task. In spite of intense concentration, performance is limited by the quality of the data. Alternatively, resource-limited tasks are those on which performance can be improved by increasing the amount of processing. Consider the earlier example of trying to take detailed notes while simultaneously trying to understand a class lecture. Most lectures (we hope) are comprehensible, but in some cases the material is sufficiently complex as to require your full attention. You cannot fully understand the lecture and simultaneously take detailed notes. Comprehension of the lecture would then be a resource-limited task.

The point of this distinction is that performance is limited by the demands a task places on the cognitive system. In the case of data limitation, we are unable to perform because of the poor quality of the information on which we are to act. Data limitations can arise due to lack of knowledge or experience, as in the example of flying an airplane, or because the physical energy received by the receptors is so degraded that sensory processing is impossible. For example, a double exposure on a photograph makes unambiguous interpretation of the picture difficult no matter how hard we try. In either case, data limitations produce poor performance for the same reason that early-selection filters do; that is, the information cannot be adequately processed. Resource limitations are analogous to late-selection filters in that performance is limited by the amount of processing devoted to the task. The sensory data are readily available, but sufficient processing resources are not devoted to the task.

Resource-limited tasks are of most direct relevance to the capacity model. Poor performance under constraints of resource limitation can be improved simply by devoting more resources or concentration to the task. In some cases, however, the primary task requires all available capacity, which implies that other tasks cannot be performed simultaneously. For example, remember when you learned to drive an automobile. Keeping the car on the road and avoiding other vehicles required such intense concentration that even simple tasks were accomplished only with advanced planning. Looking in the rearview mirror or adjusting the radio were painfully deliberate acts. The primary task of driving required all available capacity and interfered with additional activities.

In experimental studies of attention, the capacity demands of various tasks are measured by examining the amount of interference they introduce for other tasks.

Secondary Task Technique and Cognitive Effort

The amount of capacity or effort required by one task will come at the expense of capacity that can be devoted to other tasks. With this assumption, measurement of the capacity demands of a task becomes possible. The technique is quite simple; the subject is instructed to perform a task and is given the impression that this primary task is the most important aspect of the experiment. Almost as an afterthought, however, instructions to perform a secondary task simultaneously with the primary task are also given. Estimates of the capacity required by the primary task are obtained on the secondary task. The harder the primary task, the poorer will be the performance on the secondary task (*cf.* Johnston, Greenberg, Fisher, & Martin, 1970; Britton & Tesser, 1982).

For example, consider an experiment from Ellis's laboratory. This experiment (Tyler, Hertel, McCallum, & Ellis, 1979) tested the proposition that memory for words will improve as the amount of *cognitive effort* devoted to the words increases. To vary the amount of effort or capacity exerted, the words were presented as anagrams and as missing elements in sentence-completion tasks. Anagrams are words whose letters are scrambled, such as *croodt*. Can you solve this anagram? How about a different anagram for the same word, *dortoc*? The second form is easier for most people than is the first. (The word, by the way, is *doctor.*) To vary effort, one group of subjects received hard anagrams and a second group received easy anagrams for the same words. To assure that the hard anagrams required more capacity, the subjects were required to perform a second task simultaneously with the anagram task. The second task was to press a button as rapidly as possible when a tone sounded. The speed of the response to the tone was taken as a measure of capacity required by the anagram task. The more capacity required by the anagram task, the less will be available to tone detection, and the slower will be the reaction to the tone.

A similar logic prevailed in the sentence-completion task. Subjects were given sentences in which, in some cases, the word was clearly implied. For example, this sentence "The girl was awakened by her frightening _____" clearly implied the word *dream*. In this two-choice task in which two words are presented (*dream* versus *table*) the word *dream* is easy. Other sentences contained words in which the implication was not obvious and hence were more difficult.

Tone detection indeed was slower in the hard-anagram condition than in the easy-anagram condition. This outcome then permitted an interpretation of the memory data in terms of differential capacity requirements. Hard anagrams produced better memory for the words than did easy anagrams, presumably due to the greater effort required by hard anagrams. Similarly, words that did not easily fit in the sentence (high-effort condition) were better recalled than those in the low-effort condition. The basic results are shown in figure 3.3, which plots recall as a function of cognitive effort.

The remaining issue is how to explain the effects of cognitive effort on recall. Two reasonable possibilities are that the allocation of capacity or processing resources leads to a more elaborated memory trace and/or to a more distinctive memory trace. Since this issue concerns the nature of

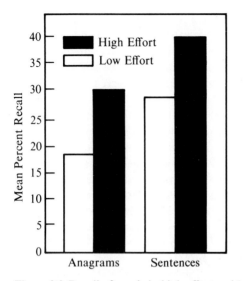

Figure 3.3 Recall of words in high-effort and low-effort anagrams and sentences. (From "Cognitive Effort and Memory" by S. W. Tyler, Hertel, P. T., McCallum, M. C., and Ellis, H. C., *Journal of Experimental Psychology: Human Learning and Memory,* 1979, *5,* 607–617. Copyright 1979 by the American Psychological Association. Reprinted by permission of the publisher and authors.)

encoding, we shall return to this topic in chapter 5. Our purpose in mentioning it here is simply to call your attention to the question of interpretation. The point of this experiment, *for present purposes,* is that the capacity demands of various tasks differ in measurable ways. Just as in the example of learning to drive, some tasks may require so much capacity that performing other tasks simultaneously is very difficult. Alternatively, some tasks, such as solving the easy anagrams or driving a car when one has years of driving experience, require little capacity. Indeed, some tasks seem to require no central processing capacity. Such tasks are said to be *automatic.*

Automatic Processing

Automatic processing is a very important concept within the capacity model. *Automaticity* refers to the apparent lack of central capacity requirements for a particular task. This is an important development because tasks that are performed automatically leave resources for other tasks; other tasks can be performed simultaneously with a task that is automatic. Driving a car has probably become automatic for you. Rarely do you have to concentrate on steering or braking, and you can leave processing capacity for carrying on conversation, listening to the radio, and thinking about other things.

The secondary task technique is used to study automaticity in the laboratory. Again, the rationale of the secondary task method involves measuring the amount of interference between two tasks. If a particular task can be performed as well with another task as it is alone, that task is assumed to require no capacity.

A very nice demonstration of automaticity is provided in an early experiment from Posner's laboratory (Posner and Boies, 1971). The primary experimental task was letter matching; the subject had to decide, as quickly as possible, whether two letters were the same or different. The letters were presented successively and were preceded by a warning signal. Specifically, the warning signal occurred to alert the subject to an up-coming letter, one-half second later the first letter appeared, and one-second later the second letter followed. As soon as the second letter appeared, the subject was to judge whether it was the same as the first letter. In addition to the letter-matching task, a tone-detection task was also included. The tone could occur at any stage of the letter-matching task, which allowed use of the reaction time to the tone to estimate the capacity requirements of each aspect of the letter-matching task.

Reaction times to the tone are shown in figure 3.4 as a function of the stages in letter matching. First note that responding to the tone becomes faster after the warning signal than before the warning signal. Presumably, the subject becomes more alert and concentrates more at the onset of the warning signal. Next, you see in figure 3.4 that the reaction to the tone is not slowed by presentation of the first letter. This is the important result for our purposes. During pattern recognition of the first letter, responses to the tone are not disrupted, a clear case of two activities being done at the same time. The tone is not filtered or blocked, as filter theory might suppose, but rather both visual pattern recognition and auditory-detection tasks are performed simultaneously. We shall return to this point after a brief discussion of the remainder of the data presented in figure 3.4. Following the first letter, reaction time to the tone increases substantially. This result is reasonably interpreted as due to rehearsal of the first letter. Rehearsal does require capacity, which disrupts responding to the tone. Reaction time increases even further following the second letter, the stage at which the decision about the letters is made. The decision process occupies even more capacity than rehearsal, which leads to this further increase in reaction time.

The major point of this experiment is that recognition of letters does not disrupt reaction time to auditory signals. Processing of the letter is automatic; little of the cognitive resources is required for this task. Of course, this result holds for college students who have had much practice in letter recognition. Imagine a young child just learning the alphabet. Letter recognition is likely to require much more effort, and only after considerable practice will it develop to an automatic skill.

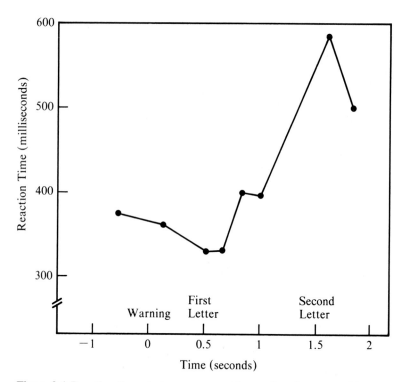

Figure 3.4 Reaction times to tone as a secondary task to letter matching. (From "Components of Attention" by M. I. Posner and S. J. Boies, *Psychological Review*, 1971, *78*, 391–408. Copyright 1971 by the American Psychological Association. Reprinted by permission of the publisher and authors.)

In a recent paper, Hasher and Zacks (1979) have extended the concept of automaticity to a variety of memory processes. The interested student should consult this important paper for further discussion of effort and automatic processing.

Automaticity and Reading

You can easily see that the development of automaticity is important for normal functioning in everyday tasks. The Posner experiment, for example, is directly applicable to reading. Reading requires rapid access to the meaning of verbal units such as paragraphs, sentences, and words. Yet, reading presumably begins with letter recognition. If each letter recognition required much effort, reading would be painfully slow. Not only is letter recognition automatic, but access to word meaning appears to occur with little effort. The primary evidence for this assertion comes from studies of the *Stroop effect.*

The Stroop effect occurs in a special kind of dual-task situation. For example, suppose you are given a list of color names, *Red, Blue, Green,* and *Orange,* but each word is printed in an ink color different from the color word. *Red* is printed in blue ink. Your job is to name the ink colors as rapidly as possible. The task in no way requires processing or even noticing the word. Nonetheless, incongruent word and ink color, *Red* printed in blue, produces slower responses than congruent conditions, *Red* printed in red. Word meaning appears to be processed and then interferes with color naming, even though the task does not require word processing. Word meaning is automatically processed and cannot be ignored.

Data such as these have led to the argument that automaticity is a very important step in learning to read. But how is it that a task becomes automatic?

Development of Automaticity

Some psychological processes never require central processing capacity. Initial sensory registration and feature analysis, for example, are always automatic processes. Neisser (1967) called these preattentive processes because they never require conscious effort. Beyond this initial stage of processing, however, we have seen that more complex tasks, such as driving and accessing word meaning, develop from effortful activities to automatic tasks. How does this happen?

Although the precise mechanisms underlying the development of automaticity are unknown, the critical ingredient in automatization clearly is practice. The importance of practice has been clear in the examples we have used thus far, driving and reading. Many other tasks, typing for example, also become automatized with sufficient practice. You must realize that we are talking about more than just increasing performance or skill with practice. Certainly good practice (not just practice per se) does make better, if not perfect, but automatization refers to performance of the task with fewer cognitive resources. A well-practiced golf swing is not only likely to be better, but it also requires less thought.

Some tasks may never become automatic, but practice still improves performance. The task posed by college courses, which we assume is the comprehension or understanding of certain material, will not be automated, but it does become easier with effective practice. We all know that you "learn how to study" as you progress through the college years. Perhaps this ability is due in large part to focusing processing capacity on the task at hand. You become more proficient at extracting salient materials from lectures and readings, not so much because "you learn what to look for," as because your ability to focus or concentrate on material sharpens. Thus, your general understanding of the material improves, with the typical result that you earn better grades as a senior than as a freshman even though you may spend less time with the books. So effective practice is important to tasks that require processing capacity, even those which do not become automated. There is no trick or necessarily a shortcut; if you want to become proficient at intellectual or motor-skills tasks, you must practice well.

Attention and Consciousness

Attention historically has been linked to the concept of consciousness. One aspect of what people mean by consciousness is that it refers to the contents of immediate experiences, be they thoughts or environmental input. We typically are aware of these events, and in that sense, consciousness and awareness are similar. We may also say that the contents of immediate experience are receiving attention in that processing capacity is devoted to these events. In this sense, consciousness may be seen as a process of allocating processing capacity, not as a place in the mind.

It would be a mistake, however, to equate attention, or allocation of capacity, with awareness. A simple example will convince you of this fact. The old joke about people who cannot walk and chew gum simultaneously reflects our belief that walking requires little or no capacity. Certainly we usually are not aware of walking. But the next time you are walking with a friend, ask that person to add two numbers which require a carrying operation, such as 63 + 49. Even the most coordinated person is likely to stop walking while computing this simple addition problem. Why? Walking does require some capacity, albeit a small amount, and solving the addition problem requires the capacity previously used by walking.

The point is that we cannot equate the use of capacity with consciousness and awareness. Perhaps it is safe to say that consciousness and awareness reflect the amount of capacity required by a task. Large-capacity allocations will be accompanied by awareness of the task, and perhaps the mysterious unconsciousness is the domain of processes requiring little or no capacity.

Summary

We began this discussion of attention with the example of the difficulty of doing two activities simultaneously. Filter theories of attention explain this situation by proposing active mechanisms to block unattended material. Early-selection filter theories argue that unattended material is blocked prior to pattern recognition, while late-selection theories suggest that responses can be organized to only one input. In either case, the limitations on processing capacity are described as rather inflexible mechanisms actively blocking unwanted input. The active blocking of information, particularly before its recognition, raises the logical problem of how we select material without knowing its meaning. But the alternative, late-selection filter, is not totally satisfying because of the many examples of the ability to accomplish two tasks simultaneously.

As a general alternative to filter theories, the capacity model is more flexible in its description of processing limitations. Attention is viewed as central processing. A certain amount of this processing capacity is available for tasks, and the number of tasks that can be performed simultaneously are limited only by the amount of capacity each requires. Thus, within the capacity approach, doing two things at once is perfectly reasonable. This is particularly the case when a task becomes automated. Automatic tasks require no central capacity either because of the nature of the task or because of extended practice of the task. Automaticity of processing frees capacity for other tasks, making simultaneous tasks even more possible. Attention becomes a decision to allocate processing resources. Automatic tasks do not require such decisions; in other cases, capacity is allotted until all of the resources are exhausted. Remaining tasks which require but do not receive capacity simply cannot be performed.

Multiple-Choice Items

1. Which theory of attention is least flexible in allowing us to do more than one task at a time?
   a. early-selection filter theory
   b. late-selection filter theory
   c. attenuator theory
   d. capacity theory

2. Experimental tests of early- and late-selection theories are very difficult because:
   a. the difference between the two theories is slight
   b. the primary task required by the late-selection theory is too rigorous to allow early selection to occur
   c. early selection would then rule out any possibility of late selection
   d. the tasks required by early-selection theory to occupy attention will also occupy attention according to late selection

3. The primary difference between resource- and data-limited tasks is:
   a. how much effort is exerted
   b. how many activities can be done at the same time
   c. whether additional effort can improve performance
   d. whether a shadowing task is used or the subject is instructed just to pay attention

4. Studies of dichotic listening show that:
   a. nonshadowed material is not processed for any meaning
   b. nonshadowed material is processed for some meaning
   c. shadowed material is not processed for meaning
   d. shadowed and nonshadowed material do not differ in degree of meaningful processing

5. In the secondary task technique, capacity is measured by:
   a. the sum of reaction times to primary and secondary tasks
   b. the difference in reaction time to primary and secondary tasks
   c. reaction time to the primary task
   d. reaction time to the secondary task

6. The primary determinant of automaticity is:
   a. the material
   b. the other tasks required
   c. the amount and kind of practice
   d. genetic

True-False Items

1. One of the reasons why we need the concept of attention is to guide selection of information from the sensory register.

2. Capacity theory of attention argues that it is difficult or impossible to do two activities at the same time.

3. If we are allocating attention or capacity to a task, we are then also aware of that task.

4. The difficulty of shadowing makes it a useful technique for testing switch models, but also makes it useless for late-selection models of attention.

5. The late-selection theory of attention suggests that we are aware or conscious of all sensory input.

6. The Stroop effect suggests that access to word meaning may be automatic.

Discussion Items

1. Describe the relationship between sensory register, pattern recognition, and attention. Be careful to include a discussion of why attention is necessary within this framework.

2. Discuss the development of capacity models of attention from the research on early- and late-selection filter models.

3. Discuss the effect that the complexity and difficulty of a task have on attention.

Answers to Multiple-Choice Items

1. (a) According to early-selection filter theory, unattended information receives no processing, and it would not be possible to do anything with the unattended information.

2. (d) Tests of early- and late-selection theories are difficult because early-selection theory requires a stringent shadowing task to ensure attention is paid to one message, and the task then makes it impossible to organize a response to unattended material, according to late-selection theory.

3. (c) Data-limited tasks are those in which the sensory information is so impoverished that no response is possible regardless of effort, while resource-limited tasks are those on which better performance results from more extensive effort.

4. (b) Shadowing studies have shown that some of the unattended information is processed for meaning.

5. (d) The capacity required by the primary task can be measured by the reaction time to the secondary task.

6. (c) Automaticity results primarily from extensive practice of a task.

Answers to True-False Items

1. (True) Since the sensory register contains more information than can be processed, some mechanism is needed to selectively process from the sensory register.

2. (False) According to capacity theory, the number of tasks which can be performed simultaneously depends on the amount of capacity required by each task.

3. (False)   Some tasks, such as walking, require such small capacity that we rarely are aware of performing these tasks.

4. (True)   A difficult task is required to ensure attention within a switch model, but a difficult task prevents the organization of a response to unattended material, according to the late-selection theory.

5. (False)   Although all input reaches the level of pattern recognition, according to late selection theory, only the attended information reaches the level of awareness.

6. (True)   The Stroop effect suggests that the meaning of words is automatically activated even when some other aspect of the word, such as ink color, is attended.

Short-Term Memory

4

Short-term memory is the first concept we encounter that is designed to explain events occurring at the conscious level. Consequently, the characteristics of short-term memory will be easily recognized as part of our everyday experience. How many times have you been introduced to a small group of people, and as soon as the introduction is completed, you turn to the first person introduced and simply cannot remember the person's name? Equally frustrating is the experience of obtaining a telephone number from Directory Assistance and having no pencil or pen to record the number. What do you do? Usually, most of us repeat the number rapidly until we dial it, but if anyone talks to us or we even think of something other than the number before it is dialed, we must make another call to Directory Assistance. A different characteristic of short-term memory emerges when you undertake a grocery-shopping errand. If the grocery list includes only a few items, you have little difficulty remembering the items, perhaps supplementing memory with some repetition. If the list is longer and has approximately five items or more, an energy-conscious shopper writes the items down.

As with the other conscious memory phenomena, we are most aware of short-term memory when it fails, as each of these examples illustrates. Failures, however, are quite instructive for students of memory in understanding the system. These examples, for instance, illustrate the two cardinal attributes of short-term memory. First, information is retained briefly, as shown in the instances of introduction to new people and receiving a number from Directory Assistance, unless the information is maintained by repetition. Second, short-term memory has quite limited capacity; long lists cannot be easily maintained.

The question now becomes: Are short-term memory and long-term memory different systems? It is important to understand the implications of either a *yes* or *no* answer in order to really understand much contemporary research and discussion of short-term memory.

To argue that short-term memory and long-term memory are completely different systems implies that the principles of memory are different for the two systems. In other words, variables or factors which affect retention, such as study time, time between input and test, and meaning and organization of material, may operate differently in short-term memory and in long-term memory. If this is so, we must then develop different theories for the two kinds of memory. Alternatively, if we argue that short-term memory and long-term memory are not different systems, then we are in the position of claiming that a unitary set of principles can explain all aspects of memory. The challenge for this position is then to describe the apparent differences between short-term memory and long-term memory without appealing to different principles.

We shall examine both approaches in chapter 4, beginning with a general theory which places short-term memory in the context of an information-processing model and argues that it is separate from long-term memory. Then we shall describe research designed to demonstrate clear differences between the systems and also the reaction to this research. Finally, we review a position which views memory as a unitary system.

The Modal Model of Memory

Richard Atkinson and Richard Shiffrin proposed a view of the entire memory system in 1968, which subsequently became so influential that it is known as the "modal" or typical information-processing model of memory. It is also known as the stage model of memory because it proposes that the flow of information moves in stages through the memory processes. Their model is particularly pertinent at this point, because it concentrates heavily upon short-term memory, including the relationship between sensory register, short-term memory, and long-term memory. A schematic view of the model is presented in figure 4.1.

According to Atkinson and Shiffrin's model, incoming information flows from the sensory register to short-term memory to permanent storage in long-term memory. The transfer of information from the sensory register to short-term memory is controlled by attention, described in chapter 3 as the decision to allocate the pattern-recognition process to sensory information. Once in short-term memory, the information is subject to *control processes,* which are operations serving a variety of memory functions. For example, the most important control process is *rehearsal.* Rehearsal serves two functions: to maintain information in short-term memory and to transfer information from short-term memory to long-term memory.

Other control processes include *coding,* which involves attaching appropriate information from long-term memory to the short-term information. For example, a telephone number is easier to remember if it is coded into larger units than to be dealt with as single digits: 1-800-555-1212 becomes one, eight hundred, five fifty-five, twelve, twelve. The rules

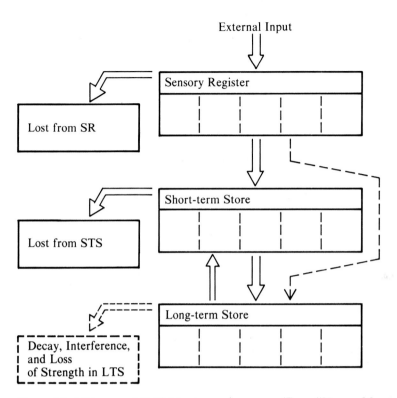

External Input

Sensory Register

Lost from SR

Short-term Store

Lost from STS

Long-term Store

Decay, Interference,
and Loss
of Strength in LTS

Figure 4.1 Atkinson and Shiffrin's stages of memory. (From "Human Memory: A Proposed System and Its Control Processes" by R. C. Atkinson and R. M. Shiffrin, in K. W. Spence and J. T. Spence, Eds., *The Psychology of Learning and Motivation: Advances in Theory and Research,* Vol. 2. New York: Academic Press, 1968. Copyright 1968 by Academic Press. Used by permission.)

for transforming the single digits are retrieved from long-term memory and applied to the string of single digits in short-term memory. The strategies for retrieving information from long-term memory are another important short-term memory control process. For example, if you are asked this question, "Who is the primary author of the switch model of attention?" your strategy may be to activate long-term information concerning "names associated with the psychology of attention." These names are then retrieved to short-term memory where you decide which is the correct answer.

You should now see that the concept of short-term memory entails much more than just memory for information after a short period of time. Short-term memory is a conceptual system which not only stores information, but also serves as a work space for rehearsing, coding, retrieving, and decision making. An important feature of the Atkinson and Shiffrin model is that the short-term memory system has a severely limited capacity. This implies not only that a small number of items can be stored, but also that the control processes require some of the limited capacity. Rehearsal, for example, may guard some information against loss from short-term memory, but this gain comes at the expense of other items. Only so much can be rehearsed at one time, as can be proved by trying to repeat rapidly the numbers 58615294 while simultaneously reading this text. In general, the control processes expedite the processing of some information, but facilitation comes at the expense of other information. This event is another instance of the assumption of limited-processing capacity discussed in chapter 3.

Much of the research surrounding short-term memory has the ultimate goal of establishing the characteristics of short-term memory, particularly to demonstrate that these characteristics differ from those of long-term memory. Such research is essential to establishing a distinction between short- and long-term memory systems, because elaborate theoretical descriptions of two different memory systems would be unnecessary if there were no evidence for two different types of memory.

Characteristics of Short-Term Memory

Three basic characteristics have been proposed to distinguish short-term memory from long-term memory. These characteristics, *trace life, storage capacity,* and *nature of the code,* also distinguish short-term memory from the sensory register. Remember that the sensory register is characterized by a very brief trace, stored in a veridical form in a large-capacity system. As the information moves on to short-term memory, the trace life increases somewhat, although it is still brief by the standards of long-term memory. The information is transformed into a phonetic code in short-term memory, and the capacity of the system is considerably smaller than either the sensory register or long-term memory. We shall now briefly consider the evidence for these characteristics, evidence which is crucial to any conceptual distinction between short- and long-term memory systems.

Duration of Short-Term Memory

Among the modern classics of experimental psychology is the research claiming to demonstrate a short-term trace. Very similar experiments were reported almost simultaneously by Brown (1958) in England and Peterson and Peterson (1959) in the United States. The experimental procedure, now known as the *Brown-Peterson paradigm,* is quite simple. Subjects are shown three items consisting of nonsense syllables or words for three seconds. Memory for these triads is then tested following a retention interval which varies from 0 to 18 seconds. Such a task does not seem to be particularly difficult: How hard can it be to remember three simple items over a period as short as 18 seconds? Indeed, the task would be no challenge at all if the subjects were allowed to repeat the items during the retention interval. This is not the case, however, because a *rehearsal prevention* task is inserted between presentation of the material and the recall test. A rehearsal prevention task is an activity which prohibits the subject from repeating the test items. For example, the subject may be required to count backward by threes from a designated number, a task which is sufficiently difficult that rehearsal becomes impossible. We are then in a position to examine memory in the absence of rehearsal.

The typical results of a Brown-Peterson experiment are shown in figure 4.2. The critical aspect of these results is the rapid forgetting that occurs over the very short retention interval. Notice that after 18 seconds, only about 10 percent of the material is remembered. Such a poor memory after such a brief period of time was a startling finding which later served as one basis for claiming a separate, short-duration memory system.

When these data first appeared in the late 1950s, they were strikingly in contrast to what was known about forgetting, mainly from studies of long-term memory. At that time, forgetting was seen as a gradual process occurring as the result of *interference*. Interference is produced by the intervention of other material between the presentation of a to-be-remembered event and the memory test. For example, suppose you have a history class immediately after your psychology class. Your memory for the material learned about psychology is subject to interference from the material learned about history. We shall discuss theories of forgetting at a later point, but it is critical at the moment to notice that interference implies that memory failure results from competition among stored information. Forgotten material does not go away, but rather loses in the momentary competition for expression.

The rapid forgetting in the Brown-Peterson paradigm challenged a unitary view of interference as the cause of forgetting. Not only did massive forgetting occur in a very short time, but also the source of interference in the Brown-Peterson task was not initially apparent. Some theorists then claimed that short-term memory is subject to *decay* of information, a position on forgetting which differs substantially from interference. Decay results from disuse, failure to rehearse in this situation, and implies that the forgotten material has disappeared from memory altogether. The important point to note here is that the Brown-Peterson data not only suggest a brief trace in short-term memory, but also seem to imply completely different principles of forgetting in short-term memory and long-term memory. It is the claim for different principles in forgetting that established these experiments as controversial in the attempt to describe memory as being successive, separate stages.

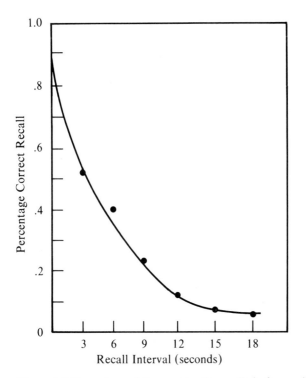

Figure 4.2 Percentage of items correctly recalled after various retention intervals. (From "Short-Term Retention of Individual Verbal Items" by L. R. Peterson and M. J. Peterson, *Journal of Experimental Psychology,* 1959, *58,* 193–198. Copyright 1959 by the American Psychological Association. Reprinted by permission of the publisher and authors.)

The Brown-Peterson paradigm also establishes the importance of rehearsal in maintaining information in short-term memory, a point later emphasized by Atkinson and Shiffrin's inclusion of rehearsal among the important control processes. Rehearsal not only serves to counteract the short-term trace, but also serves as the mechanism of transfer to long-term memory. In this regard, a useful distinction can be drawn between two types of rehearsal.

Rote or *maintenance rehearsal* functions primarily to keep information active in short-term memory. Maintenance rehearsal corresponds to simple repetition of information. *Elaborative rehearsal* involves relating the information to other known information, a process involving meaning. For example, if the words *dog, tree,* and *cat* are to be remembered, elaborative rehearsal might involve the construction of a relationship among the words, even to forming a visual image of a dog chasing a cat up a tree.

Elaborative rehearsal functions to quickly transfer information to long-term memory. Thus, the two types of rehearsal extend the trace life of short-term information but in different ways. In either case, you also should keep in mind the trade-off between rehearsal and capacity. The rehearsal process may increase the duration of some information, but rehearsal requires some of the limited capacity which is then unavailable to other items. We now turn to a discussion of studies designed to demonstrate the limitations on capacity of short-term memory.

Capacity of Short-Term Memory

In an influential paper Miller (1956) argued that the capacity of short-term memory ranged from five to nine items, with the average being seven items. These estimates were obtained from Miller's study of immediate memory span performance. Immediate memory span is measured by presenting a list of items, digits, letters, or words and determining how many items can be recalled in their correct serial order immediately after presentation. In this task, Miller noticed that most people remembered between five and nine items, which suggested that short-term memory has quite limited capacity. It is no accident, by the way, that the standard telephone number is seven digits; the telephone company takes Miller's estimate quite seriously in its effort to reduce the number of calls to Directory Assistance.

Seven items may seem an unrealistically small number, especially when we consider that short-term memory must funnel vast amounts of information from the sensory register into long-term memory. Notice, however, that "item" has not yet been defined. An item is a *chunk* of information ranging from a single letter to an idea expressed by a paragraph. At this point, another of Atkinson and Shiffrin's control processes becomes important. As information arrives in short-term memory, relationships may be detected among individual items which allow the items to be organized or "chunked" into a single unit. Simple examples of chunking include grouping individual letters, *c-a-t,* into a single unit, *cat.* More complex chunking involves detailed linguistic descriptions that are organized into single idea units. For example, this description "The man, whose skin was wrinkled and leathery, had silver-white hair and supported his slow, limping walk with a cane" might be reduced to a single idea, "The man is old."

Regardless of the complexity of chunking, the process of integrating or organizing discrete items into larger units is actually an example of elaborative rehearsal. To form a coherent unit, it is necessary to detect a relationship among the discrete items based on what is known about the items. What is known about the items is stored in long-term memory. Thus, chunking must require retrieving information from long-term memory to aid organization of items in short-term memory.

Chunking is a useful process which can serve to offset the extreme capacity limitations of short-term memory. More information can be stored by increasing the information in each unit, thus making the limited number of chunks rich in information value. As with rehearsal, however, the chunking process consumes short-term memory capacity, and the advantage of chunking certain information comes at the cost of other information, which may be lost due to lack of rehearsal. To illustrate this point, consider the difficulty of coding 7-3-1-9-8-0 as a single number while simultaneously repeating or rehearsing the words, *horse, justice,* and *green.* Again, we see that critical decisions concerning allocation of processing capacity must be made in short-term memory.

The limited capacity of short-term memory contrasts sharply with the large storage capability of long-term memory. Everything we know is assumed to be stored in long-term memory, a very large amount of information indeed. This marked difference in storage capacity is then taken as additional evidence for separate systems of short-term memory and long-term memory.

Coding in Short-Term Memory

Another distinction between short-term memory and long-term memory is the memory code of each system. Long-term memory is assumed to be based on a semantic code, and short-term memory is acoustically or phonetically coded. Information is stored in long-term memory in terms of its meaning, whereas sound patterns are remembered in short-term memory. Research supporting these assumptions has demonstrated greater confusion among semantically similar words in long-term memory and greater confusion among acoustically similar words in short-term memory.

For example, Baddeley (1966, a, b) describes experiments in which subjects were asked to remember either a five-word list or a ten-word list. The shorter list is within the capacity of short-term memory, while the longer list exceeds short-term capacity and must reflect the operation of long-term memory. In both the five-word and ten-word lists, all of the words either sounded alike (e.g., *bat, hat, cat*), had a similar meaning (e.g., *tiny, small little*), or were unrelated (e.g., *bat, desk, tiny*). The five-word lists were poorly recalled when all of the words sounded alike, but similarity of meaning produced recall much like that of unrelated words. With the ten-word list, however, semantic similarity produced poor recall, and acoustically similar words were recalled as well as were the unrelated words. This outcome can be understood by assuming that similar memory codes produce confusion among the items. Since acoustic similarity but not semantic similarity disrupted memory for short lists, Baddeley argues that short-term memories are acoustically coded. Semantic confusion in the longer lists suggests existence of a meaning code in long-term memory. Thus, studies such as Baddeley's are offered as further evidence that different kinds of information are stored at different stages in the retention interval. If it is valid, such a conclusion would suggest a useful distinction between short-term memory and long-term memory.

Additional Evidence for Short-Term Memory

Short-term memory has a brief trace and small capacity and is acoustically coded, whereas long-term memory is assumed to be permanent, to have a large capacity, and to be semantically coded. These characteristics are the primary distinctions between short- and long-term memory systems. These distinctions, however, can also be used to interpret other situations, and to the extent that the interpretation is reasonable, additional evidence is provided for the short-term-long-term distinction. Simply stated, if a particular phenomenon can be better understood by the assumption of a difference between short-term memory and long term memory, we have another reason for accepting the distinction.

The Serial Position Effect

A good example of this approach is to apply the short-term–long-term distinction to the *serial position curve*. The serial position curve depicts the accuracy of recall of an ordered list as a function of the input position of an item in the list. Early items are recalled well and so are the last items, but the middle items are remembered poorly, resulting in a U-shaped function such as that depicted in figure 4.3. Examples of the serial position effect are quite common. Consider a young child learning the alphabet; *A B C* and *X Y Z* are not a problem for the child, but the middle letters are the last added to the child's knowledge. Many children in the initial stages of alphabet learning even treat *L M N O P* as a single letter. Knowing about the serial position effect can help you prepare for serial rote memory tests. Whether you are faced with remembering a long grocery list or the names of the bones in the hand for a biology test, you can be sure that the first and last items will be best remembered. Thus, you may want to give special attention to the middle items in preparing for a test involving serial retention.

Why does the serial position effect occur? One explanation is based entirely on the distinction between short- and long-term memory systems. The early items are recalled well, which is called the *primacy effect,* because they are the first to enter short-term memory and thus allow adequate opportunity for rehearsal and subsequent transfer to long-term memory. The middle items, however, enter short-term memory while the

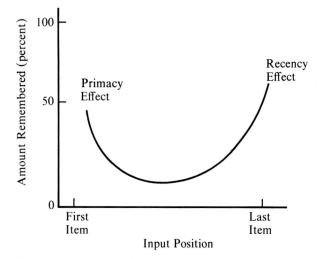

Figure 4.3 An idealized version of a serial position curve showing memory as a function of the input position of the material.

first items are being rehearsed, and hence little capacity is available to rehearse the middle items. Therefore, the middle items are not likely to be transferred to long-term memory. The last items in the list are also well remembered, a finding called the *recency effect,* presumably because these items are still in short-term memory at the time of recall.

This explanation of the serial position curve was tested by Glanzer and Cunitz (1966) in an experiment which demonstrated that the primacy and recency effects can be manipulated independently. In one condition, subjects were given a list of twenty words to remember, but after the words were presented and before the memory test, the subjects were required to perform a rehearsal prevention task. After the rehearsal prevention activity, the normal recency effect did not occur, presumably because rehearsal prevention allowed time for the last items to decay from short-term memory prior to the recall test. The primacy effect was unchanged by rehearsal prevention as should be the case if the early list items are recalled from long-term memory. In the second part of the same research, the primacy effect was reduced by increasing the rate at which the items were presented. Faster presentation rates decrease the time available for rehearsal and thus should reduce the probability of items entering long-term memory. Since the primacy effect is due to the early list items reaching long-term memory, the decrease in primacy effects with faster presentation rates is consistent with interpretation of the serial position curve as the joint operation of short-term memory and long-term memory.

Clinical Case Studies

Another indirect argument for the distinction between short-term memory and long-term memory comes from the study of persons who suffered serious head injury resulting in *amnesia*. In some cases, these patients demonstrated normal performance on a memory span task, but had trouble learning new information. This pattern suggests that short-term memory is functioning normally, but that long-term memory is impaired (e.g., Baddeley & Warrington, 1970; Milner, 1970). In other cases, memory for preinjury information remains intact and new, long-term learning is possible, but immediate memory span is far below normal (e.g., Shallice & Warrington, 1970; Warrington, Logue, & Pratt, 1971). In at least one case, the patient had an immediate memory span of one item!

These reports seem to provide a physiological basis for the distinction between short- and long-term memory systems. Certain cases involve the loss of long-term information, whereas others result in inability to retain new information. It is easy to imagine that the former cases reflect damage to brain mechanisms corresponding to long-term memory, and the latter cases indicate that short-term memory mechanisms have been damaged.

Summary of the Short-Term–Long-Term Distinction

To this point what emerges from the theory and research is the suggestion of two distinct memory systems which obey different principles and produce differential retention. Immediate memory for new events is very fragile because short-term memory decays rapidly and has small capacity. In contrast, the information which progresses through short-term memory is stored permanently in long-term memory. Long-term memory has a huge capacity, storing all of the knowledge we have of the world. Whatever forgetting occurs in long-term memory is the result of interference produced by intervening events. The rapid forgetting in short-term memory occurs due to decay or disuse, a condition which can be prevented with constant rehearsal. Rehearsal, however, requires a code which is easily repeated. Sound patterns satisfy this requirement, and therefore a phonetic code in short-term memory becomes highly adaptive. It is much more difficult to imagine rote repetition of visual images and of meaning codes, yet these codes would be quite efficient in long-term memory where decay is no problem and rehearsal is unnecessary.

In summary, the stage model assumes that a different set of principles is required to understand both short-term memory and long-term memory. Since the major demarcation between the memory systems is the length of time after presentation of the material, the laws of memory would differ as a function of the length of the retention interval. As plausible as this theory seems, it is not perfectly clear why the memory system would operate completely differently for recent versus past events. Therefore, concern over this issue led to critical reexamination of the evidence for separate short- and long-term memories.

One Memory System or Two Memory Systems?

The examples of short-term retention given at the beginning of the chapter are real enough, and the experimental work just discussed may seem to require that there be separate short- and long-term memory systems. If we accept this distinction, we must then try to establish at least two, and probably three, completely different sets of principles governing memory, one each for the sensory register, short-term memory, and long-term memory. Furthermore, we also need to try to understand the relationships among the systems. It is not difficult to imagine what a complicated activity this becomes. Consequently, psychologists have carefully examined the short-term-long-term distinction to ensure that it provides the best description of memory. As a result, many theorists now contend that two separate systems are unnecessary and propose an alternative which assumes only one memory system. Let us now examine the arguments against separate memory systems or stores. We will see serious objections to the stage model and to the idea of distinct memory systems.

Forgetting in Short-Term Memory

We have seen that a major distinction between long-term memory and short-term memory is the duration of the trace. The Brown-Peterson data show rapid forgetting for recent experiences if rehearsal is prevented, and this rapid forgetting is explained by assuming that unrehearsed information decays rapidly. Long-term memories, however, remain available in the absence of any use or rehearsal, as is evident by consulting any of myriad facts we know but have not thought about recently. Decay, then, must not be operating in long-term memory; consequently, some other principle of forgetting must control failure of long-term memory. Thus, we now see that the differences in the duration of short- and long-term memory traces points to a more fundamental difference: the principles of forgetting differ in the two systems. This fundamental difference in the laws of forgetting is proposed as a major distinction between short- and long-term memory systems.

If we look more closely, however, we see that the original decay interpretations of forgetting in the Brown-Peterson paradigm were influenced by the inability to identify interfering events. *Interference* is forgetting caused by events intervening between exposure to the to-be-remembered material and the test for that material. If such interfering events could be identified in the Brown-Peterson paradigm, differences in forgetting from short-term memory and long-term memory would be less apparent, and an important basis for the distinction between the two systems would be undermined.

As we discussed the Brown-Peterson paradigm and the issue of interference and decay, you may have already identified the rehearsal prevention task as a potential source of interference. Counting backward, or any of the other activities used to prevent rehearsal, intervenes between exposure to the material and the memory test and may induce forgetting through interference. Decay theorists argued that the rehearsal prevention activities do not produce sufficient interference to account for the enormous forgetting normally found in the Brown-Peterson paradigm. This argument is based on the fact that interference increases with the similarity between target (to-be-remembered) and interfering materials, and the similarity between the target and the rehearsal prevention materials is minimal. Counting backward requires the use of numbers which are not similar to the words the subjects are to remember. Nonetheless, the suspicion that the rehearsal prevention task may cause interference remains. You should also notice that a real dilemma is introduced when we try to decide between decay and interference theories. To establish a situation in which decay can occur, rehearsal must be prevented, but anything done to prevent rehearsal may actually introduce interference. Hence, it becomes extremely difficult to decide whether the forgetting is due to interference or to decay.

In addition to the rehearsal prevention task, another source of interference in the Brown-Peterson paradigm was identified by Keppel and Underwood (1962). In the typical Brown-Peterson experiment, the subject faces a number of recall trials. After the very first trial, each succeeding trial is subject to interference from the preceding trials. If only memory on the first trial is examined, the length of the retention interval seems to make little difference. Only after a long series of trials does the decline in performance over the 18-second retention interval appear. Thus, it appears that interference is present in the experimental situation.

The most recent ideas about forgetting in short-term memory represent a compromise between interference and decay. For example, Reitman (1971, 1974) suggests that we think of retention of recent experiences as being similar to the detection of a signal against a background of noise. For example, your ability to hear the radio is obviously related to the amount of additional noise in the immediate surroundings as well as to the loudness of the radio. If we consider the to-be-remembered event as the signal and interference as the background noise, we see that memory will be determined by the strength of the memory trace and the amount of interference. Moreover, the strength of the trace declines as the length of the retention interval increases, a statement of the decay principle of forgetting. As the retention interval lengthens, the memory trace weakens and becomes more difficult to detect. Detection, of course, depends upon the existing level of interference, but a constant level of interference has different effects, depending upon the decay of the target signal. In this way, Reitman argues that short-term forgetting involves the principles of both decay and interference. Just as the ability to hear the radio depends upon both how loud the radio is and how much other noise is around, so the ability to remember a recent experience depends upon both how long it has been since the event was experienced and how much interference is present.

Reitman's theory exemplifies the increasing complexity in ideas about forgetting as we learn more about memory. Simple descriptions of forgetting in short-term memory and long-term memory as due, respectively, to decay and interference no longer seem adequate. We must begin to wonder whether the theoretical distinction between short-term memory and long-term memory is really as necessary as it once seemed.

The Question of Different Codes

Another of the primary distinctions between short-term memory and long-term memory which has been seriously questioned is the nature of the code. Remember it is assumed that short-term memory is stored as a phonetic code, whereas long-term memory is stored semantically. While both of these assumptions are possible, recent evidence clearly indicates that *no one code exclusively characterizes either short-term memory or long-term memory.* Some experimenters report that short-term memory can be based on visual codes. In the discussion of pattern recognition in chapter 2, we mentioned the experiment on mental rotation. A letter is shown briefly and the subject then has to decide whether the normal orientation or the mirror image of the letter is shown. Since the decision must be made rapidly, such an experiment qualifies as short-term retention. If, as the accepted interpretation implies, subjects do rotate mental images to reach their decisions, the short-term code is the visual image of the target letter. In addition to other reports of visual codes in short-term memory, some investigators have even reported the existence of semantic codes in short-term memory.

Long-term memory also can be coded in less rigid ways. Abundant evidence is available to suggest the presence of visual codes in long-term memory. For example, consider this question: In your room is the doorknob on the left or right as you exit the room? To answer this question, most people claim to retrieve "a picture" of the door. Phonetic codes also are much in evidence in long-term memory, as is clear from the evidence of our ability to remember any of a range of sound patterns as well as from the evidence of experimental work.

Again, as with the distinction between the types of forgetting, short- and long-term retentions cannot be neatly distinguished on the basis of codes. The ability to remember material may well depend upon whether we attend to the way it looks or sounds or to its meaning, but certainly we are not constrained to code recent experiences in one way and longer-standing memories in some other way.

Additional Evidence on Serial Position Effects

We saw that one source of support for the distinction between short-term memory and long-term memory is the way the stage model interprets the serial position curve. Particularly convincing is the research showing that recency effects are reduced by adding a rehearsal prevention task to a serial recall test and that primacy effects are reduced by increasing the rate of item presentation. If recency effects are due to recall from short-term memory, rehearsal prevention should eliminate the recency advantage; if primacy effects are attributed to the amount of rehearsal devoted to initial list items, increasing the rate of presentation should reduce the time for rehearsal and consequently the primacy effect. Equally important are the facts that rehearsal prevention does not affect primacy nor does rate of presentation reduce recency effects, which suggests that information is in either short-term memory or long-term memory but not in both.

More recent research raised several difficulties for this interpretation of serial position effects. For example, a number of researchers found recency effects in situations where short-term memory should be eliminated, an event that should never happen according to the stage model. Further problems are posed by the research of Bernbach (1975) who showed that under certain circumstances rate of presentation reduces recency effects. One simple situation producing such results occurs when subjects do not know the length of a list. Denied such knowledge, the subjects continue rehearsing all items, but when they know how long a list is, rehearsal can be stopped near the end of the list and immediate recall of the last items can occur.

The results of Bernbach's experiments are obviously inconsistent with the stage-model interpretation of the serial position curve. His idea is that the strategy the subject adopts determines the serial position curve. This idea foreshadows what can be described as the major alternative to the stage model, namely, *memory can be best understood in terms of what a person does to incoming information.*

Clinical Case Studies Reconsidered

Some patients who suffered severe head injuries have considerable difficulty with short-term memory tasks, but little trouble with new long-term learning. Although this observation may appear highly consistent with there being distinct short- and long-term memory systems, it is actually quite difficult to reconcile with the idea that all incoming information must pass through short-term memory in order to reach long-term memory. If the short-term system is damaged or destroyed, how can new long-term memories be formed? What then appears to be strong evidence for the difference between short- and long-term memory systems from clinical cases turns out to be much less convincing.

Summary of Objections to the Stage Model

The fundamental premise of the stage model is that memory is determined by *where* the to-be-remembered information is in the processing sequence. Each of the stages (sensory register, short-term memory, and long-term memory) has characteristics which theoretically determine the probability of remembering information. Chief among these characteristics, of course, is duration of the trace. Thus, all other things being equal, the probability of retention increases as we move through the system because each succeeding stage has longer trace life. If retention is determined by the stage in which the information resides, the question now becomes: what factors determine in which stage the information will be?

The two critical factors seem to be the length of time after presentation of the material and the type of processing performed on the material. For example, incoming information may be in the visual sensory register for up to 250 milliseconds after presentation, but only moves on to short-term memory if it is selected by the process of attention. Information may remain in short-term memory for up to 30 seconds, but rehearsal must occur to move the information to long-term memory. If we now consider this system, we realize that the length of time after presentation is much less critical for memory than is the *activity or process* imposed on the material. Transfer from one stage to another is always determined by a process, never by mere passage of time. Moreover, memory for information within a system is also under the influence of processes. Rehearsal allows information to be maintained in and recalled from short-term memory. Recall from long-term memory requires, among other factors, the operation of the retrieval process. The point to see here is that, even from the view of stage models, memory is primarily a function of the processes imposed upon the information.

We must now ask why various stages should be considered, rather than concentrate solely on processes. The only reason to propose discrete stages of memory would be if each stage included different processes. This was the original assumption of the stage model—that certain processes occur only at a particular stage. For example, semantic coding occurs only in long-term memory. However, we have just reviewed evidence contrary to this assumption; identifying the stage as best we can based on the length of the retention interval, neither the principles of forgetting nor the type of coding seems to differ. *What again emerges is that memory is determined by what is done to the information, but now the important point is that what is done does not seem to be constrained by how long it has been since the information was presented.* Hence, there seems to be little compelling reason to think of memory as occurring in stages. *Memory is determined by what is done to the information, not by where the information is.*

Arguments of this type have convinced most researchers that the stage model may not be quite as useful as once thought. Nonetheless, the stage model made a real contribution to theories of memory by focusing upon short-term retention, which clearly has characteristics which must be explained. We now shall consider alternatives to the stage model, with the full realization that these alternatives build upon the foundation laid by the stage model.

Working Memory

The stage model was proposed to account for certain fundamental facts, and if we reject the stage model, we must provide an alternative account for these facts. Among the basic facts, two important issues stand out. The first fact concerns our awareness of the contents of memory; we are usually aware or conscious of immediate experiences. In other words, certain events occupy our thought processes at any given moment, but at the same time, many other facts are also known but not thought about, although they could be. In a sense, this is the distinction between currently active and inactive memories, and historically active memory has been ascribed to short-term memory and inactive memory to long-term memory. If we abandon the short-term–long-term distinction, we must have an alternative account for the active-inactive memory phenomenon.

The second fundamental fact is the limitation on retention of recent experiences, which were discussed extensively. Even if we cannot find convincing differences between the principles of forgetting, the limitations on short-term retention are real enough, as evidenced by both experimental work and everyday experiences. In the absence of a short-term memory system, how are we to account for this important observation?

The processing of immediate experiences was recently described by Baddeley and Hitch (1974) as *working memory*. Actually, *working memory* refers not only to the processing of recent events, but also to operations and computations based on information from long-term memory. For example, when you are asked to multiply 55 × 5 "in your head," you must retrieve rules of multiplication from long-term memory, perform the computations, and store partial products. All of these events occupy working memory. In part, then, working memory is a description of current thought processes, but the contents of working memory cannot be strictly equated with conscious thought.

The reason that working memory is not synonymous with consciousness is clear on reconsideration of the earlier discussion of attention and consciousness. *Attention* was described as the allocation of processing capacity and *consciousness* or *awareness* as a psychological state accompanying the allocation of a certain amount of capacity. Working memory describes the active processes involved in retention, processes such as rehearsal, chunking, and other processes to be described in chapter 5. We may be conscious or aware of some of these processes, but as previously suggested, processing may occur below the level of awareness. For example, when you are introduced to a new person, the friend making the introduction includes the information that the person is her grandmother. You may be quite aware of noting this information and perhaps even think that the lady looks remarkably young for a grandmother. In order for you to make the observation, however, you must retrieve your general knowledge of "grandmother" from long-term memory and compare at least some portion of that knowledge with the grandmother to whom you are introduced. All of these activities occur in working memory, and the point is that you may be aware of some of the processes and not of others.

In other respects, however, working memory shares some of the characteristics of short-term memory. As discussed in chapter 3, the processing capacity is limited such that insufficient capacity is available to deal simultaneously with all information. Although more extensive processing produces better memory, it also requires more capacity. Recall the experiment on cognitive effort and memory discussed in chapter 3. Using the secondary task procedure to measure capacity, Tyler, Hertel, McCallum, and Ellis (1979) found that memory is better when more capacity is devoted to the material. These results are consistent with the view of memory as a single processing system, with retention determined by the amount of processing resources devoted to any material. Such a position now allows us to account for the limitations on retention of recent experiences. As we have stressed repeatedly, processing capacity is limited. Retention of new information requires a considerable amount of the available capacity, and the limitations on processing capacity limit the retention of recent experiences.

As an alternative to short-term memory, working memory does not propose separate principles for long- and short-term memory systems. All retention is determined by the amount and type of processing devoted to the material. New events require extensive processing, and as extensive processing produces awareness, we are likely to be conscious of memory for recent events. Since processing capacity is limited, however, a limitation is imposed on the amount of new information which can be retained. Thus, the concept of working memory deals effectively with the basic facts of retention of immediate experiences and is compatible with the general view that retention is a function of processing.

Improving Memory for Recent Events

William James, a distinguished American psychologist, many years ago claimed that attention is the key to better memory. Assuming attention to be the allocation of processing capacity through rehearsal or semantic elaboration, James's suggestion has considerable merit for improving memory of recent events. Take the simple case of meeting new people and remembering their names shortly after an introduction. First, be sure you hear each name. Many times we simply do not listen carefully when a name is mentioned. Look at the person being introduced and then use his or her name immediately when expressing your delight at meeting the person. After that, continue to use the name frequently when addressing remarks to that person. As simple as this technique is, most of us rarely use it and all too often find ourselves in the embarrassing situation of forgetting a name immediately after an introduction. If you should forget, ask the name again; most people would rather be asked than be addressed impersonally. People want you to know and use their names, and in some professions such as sales, it is an important skill.

Other techniques for improving long-term retention are discussed in chapter 5. A final hint concerning retention of recent experience is suggested here. Now that you are aware of the limitations on processing capacity, be prepared to write long lists of items and events you know you are going to have to remember. A complex event or a long list of items is impossible to remember with complete accuracy when you are only briefly exposed to it. Knowledge of the limitations of memory is a very important step toward better retention, because with this knowledge you can take appropriate steps to supplement your memory with written records.

Summary

Memory for recent experiences characteristically is quite fragile. We seem to remember only a small proportion of this information, and the information is remembered for a short period of time. Observations such as these have led to the concept of short-term memory which some researchers regarded as a system separate from long-term memory. The implication of this distinction between short-term and long-term memory systems is that different processes determine retention in the two systems. If this is the case, it should be possible to discover that the same variables will have different effects upon memory, depending upon where the information is in the system. Thus, in chapter 4 we reviewed a good deal of research which was designed to argue for differences in the capacity, duration, and nature of the codes in the short-term and long-term memory systems.

We also saw that the primary determinant of retention, even within the modal model of memory, is what is done to the information. A strong delineation of short-term memory and long-term memory is then necessary only if it is believed that the processes which can be imposed on the material are different for the short-term and long-term memory systems. More recent research questioning this assumption was then reviewed. Consequently, the current view of short-term memory is that it is much less like a separate storage system, distinct from long-term memory, and more like a work space during which information may be elaborated upon. Hence, the change from short-term memory to working memory.

In chapter 5, we will see that another view of memory, called the levels-of-processing approach, also strengthens the idea that memory is a single basic system, rather than two systems having separate structures.

Multiple-Choice Items

1. The characteristics which best describe short-term memory are
   a. large capacity and long duration
   b. small capacity and long duration
   c. large capacity and short duration
   d. small capacity and short duration

2. The results from the Brown-Peterson paradigm were important in establishing
   a. temporal limitations of short-term memory
   b. capacity limitations of short-term memory
   c. coding characteristic of short-term memory
   d. physiological distinctions between long-term memory and short-term memory

3. The fundamental objection recently expressed to the distinction between short-term memory and long-term memory is based on
   a. the failure to replicate the Brown-Peterson data
   b. the lack of attention to processing assumptions in the modal model
   c. the lack of any convincing evidence that the principles of memory differ as a function of the retention interval
   d. the failure to locate precise physiological mechanisms corresponding to the two memory systems

4. Rehearsal represents a trade-off in short-term memory because
   a. it can use either maintenance or elaborative rehearsal
   b. it extends the trace life, but also requires capacity
   c. it reduces both the primacy and recency effects
   d. it requires different physiological mechanisms than does chunking

5. The serial position curve has been important in distinguishing short-term memory and long-term memory because
   a. the primacy effect may be explained as long-term memory and the recency effect as short-term memory
   b. chunking explains the primacy and recency effect.
   c. rehearsal is very important in explaining both the primacy and recency effects
   d. memory for primacy and recency items is about the same, but the middle items are poorly recalled

6. The two fundamental facts associated with memory for recent events which must be explained by any theory of memory are
   a. primacy and recency
   b. awareness and poor retention
   c. rehearsal and chunking
   d. phonetic codes and small capacity

True-False Items

1. The primacy effect in the serial position curve is due to short-term memory.

2. In the theoretical analysis of memory, the process imposed on the material is more important than the amount of time elapsed since the material was seen.

3. Working memory is more similar to the concept of long-term memory than to that of short-term memory.

4. The different trace life in short- and long-term memory systems implicates different principles of forgetting in the two systems.

5. Considering all available research, it is now clear that only phonetic codes are available in short-term memory.

6. Working memory suggests that all aspects of short-term memory are conscious.

Discussion Items

1. Describe the argument for separate systems of short- and long-term memory.

2. Why have many theorists become increasingly skeptical of the structural distinction between short- and long-term memory?

Answers to Multiple-Choice Items

1. (d) The short-term trace lasts for a brief period, and the limits of capacity are quite small.

2. (a) The Brown-Peterson paradigm shows very rapid forgetting.

3. (c) The distinction between short-term memory and long-term memory requires different processes operating at different times after presentation, and the evidence for this assumption is quite limited.

4. (b) Rehearsal helps by extending the trace life, but the help comes at the expense of capacity.

5. (a) The short-term–long-term distinction provides an explanation of the serial position function which lends credibility to the distinction.

6. (b) Memory for recent events is different from memory for less recent events in that we tend to be thinking about the recent events, but the information is poorly retained relative to long-term memory.

Answers to True-False Items

1.   (False)   The primacy effect is due to the operation of long-term memory.

2.   (True)   Memory seems to be determined by what is done to the material regardless of how long it has been since the material was seen.

3.   (False)   Working memory is a concept designed to account for many of the characteristics of short-term memory.

4.   (True)   The different trace life simply indicates there are different rates of forgetting.

5.   (False)   Evidence exists suggesting both visual and semantic codes in short-term memory.

6.   (False)   Much of the activity of working memory may be conscious, but not all.

Encoding in Long-Term Memory

5

Much of the previous discussion centered on the fragile status of short-term memory. At one level, we have all experienced the frustration of failure of short-term memory. At another level, performance of even the most mundane activities, tying a shoe or preparing a simple meal, requires memory for events and information that occurred in the past. Indeed, our very survival depends upon long-term memory. Thus no matter how limited short-term memory is, a lot of information must survive from past experience to form the basis of long-term memory.

Long-term memory is the concept which represents the vast store of knowledge we have about the world, ranging from everyday events such as how to use a knife and fork to more esoteric information such as axioms of geometry. In addition to the concept of the vast amount of information in long-term memory, many researchers hold the assumption that long-term memory is permanent: that is, once information enters long-term memory it remains there. Any forgetting which occurs is due to inability to retrieve the information and not to a decay process. The permanence assumption was, however, recently questioned by Loftus and Loftus (1980). Regardless of its permanence or nonpermanence, long-term memory remains a critical concept for human information processing. In chapter 5 we concentrate upon the processes important to the input stage of long-term memory.

Long-term memory has always been of interest to psychologists, and a vast amount of information concerning its function has been accumulated. Since it is not reasonable to review all of this information, we shall concentrate on recent ideas about long-term memory processes in chapters 5 through 7. One such idea which has been quite helpful is to distinguish between long-term memory for specific events and for more general knowledge.

Event Memory and General Knowledge

The distinction between event memory and general knowledge refers to different types of information in long-term memory. General knowledge, or *semantic memory,* represents knowlege of the world. For example, semantic memory is knowledge of who was the first president and even of the concept of president. Semantic memory does *not* include, however, memory for specific events. Tulving (1972), who proposed this distinction, called specific event memory *episodic memory* since it refers to specific episodes experienced by an individual. For example, memory for what happened at 2:00 P.M. yesterday is episodic memory.

Both episodic memory and semantic memory are components of long-term memory, but are different types of memory information. For example, perhaps the most important function of memory is to enable us to plan and predict. When you think about having dinner, you draw on both semantic and episodic information in long-term memory. You know the kinds of food generally thought to be dinner food, information from semantic memory. You also probably consider what you had for dinner the night before, information from episodic memory. Taken together, the two kinds of information are invaluable aids in planning tonight's dinner. The reason behind this distinction is discussed more thoroughly in chapter 6, which concerns retrieval, and the remainder of this chapter is devoted to event or episodic memory. Semantic memory is considered in chapter 7.

Encoding, Storage, and Retrieval

Psychologists interested in event memory also find it useful to distinguish between encoding, storage, and retrieval. The general idea here is to model the psychological processes in event memory after a computer. *Encoding* refers to the input stage in memory. Beginning with contact with sensory information, the environment provides the initial information to the system much the same way that a computer programmer provides the initial information to the machine. Encoding also entails the *transformation* of the initial input into a form suitable for storage. Just as the storage mechanism of the computer requires transformation of the form of initial input, so the human brain requires changes in the input in order to use it. We describe these changes at the behavioral level, not at the physiological level, and the description focuses on three aspects of encoding transformation: the addition of information to the event, the deletion of information from the event, and the particular change in information from verbal to visual form.

The encoded information is then stored as a *representation* of a particular event. The storage system is a highly organized register of past events from which information is drawn as needed. The process by which information is secured from storage is called *retrieval*. Retrieval is usually assumed to be like a search process; information in storage is sorted through until the appropriate representation is uncovered. Retrieval thus refers to the output process from memory.

Although the distinction among encoding, storage, and retrieval is quite useful, a thorough understanding of event memory requires an understanding of the interaction among these processes. Obviously you cannot retrieve information which has never been encoded and stored (although you may retrieve information that you "think" you have stored), and perhaps less obvious but equally important, the encoding process is effective through its impact on retrieval. That is, anything occurring at input which makes subsequent memory better also facilitates retrieval. The point is that the interaction between input and output must be considered in understanding memory.

Overview of Encoding

Encoding refers to psychological processes which transform incoming information into the form we remember. When we experience a particular event, we are likely to remember certain aspects of the event rather than all of the details. For example, recall the specific events of lunch yesterday. Did you have lunch? What did you have? With whom did you eat? Where did you eat? What was the conversation? What were you thinking? Certainly you can answer some, perhaps all, of these questions, but you may have difficulty reconstructing all the details of yesterday's lunch. In many cases, what is remembered or not remembered is the result of *selective attention*. We concentrate on some aspects of an event and not on others. This process sounds very much like the process of selective attention discussed earlier, and indeed selective attention is a very important component of encoding. Very simply, if you do not pay attention to something, you will not remember it, and this is not a trivial point. Selective attention implies that only part of a stimulus event is actually processed for long-term memory. In this selective sense, memory for a situation represents a transformation of the original experience.

Another aspect of active encoding is the *elaboration* of a particular event with other facts we know about the event. Memory for any particular event invariably involves *relating* that event to other facts we know. Suppose you arranged to meet a friend for coffee immediately after her morning class. Your friend has an examination scheduled for that class, and you know that she has studied very hard and is quite concerned about doing well on the exam. When you meet her outside of her class, she emerges from the classroom, walks past you without saying a word, and leaves the building, slamming the door behind her. You immediately assume that the examination did not go well and decide to have coffee alone.

Your later memory of this event will include not only the action of your friend, but also your assumption that she did poorly on the examination. Note that at this point you do not know that she had a bad examination, but based on everything else you know, you decide that this assumption is the key to making sense of what happened. You elaborate upon the event with information you know in order to give the event *meaning*. In essence, you enrich or elaborate the event from your prior knowledge, and in adding additional information, you increase the meaning of the event.

A slightly different form of elaborative encoding occurs when knowledge is used to *organize* the discrete events making up a particular episode. Rather than enrichment of a single event with other information, the process now is to detect relationships among separate events which will allow organization of the events into a single unit. A simple example is not to rote memorize a list of grocery items, but rather to employ a form of organization to facilitate memory for the items. Several schemes can be used, but one effective organization is to categorize by *meal*. If, for example, orange juice, cereal, eggs, and coffee are needed, these items can all be grouped as breakfast food. A shopper remembers breakfast food when arriving at the grocery and then can remember specific items. Organization, like elaboration, serves a helpful function in long-term retention. Both activities are viewed as active psychological processes operating at the time an event is experienced.

The final encoding process to be discussed is the transformation of verbal information to a visual form, a process known as *imagery*. Suppose someone tells you about spending a day sailing on a beautiful mountain lake. It is quite easy to transform this verbal description into a vivid mental image. Some evidence suggests that conditions favoring the development of mental images produce better memory, a result which has led to controversy about whether we remember "pictures in the head." Presently both the evidence and controversy surrounding imagery in encoding will be examined.

First, the research on organizaton and elaboration is discussed in detail and attention is given to how these processes are related and their impact on retrieval.

Organization

Organization is the process which groups discrete, individual items into larger units based on a specific relationship among the items. The relationship can be based on a number of different dimensions such as conceptual (e.g., animals, vegetables, breakfast foods, tennis equipment) or perceptual (e.g., big objects, green objects, round objects) or functional (e.g., things to sit on, things to eat with, things to smoke) or even alphabetic (e.g., things beginning with the letter *a*). Although some types of groupings are better than others in aiding retention, any form of organization seems better than no organization. Much of the research was designed to demonstrate this point. Furthermore, the research distinguished between *material-induced* and *subject-induced* organization. Since organization is the psychological process of relating several to-be-remembered events, the process may be engaged or suggested by the materials to be remembered or may be imposed subjectively.

Material-Induced Organization

The majority of laboratory studies of organizations and event memory use *categorized* word lists. The lists consist of words drawn from the same natural category, such as *dog, cat, horse, pig,* and *cow* from the category *animal*. In most experiments several categories are used to represent the words; for example, a list might contain twenty words having four words from each of five categories. Compared to uncategorized lists, subjects remember categorized lists very well.

Furthermore, categorized lists are better remembered when presented in *blocked* form than when presented *randomly*. Blocked presentation refers to the presentation order in which all items from a particular category are presented one after another before items from another category are presented. With random presentation, the items from different categories are mixed in the presentation order. The superior memory for blocked presentation again suggests the important role of organization in memory, because blocked presentation is much more organized than is random presentation.

Further indication of the importance of organization is obvious from the finding of active rearrangement of randomly presented lists. That is, even though items from various categories are presented in random order, subjects group the items into their appropriate categories at recall. That is, the items are recalled by category in spite of having been presented randomly. This regrouping is known as *clustering in recall*. Clustering is an important indication of the active encoding process of organization in that the materials are rearranged from the random presentation order to an organized output order.

The importance of the relationships among separate elements also has been illustrated with nonverbal materials. Palmer (1975) has shown that simple line drawings of parts of the face are difficult to recognize when presented separately. Examples of these drawings are presented in figure 5.1. The same drawings, however, are quickly recognized when presented in the context of a face. Additional information is provided by the context,

A   In Context   B   Out of Context

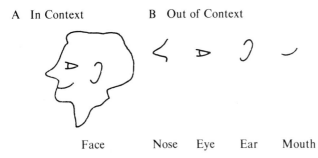

Face   Nose   Eye   Ear   Mouth

Figure 5.1 Materials used by Palmer to assess memory for facial features following presentation of certain features of the face in context (*A*) and out of context (*B*). (From *Explorations and Cognition* by Donald A. Norman and David E. Rumelhart and the LNR Research Group. W. H. Freeman and Company. Copyright © 1975.)

the face in this case, which aids the recognition of each separate element. Again, organization in the form of relationships among elements is important to the encoding process.

Subjective Organization

Organizational effects are obvious when categorized lists are compared to uncategorized lists, but careful examination of performance on uncategorized lists also reveals persuasive evidence of organizational activity. When subjects are asked to remember lists of words unrelated in any obvious way, they find idiosyncratic relationships which result in consistent output groupings. Although clustering scores based on some category grouping cannot be obtained from uncategorized lists, Tulving (1962) outlined a method for detecting organization of presumably unrelated lists. Tulving's measure of *subjective organization* requires multitrial recall. That is, the subjects receive several presentations and recall tests of a list. Subjective organization is measured by the *consistency of output order* over the recall tests. As the tests progress, the order in which the words are written on the tests becomes progressively more consistent. The particular order differs for different individuals, since the groupings are based on idiosyncratic relationships. Nonetheless, subjective organization is a stronger indication of the prevalence of organizational activity in encoding than is material-induced organization. It is important to remember that even when the words appear to be unrelated and the input order changes on each presentation, the output becomes highly organized.

Subjective organization is yet another example of using previous knowledge to interpret a current situation. Individual experiences allow us to relate the apparently unrelated words and to bring order to an otherwise chaotic event. Analogous situations exist in everyday experiences, perhaps more commonly than not. When we are confronted with actions which seem to make little sense, most of us try very hard to bring whatever information possible to bear on such situations to interpret and organize them. Consequently, the discrepancies among different persons' memory for the same event are not at all surprising. Based on differences in knowledge of it, an event may be organized and remembered in very different ways by different observers, just as unrelated lists are subjectively organized in very different ways by different persons. This phenomenon is enlarged on later when comprehension and memory are discussed. For the moment, it is important to see the pervasiveness of organization in memory, which is perhaps best illustrated by subjective organization.

Locus of Organizational Effects

The question of how organization affects memory is a very important and also a very complex situation. In studies of both material-induced and subjective organization, good memory is accompanied by good organization, but measures of memory and measures of organization are measuring two different processes. Memory is measured by recall and organization by clustering or subjective organization. When these two measures are correlated, that is, good memory is accompanied by high clustering, it is tempting to assume that organization causes good memory. We must consider, however, that the relationship is correlational, and we cannot be absolutely sure that organization *causes* good memory. Indeed, the relationship may indicate just the opposite: good memory may cause organization. How can this be? Very simply, the more you remember the more capable you are of detecting the relationship among the items at output. In other words, as you recall a lot of the items, you see the relationships among them and organize them according to those relationships in the test. This interpretation of the relationship between clustering and recall implies that memory leads to organization. Although such a view cannot be completely dismissed, it just does not make much sense. Why would organization be so prevalent? What is the function of organization? Why should we bother to organize the information *after* we remember it?

In the absence of persuasive answers to these questions, the relationship between recall and clustering becomes much more sensible if *it is assumed that organizational processes contribute to good memory*. With this assumption, it now becomes important to ask how organization affects memory. Why does organization improve memory? Two related answers to this question have been offered.

On the one hand, Mandler (1967) suggested that organization is effective because of *economy of storage*. Organization of discrete units into one holistic unit reduces the number of items to be stored. *Dog, cat, horse, pig,* and *cow* can be stored in the category *animal,* just as eggs, *bacon, juice,* and *coffee* can be stored in the category *breakfast items.* Reminiscent of the short-term memory work on chunking, Mandler then argues that organization improves memory because the amount of information per stored unit is increased. This approach assumes that the organization occurs as the information comes in and thus occurs during encoding.

Alternatively, Tulving argued that organization benefits memory because of its *effect on retrieval.* Tulving agrees with Mandler that organization occurs as an encoding process of integrating separate items into holistic units; the benefit to memory then derives from the ability to access the whole unit at retrieval. Once the unit is accessed, all of the information within the unit can be retrieved. For example, while viewing a categorized list, you may notice that some words are categorized as *animals,* some as *vehicles,* and so on. At retrieval you remember seeing *animals* and *vehicles,* which gives you access to all of the individual items. Organization then is assumed to work because the integrated unit formed at encoding can be retrieved with all of the information of the individual units.

Tulving's retrieval argument is not really at odds with Mandler's encoding position. In fact, Tulving assumes that organization occurs at encoding as Mandler does, only Tulving goes further to suggest why organization at input facilitates output.

Many questions remain concerning the precise mechanisms of organizational effects. For example, how are the similarities among items detected and why does organization improve retrieval? In chapter 8 on comprehension and memory we shall see that organization is very important to understanding what is read and heard. Even though we may perfectly understand an individual sentence, we must be able to detect the relationships among the sentences in order to understand the passage or conversation. Thus, organization is one of the most important processes in human cognition, and its effects can be seen throughout the system from perception of visual scenes to comprehension of prose passages and discourse.

Perceptual Grouping, Organization, and Memory

In this section another type of organization involving the discovery of higher-order structure in materials to be remembered is considered. This type of organization is called *perceptual grouping* and it emphasizes that the way events are grouped perceptually determines the way they are eventually organized in memory. Information in the environment is sometimes spatially or temporally organized and this organization is used to encode and store the information. For instance, telephone numbers are grouped in digit sequences of three and four digits. Melodies have particular temporal groupings which facilitate memory. More generally, the basic idea of perceptual grouping is that discrete stimuli in the environment are not responded to as such, but are organized perceptually into structured patterns or sequences.

One approach to studying perceptual grouping has been to present strings of digits auditorially, breaking the digits into groups by pauses (Bower & Winzenz, 1969; Bower, 1970): for example, the digit sequence 418–35–9472–6257 in which the dashes represent pauses breaking the digits into groups or chunks. Subjects can learn a digit sequence when the groups or chunks remain constant or identical on subsequent presentations. In contrast, when the grouping structure varies on successive presentations, such as 41–8359–4726–257 and 4183–5947–26–257, subjects show little mastery of the sequence. In short, human beings must have some consistency in grouping or they will be unable to encode and store sequences. This generalization holds where the sequence to be learned has no obvious higher-order structure, that is, where a hidden sequence of digits or letters easier to encode than the sequence presented for study cannot be detected.

In contrast, if the series to be learned does have a higher-order structure, then varied rather than constant groupings actually facilitate recall of the sequence. This finding is known as the *variability effect in recall* (Ellis, 1973; Ellis, Parente, Grah, & Spiering, 1975). Consider, for example, a letter sequence such as *CU PN ET,* which is derived from the word pair *CUP-NET.* When the letter sequence is shown in varied fashion, such as *CU PN ET, C UPN ET* or *CU PNE T,* on successive presentations, recall of the entire letter sequence is much better than when a constant grouping of letters is shown. In this case the intact words *cup* and *net* are never actually seen. Thus varied input in the form of varied spatial groupings allows the information to be organized more effectively, but *only* if there is some *overall structure* in the material to be learned. A more general implication of these findings may be that varied stimulus presentations provide for a deeper level of processing because a person is forced to work harder with the information. Another possibility is that varied input encourages a person to look for structure or groupings which are more meaningful, and as a by-product causes the person to allocate more cognitive capacity or effort to the task (cf. Tyler, Hertel, McCallum, & Ellis, 1979).

In summary, we have just seen how important organization is in memory, but there is reason to believe that other processes are also necessary for optional retention. Some of these processes even appear to be diametrically opposed to organization. For example, organization argues that good memory results from noticing *similarities* among items. We shall now review research which suggests that good memory also results from noticing *differences* among items.

Elaboration of Individual Items

Elaboration, like organization, is a process of relating the to-be-remembered event to other facts related to that event. Unlike organization, however, elaboration refers to *relationships among the to-be-remembered event and additional information which is not to be remembered.* Organization is reserved for the relationship just among the to-be-remembered events.

A simple example clarifies this distinction. Suppose you are given the common laboratory task of remembering a list of words. Some of the words refer to *animals: dog, cat, camel,* and *tiger.* You detect the relationship among the four words and *organize* them under the category *animal.* In addition, however, you also may encode information about each word that is not relevant to the other words. For example, you may elaborate *tiger* by including such information as *stripes, India,* or maybe *nickname of football team.* Elaboration, then, *adds information unique* to the individual item. In both processes, organization and elaboration, the *meaning* of the word is being encoded; that is, facts we know about *tiger* include it is an animal, lives in India, and has stripes. The distinction between organization and elaboration, however, is that with organization what is encoded is information shared by the meaning of the to-be-remembered events, whereas with elaboration what is encoded is information unique to the meaning of one of the events. As with organization, a considerable amount of research supports the importance of elaboration.

Levels of Processing

The concept known as *levels of processing* was proposed by Craik and Lockhart (1972). Two fundamental assumptions underlie the concept of levels of processing. The first assumption, about encoding, states simply that the memory trace is a by-product of perceptual analysis. In other words, what is remembered about a particular event will be what was attended to when the event was experienced. When introduced to a new person, you may concentrate on the person's face, hair, clothes, names, or any of a number of other features. The point is that whatever you attend to will constitute the basis for a memory trace for that person. The second assumption of levels of processing concerns the differential retention of an event based on what is encoded. Very simply, semantic or meaningful features support better retention than do nonsemantic features. If what you notice or encode is an aspect of the *meaning* of the overall event, you will remember the event better than if what you notice are superficial aspects of the event.

The two fundamental assumptions are easily captured in an experiment requiring special processing of each individual word in a list. The special processing comes in the form of an *orienting task,* which is a simple activity performed on each word. For example, the subject is told to rate each word for its pleasantness. Alternatively, the subject might be asked to write the middle letter of each word. The first task is designed to direct attention to the meaning of the word, a semantic task. Consider making a pleasantness judgment of the word *rape*. Most persons rate this word as quite unpleasant. Why? It is not a particularly ugly-looking word, and its sound is very much like *grape*, a word usually rated as quite pleasant. Clearly, the unpleasantness of *rape* stems from its meaning. Thus, pleasantness ratings serve as a semantic orienting task because a pleasantness judgment requires determining the meaning of a word. Writing the middle letter of a word, however, does not require determining its meaning and hence is a nonsemantic task. Any task that can be performed without determining the meaning of a word is nonsemantic orientation. Nonsemantic tasks usually require a judgment about the letter patterns or sound patterns of a word, such as estimating the number of rhymes for a word.

The orienting task is designed to control the subject's attention. (For a discussion of the effectiveness of orienting tasks in controlling attention, see Hunt, Elliott, & Spence, 1979.) Regardless, levels of processing argues that memory is based on what is attended to, and furthermore that attention to semantic attributes produces better memory than attention to nonsemantic attributes. In addition, these experiments are usually conducted under *incidental memory* instructions. Incidental instructions mean that the subjects are not told to remember the words, but rather are led to believe that the purpose of the experiment is something other than to test memory, usually something to do with their orienting response. After all the words have been seen, a surprise memory test is administered. The incidental instructions are designed to strengthen the attentional control of the orienting task.

Imagine that you are a subject in one of these experiments and are given a nonsemantic orienting task. For example, you are told to check all of the *e*'s in the words you see and are given memory instructions that are *not* incidental but *intentional*. That is, in addition to checking *e*'s you are told to remember the words. In all probability, you will not restrict your attention to the letter *e*, but will also engage in processes you normally use to remember. In this situation, we have no assurance that what you remember is under the control of the orienting task. However, when you are not told of the memory test but rather are told that the interest is in how quickly and accurately a person can detect particular letters, our confidence is greater that the orienting task affects your attention. You have little reason to attend to anything other than the orienting task if you are not told of the impending memory test. In summary, the subject in these experiments sees a list of items—words, pictures, even sentences—and is asked to perform a task on each item, either a task requiring that the meaning of the item be detected or one that does not require the meaning to be detected. The sole purpose of the experiment is to determine whether more items are remembered following semantic orientation than following nonsemantic orientation.

The answer to this question is a resounding yes! Regardless of the semantic task, be it pleasantness rating, free association, sentence completion, or whatever, semantic orienting tasks produce better memory for the items than do nonsemantic tasks. Using pictures of human faces, Bower and Karlin (1974) showed that judgments of honesty produce better memory than do judgments about physical features of faces. The honesty judgment is seen as a semantic orienting task. This experiment is widely quoted as evidence that levels of processing applies even to memory for faces. But why should semantic tasks produce better performance than do nonsemantic tasks?

Craik and Lockhart's original answer was that semantic information lasts longer than does nonsemantic information. Notice the similarity to the stage model where phonetic (nonsemantic) information is assumed to be stored in short-term memory and semantic information in long-term memory. Short-term memory has a shorter duration than does long-term memory. In spite of many other differences between the descriptions of encoding, the stage model and levels of processing agree that storage duration is nonsemantic information is briefer than in semantic information. Unfortunately, this particular assumption appears to be incorrect.

Doubts about Depth

Why should semantic orientation support better memory than nonsemantic orientation? Is it really true that semantic information lasts longer than nonsemantic information? The answer seems to be no, as illustrated by an experiment by Stein (1978) (see also Hunt & Mitchell, 1978; 1982). In this experiment, subjects were given a list of words in which one letter in each word was capitalized. After each word, the subject had to make a yes-no decision requiring either semantic or nonsemantic information. The semantic decision was to judge whether the word fit in a sentence frame. For example, with the word *roCk,* the sentence frame was "The _____ rolled down the hill." The nonsemantic decision required a yes-no response to a statement such as "The letter *c* is capitalized." After presentation of all the words, subjects were given a recognition memory test to tap their semantic or nonsemantic retention. The semantic test required that the subjects select the words on the original list from a larger group of words. The nonsemantic test required that the subjects select the version of the original word which had the same letter captialized: for example, "Among *Rock, rOck, roCk,* and *rocK,* which one was presented earliest?" Subjects whose orienting task required a semantic decision performed better on the semantic recognition test, but subjects who performed the nonsemantic orienting task did much better on the recognition of capital letters.

The important message of this experiment is quite clear. Nonseman- tic information is retained as long as is semantic information. Conse- quently, the superior retention for words following semantic orientation cannot be due to more rapid decay of nonsemantic information. Again, why does semantic orientation produce better memory than does nonsemantic orientation?

Elaboration Hypothesis

One answer is a modification of the depth hypothesis proposed by Craik and Tulving (1975). They suggested that semantic processing produces more *elaborate* encoding than does nonsemantic processing. As noted earlier, elaboration is a process of relating the to-be-remembered event to other information that may be known about the event. Elaboration serves to broaden the stored information of the to-be-remembered event. The elab- oration hypothesis was actually proposed to explain the effects of different semantic orienting tasks.

In particular, the phenomenon known as the *congruity effect* posed some difficulty for the original depth hypothesis. Many of the earlier ex- periments using the levels-of-processing paradigm presented semantic ori- enting questions which were either true or false. For example, the subject was given a sentence such as "A DOG is an animal" or "A STONE is an animal" and asked to respond yes or no, depending upon whether the state- ment was true. Later, the subject was asked to remember all of the capi- talized words. Memory in this situation was much better for all the sentences to which the yes response was given. Why should this happen? Both true and false sentences require semantic processing of the target word. In order to say no to the assertion that "A STONE is an animal," you must deter- mine the meaning of *stone*. The difference in memory cannot then be solely a matter of depth or semantic processing.

Craik and Tulving argue that the true statements leading to the yes response are more congruent than are the false statements. That is, the elements of the true sentence make sense, while the elements of the false sentence are incongruous or nonsensical. Congruent sentences provide elaboration on the basic meaning of the target word, whereas incongruous sentences do not. Semantic processing then produces better memory than nonsemantic processing because the semantic encoding is more elaborate, but within the realm of semantic processes, certain situations can produce more elaborate encodings than others.

The heart of elaboration is embodied in the suggestion that something is remembered better if it is related to other known facts. Certainly this suggestion can be appreciated by reflection on personal experiences. For example, material in a totally new course may be difficult, not only to understand but also to remember. The reason for this is not surprising; very little about the material is known and little related information is available. Most introductory courses devote a great deal of time to definitions of basic concepts in order to provide the foundation upon which more advanced courses may elaborate. But let us return to the original question: Why does semantic processing, now in the form of elaboration, improve memory?

Perhaps elaboration comes closer to providing the answer than does depth. Relating material to a number of other known facts increases the number of potential retrieval cues. Elaborate processing may improve memory, because the number of events which may remind us of the target item have increased. This explanation of the influence of elaborate encoding on subsequent retrieval is quite plausible, but it implies that the encoded information is widely spread, perhaps to the point of not specifying the to-be-remembered event clearly. That this need not be the case is illustrated by yet another idea about why semantic processing and elaboration aid memory.

Distinctiveness Hypothesis

Suppose we take quite literally the first assumption of levels of processing that the memory trace consists only of the attended portion of an event. That is, what is encoded and remembered is that collection of attributes, only a subset of the total number available, that is concentrated upon during the experience. At the time the event must be recalled, only what is available can be worked with, and the entire event must be reconstructed from the encoded subset of features. The ability to reproduce faithfully the original event will depend in large part upon how well the encoded features specify that event. A simple example clarifies this suggestion. Suppose you are asked to remember a list of words, one of which is *elephant*. If the task requires a semantic orientation, the encoded trace might contain information corresponding to "very large, gray animal with large ears and nose living in Africa and India." If you retrieve this information at the time of recall, *elephant* is an obvious response. However, if your task is nonsemantic orientation, for example, to check all the *e*'s in the word, the encoded trace might contain information that the word has two *e*'s. Reconstructing the word *elephant* from just that information seems to be quite unlikely. Most of us know a large number of words which contain two *e*'s.

This illustration is designed to introduce the distinctiveness hypothesis. According to the *distinctiveness hypothesis,* memory is determined in part by how well the information encoded specifies the event being reconstructed. As in the earlier discussion of pattern recognition, it is as if the cognitive system were playing a game of twenty questions. What is required here is the best guess possible, based on all available information concerning the event. In the case of event memory, part of the available information is what was encoded at input. Semantic information is likely to be much more specific and thus much more useful than nonsemantic information, as illustrated in the example of remembering *elephant.* Nonsemantic information such as letter combinations and sound patterns are considerably more redundant than semantic information. Simply put, the meanings of different words are less likely to be shared than are the letter combinations or sound patterns. Semantic orientation then produces superior performance because semantic features more distinctively represent the event. Semantic features are simply more useful in the game of twenty questions with past events.

The distinctiveness hypothesis shares with levels of processing the assumption that the memory trace is a by-product of attention and pattern recognition, but the two ideas differ in their descriptions of what constitutes effective information. Rather than semantic information, the distinctiveness hypothesis emphasizes distinctive information.

This difference has interesting implications, among which is the prediction from the distinctiveness hypothesis that nonsemantic information can be useful in memory (Hunt & Elliott, 1980). If the nonsemantic information is distinctive, attention to that information should facilitate memory. Consider an experiment by Eysenck (1979). Subjects were asked to attend to the sound patterns of words as an orienting task. In one condition, however, the subjects were given very unusual, atypical pronunciations of the words. Since these pronunciations are not likely to be shared by other words, the distinctiveness hypothesis predicts that they should facilitate memory. In fact, subjects attending to atypical pronunciations remembered the words as well as did a group given semantic orientation. This should not happen if nonsemantic information decays more rapidly than does semantic information, as originally supposed by the depth hypothesis. The distinctiveness hypothesis, however, predicts that *unique features* aid memory for an event, regardless of whether the features are semantic or nonsemantic. Thus, Eysenck's results are more consistent with a distinctiveness explanation.

Distinctiveness may be preferable to depth, but what about elaboration? Elaboration, with its concern for the spread of encoding, seems diametrically opposed to distinctiveness, with its concern for highly specific encoding. For example, consider an experiment by Winograd (1981) on memory for faces. This experiment asked the question "Is memory for faces better if you encode the most distinctive feature?" To induce elaborative encoding of a number of features, subjects were asked to scan the pictures and rate the most distinctive feature. In the process of scanning, the subjects presumably would encode a large number of features. For the distinctive encoding condition, Winograd had a group of people rate the pictures prior to the experiment and select the most distinctive feature. Subjects in the experiment then focused on this feature of each picture, be it eyes, nose, mouth, and so forth. Thus subjects in the elaboration group encoded a number of features, while subjects in the distinctiveness group encoded only one feature. As it resulted, both groups were equally proficient at recognizing the faces. Winograd interpreted this finding as indicating that the function of encoding a number of features is to increase the distinctiveness of the encoding. One feature will do as well *if* it is highly distinctive. This interpretation suggests that elaboration is effective because it produces distinctiveness.

A bit of reflection may persuade you that this position is sensible. As Craik and Jacoby (1979) suggest, the more elaborate the encoding, the more will be remembered about an event. Not only does elaboration increase the probability of sampling a single distinctive feature, but also the more that is known about something the less like other things it will appear. For instance, if all you can remember is that one of the words in a list was an animal, you may have trouble producing the precise word. If you have more elaborate information, such as "a large grey animal with large ears and nose living in India and Africa," you will have little trouble producing the correct response. Elaborate information increases the distinctiveness of any event *because the more that is known about something, the less like other things it will seem.*

Distinctiveness and Organization

Let us agree for the moment that something like distinctiveness is important in encoding event memories. That is simply to say that memory benefits from attending to differences among separate events. The more distinctive the memory is, the less it will be confused with other events. We must now reconcile the importance of attending to differences among the items with what was said previously about organization. Organization, with its emphasis upon integration of discrete events, suggests that encoding of similarities is very important to memory. We now seem to be confronted with diametrically opposed prescriptions for good memory. Organization argues for the encoding of similarities, whereas levels of processing emphasizes encoding of differences.

One resolution of this apparent dilemma is to assume that *both types of information* are important to memory (Einstein & Hunt, 1980; Hunt & Einstein, 1981). Some evidence indeed suggests that this is the case. Consider the following experiments reported by Epstein, Phillips, and Johnson

(1975) and by Begg (1978). Subjects were given either highly related word pairs (*beer-wine,* for example) or unrelated pairs of words (*beer-dog,* for example). For each pair the subjects had to list either the similarities between the members of the pair or the differences between the members of the pair. Memory for the pairs was then tested. Related pairs were better remembered when subjects oriented to the differences between the words, and unrelated pairs were better remembered when similarities were processed. Why should this be? It appears that both similarities and differences are important. Related pairs command attention to similarity, but the similarity may produce confusion in memory. Subjects may remember "alcoholic beverage," but be unable to decide whether they saw *beer, wine, vodka* or *scotch.* Noticing the differences among similar items aids in this discrimination. The opposite problem occurs with unrelated items. The differences are obvious, but no relational structure is available to help generate the items. This relational structure or similarity among events seems to be very important in initiating the retrieval process. Remembering an event, whether it be a word in a list or what was done last Tuesday, seems to start at the general level of shared information, such as "words in the list" or "events of last Tuesday," and proceed to finer discriminations.

This interaction between similarities and differences is illustrated in figure 5.2. If each of the circles represents what is known about a word, the overlap or intersection of the circles represents their shared meaning and the nonoverlapping portions represent the meaning of each that is not shared. For example, *beer, wine,* and *vodka* all share *alcoholic beverage* as part of their meaning, but we also know that they have different colors. Color, then, is part of the information which does not overlap.

Thus, the encoding process involves attention to certain aspects of events. Some of this information will be shared among the events and some of the information will differ. Optimal verbatim memory requires both, a point that will be more appreciated when retrieval is discussed in chapter 6.

Cognitive Effort and Memory Revisited

You may recall that in the discussion of attention (chapter 3) we saw that memory of words presented in an anagram or sentence-completion task was better when the words were in a high-effort condition than in a low-effort condition (Tyler, Hertel, McCallum, & Ellis, 1979). In brief, memory for words was better when more capacity (cognitive effort) was allocated to the task. Cognitive effort was manipulated by varying the effort involved in deciding whether a word was correct and was *independently* measured by obtaining reaction time measures during processing of the items. Thus

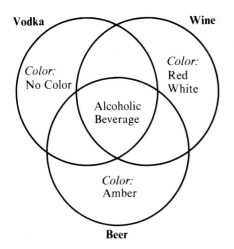

Vodka ... **Wine**

Color: No Color

Color: Red White

Alcoholic Beverage

Color: Amber

Beer

Figure 5.2 Representation of shared information (*alcoholic beverage*) and distinctive information (*colors*) among the concepts *beer, wine,* and *vodka.*

the procedure involved using the secondary task technique in studying attention. But do the memory results mean that effort directly produces better memory? This raises the question of whether "hard work" in studying directly effects memory or whether some other processes are operating.

What the results mean is that there is a *correlation* between cognitive effort and memory, but not necessarily a causal relationship. Thus the issue is, what mechanisms or processes account for the effects of effort memory? Tyler, Hertel, McCallum, and Ellis (1979) have indicated that several possibilities may exist. One is that with greater effort there is a greater tendency to integrate the context (or task environment) and the target word, thereby facilitating later retrieval. This type of explanation emphasizes elaboration. It is also possible that effort produces a more distinctive trace. The point is that, whatever explanation, the effects of cognitive effort on memory are likely to be explained in terms of processes, such as elaboration or distinctiveness rather than in terms of a direct causal effect of effort. But this issue remains to be explored.

Let us now turn to a third encoding issue, imagery.

Imagery

Think about your room when you were ten years old. As you left the room, was the doorknob on the left or right side of the door? In answering this question, many people report that they visualize the room including the door. The answer requires information from long-term memory, and the visual representation reported by many people suggests that long-term memory may store *images*. Imagery is an instance of an analogue representation. Analogue representations directly mirror the world; analogues contain a point-for-point correspondence with the object they represent. For example, a photograph is an analogue; a verbal description of the same object is not an analogue. Considerable debate has arisen over the existence of analogue repesentations in memory, particularly as they refer to visual memory. We shall examine the debate shortly, but first let us review the evidence for imagery encoding in memory.

Evidence for Imagery

The old saying that a picture is worth a thousand words has considerable validity when applied to memory. Pictures are much better remembered than are words in recognition tests. Of the many experiments demonstrating this fact, consider the work of Standing, Conezio, and Haber (1970). Subjects were shown 2,560 pictures of complex visual scenes, each picture available for inspection for only 10 seconds. In the recognition test the subjects were able to remember correctly 93 percent or a total of 2,380 pictures. This remarkable level of performance is much higher than is usually obtained with verbal materials. Moreover, the rapid rate of presentation and the complexity of the visual scenes make it unlikely that the pictures were verbally recoded. One interpretation of these data, then, is that pictures are stored in a visual form which somehow facilitates memory.

Further evidence for direct storage or visual information comes from Kosslyn's work on "mental travel" (Kosslyn, Ball, & Reiser, 1978). Subjects are shown a simple map containing several important landmarks. The map is drawn so that the distance between the points differs, and these distances are labeled, for example, A to B = 10, B to F = 20, F to A = 30. An example of such a map is shown in figure 5.3. Subjects are asked to remember the map, an easy task given its simplicity. With the map absent, the subjects are then asked to go from one point to another based on their memory of the map. The request is for mental travel, and when the person reaches the designation point, a button is depressed to signify the end of the journey. The button actually stops a clock which was started when "travel" began. The measure of interest in this research is the amount of time to mentally travel the map as a function of the actual distances listed on the map. Interestingly, the times are directly correlated with the distances. If A to B = 10 and B to F = 20, the subjects take much longer to mentally scan from B to F than from A to B. Kosslyn suggests this result indicates that subjects actually use visual representation to perform this task, much as a person might visualize a familiar route when giving directions. As with the previously mentioned picture superiority in memory,

Figure 5.3 A map used in the studies of mental travel. (From "Visual Images Preserve Spatial Metric Information" by S. M. Kosslyn, T. M. Ball, and B. J. Reiser, *Journal of Experimental Psychology: Human Perception and Performance*, 1978, *4*, 47–60. Copyright 1978 by the American Psychological Association. Reprinted by permission of the publisher and the authors.)

Kosslyn's work, along with the mental rotation phenomenon discussed in chapter 2, suggests that visual stimuli may be stored in a visual form.

The argument for an active imaginal encoding to memory, however, is easily illustrated with materials other than pictures. For example, do we imagine an object or scene represented by words and then store the visual scene in memory? If this is so, imaginal encoding would be a very active process of converting an abstract symbol, the word, into a completely different representation. Paivio (1971) has vigorously pursued this issue with a very interesting research program. At the basis of Paivio's research is his discovery that concrete words are better remembered than are abstract words. Concrete words refer to real-world objects and are words such as *cigar, bicycle,* and *dog;* abstract words have less clear real-world referents and are words such as *belief, justice,* and *knowledge.* Paivio and students clearly demonstrated that concrete words are better remembered than abstract words. What does this fact have to do with imagery?

To illustrate Paivio's answer to this question, close your eyes and attempt to visualize *cigar.* Most people find it rather easy to obtain a vivid image of cigar. Now close your eyes and try to get a mental picture of *knowledge*. This is a much more difficult matter, and whatever you may imagine, the image is likely to be hazy and only related to *knowledge* in some fashion. There really is no single concrete instance of knowledge. Abstract words then are more difficult to encode in an imaginal form. Paivio suggests that this fact may account for the difference in memory for concrete and abstract words. The more important question now becomes, How does imagery influence memory? Paivio's dual-code theory provides one answer to the question.

Dual-Code Theory

Paivio suggests that information in memory may be stored in two forms, *verbal codes* and *imaginal codes*. Any event or object which can be described may be stored in a verbal code, and any event or object which can be visualized can be stored in an imaginal code. Thus, most events can be remembered through either a verbal code, an imaginal code, or both. For example, a picture can be labeled and remembered as the verbal code implied by the label. Alternatively, the picture can be remembered through the image code, which Paivio argues will produce better memory because the visual image retains more detail than does the verbal code. Thus, superior memory for pictures is due to the ease with which they are visually stored and the amount of detail maintained in the image.

With words, a verbal code may be more probable, but words may also be transformed in encoding to a visual image code. If a word is remembered both by verbal code and image code, the probability of retrieving one of the codes is higher than if only one code is available. Very simply, two codes are better than one. Abstract words, which are difficult if not impossible to code visually, will then be at a disadvantage compared to concrete words. Concrete words can be encoded verbally and visually, whereas abstract words can only be encoded verbally.

As plausible as Paivio's ideas are, a great deal of controversy developed around the concept of imagery. No one doubts the validity of the experimental effects of imagery on memory. Rather, the dispute centers on the idea of a visual long-term memory. Let us briefly examine these arguments.

Are Visual Images Stored in Memory?

Among the most persistent critics of imagery is Pylyshyn (1973), who is, interestingly enough, a colleague of Paivio's at Western Ontario University. The thrust of Pylyshyn's argument is that the experiments just discussed *do not require* a mental imagery interpretation. Furthermore,

Pylyshyn and others do not believe that memory contains anything resembling a "picture." For example, consider the work on rotation of mental images. Pylyshyn points out that beliefs and knowledge can affect the way this task is performed, but beliefs and knowledge exert little effect on the rotation of an actual physical picture.

In the same vein, Richman and colleagues (Mitchell & Richman, 1980; Richman, Mitchell, & Reznick, 1979) have criticized Kosslyn's work on visual memory for maps. In a series of papers entitled "Reservations on Mental Travel" and "Confirmed Reservations on Mental Travel" they argue that the correlation between reaction time and distance in Kosslyn's work reflects the subjects' perception of the task demands. That is, the subjects guess that the experimenter expects longer distances to require more time to traverse, and they comply with the expectation.

Again, the argument is that human beings do not really store "pictures" of the world in memory. Neisser and Kerr (1973) provided the opportunity to directly confront this question experimentally. If the mental image is like visual perception, an object hidden in the image should not be remembered. If you are actually looking at a piano and a ball is hidden behind it, you will not see the ball. By the same token, you should not be able to "see" hidden objects in a mental image if the image is like visual perception. Neisser and Kerr instructed people to visualize scenes described by sentences such as "A harp is hidden inside the torch of the Statue of Liberty." Later the subjects were given a cue such as "torch" and asked to recall the sentence. Will they remember *harp* which should be concealed in the torch? In fact the subjects remembered *harp* as well in the hidden condition as they did in conditions where the harp was blatantly exposed "on top of the torch." Neisser and Kerr conclude that mental images, whatever they are, cannot be two-dimensional snapshots of the world.

More recently, however, Keenan and Moore (1979) repeated Neisser and Kerr's experiment with much stronger instructions about hidden objects. Keenan and Moore report that their subjects remember fewer of the hidden objects than of the exposed objects. Such results, of course, suggest that the image may be like visual perception. This issue continues unresolved at the moment.

The critics of imagery offer an alternative account of encoding processes which involves a common, underlying propositional code. A *propositional code* is an abstract representation (some theorists call it the language of thought) of both verbal and pictorial materials. According to this approach, all types of incoming materials are encoded in the propositional code. Certainly we do experience images, but not because images are stored in memory. Rather the images are generated or created from the underlying propositional representation. How would this position account for some of the data on imagery, for example, the difference in memory between concrete and abstract sentences? As it turns out, abstract sentences are more complex and difficult to understand than concrete sentences. One effect of this additional complexity may be increasing difficulty with propositional encoding, leading to poorer memory.

Regardless of the outcome of the continuing disagreement over imagery, the debate represents a healthy concern for understanding the effects of variables such as pictures, concrete words, and instructions to image upon memory. Again, there is no disagreement that these variables can help to improve memory, as can be illustrated with mnemonic techniques. The argument is in how *to conceptualize* these effects.

Imagery Mnemonics

Almost everyone who claims to have new tricks for better memory will encourage the use of an imagery mnemonic. One of the oldest uses of this technique is known as the *method of loci* and was used by early Greek orators. The method of loci involves associating certain ideas and points with certain parts of the room in which a speech is made. The method can be modified for remembering lists of things by imagining a familiar walk, say from your room to a classroom. Imagine notable landmarks along the walk: a fence, a particular tree, a rock, or anything you might notice on this walk. Now take the list of things you want to remember—grocery items, chemical elements, names of people doing imagery research, or whatever— and place one item at each of the familiar landmarks. When the time for memory comes, you take a mental walk along the route, noticing each landmark and the associated item. Regardless of whether images are visual or propositional codes, the method of loci is an effective technique for improving memory.

Summary

Encoding processes are the psychological activities which determine the type of information available for later memory. Encoding generally involves the transformation of the incoming information, either through addition or deletion of information. An important source of additional information is the relationship between an event and other known facts. The relational information can serve to organize a set of discrete events into a single, higher-order unit by detecting similarities among the events. This, of course, is the encoding process described as organization. Relational information can also serve to elaborate a single event with additional information not contained in the episode. Such elaboration serves to enrich memory for the given event, probably by making it distinct from other events. Finally, encoding may involve the transformation of information from one form to another, for example, from verbal to visual form or vice versa.

Encoding processes are important to understand because they determine what is *potentially* remembered about an event. What is *actually* remembered, however, is determined by the ability to access or retrieve the information stored in encoding. The effect of any variable on encoding must also be explained through its impact on retrieval, which is the topic of chapter 6.

Multiple-Choice Items

1. The difference between semantic memory and episodic memory is
   a. semantic memory is short-term and episodic memory is long-term
   b. semantic memory is event memory and episodic memory is general knowledge
   c. semantic memory is less likely to include images
   d. semantic memory is memory for general knowledge and episodic memory is for specific events

2. A consistent ordering in the output of unrelated items is referred to as
   a. material-induced organization
   b. subjective organization
   c. elaboration
   d. distinctiveness

3. It is difficult to decide conclusively whether organization causes good memory because
   a. clustering scores and recall scores can only be correlated
   b. organization does not always improve memory
   c. we do not know how retrieval is influenced by organization
   d. we do not know whether organization affects short-term memory or long-term memory

4. The primary difficulty for the original levels-of-processing hypothesis was
   a. nonsemantic processing normally does not lead to poorer memory than does semantic processing
   b. orienting tasks really do not control encoding
   c. nonsemantic information does not decay more rapidly than does semantic information
   d. semantic information is usually less distinctive than is nonsemantic information

5. The relationship between distinctiveness and organization suggests that
   a. neither are important to memory
   b. both are important to memory
   c. organization is more important to memory
   d. distinctiveness is more important to memory

6. The most direct experimental evidence on the question of whether images are stored in memory comes from studies
   a. on imagination of hidden objects
   b. on concrete versus abstract words
   c. on mental travel
   d. on words versus pictures

True-False Items

1. Encoding processes are an important determinant of retrieval.

2. Material-induced organization requires no psychological process because the organization is in the material.

3. The experiments on clustering and recall clearly show that organization occurs only during encoding or input.

4. Semantic orienting tasks *always* produce better recall than do nonsemantic orienting tasks because semantic information lasts longer.

5. The distinctiveness hypothesis predicts that under some circumstances nonsemantic information can produce better memory than can semantic information.

6. There is much disagreement about whether imagery effects occur in memory.

Discussion Items

1. Describe the relationship between organization and distinctiveness.

2. Why is the research on hidden objects in images crucial to the question of images in memory?

3. Trace the development of the levels-of-processing approach to memory.

Answers to Multiple-Choice Items

1. (d)   Semantic memory refers to general knowledge, while episodic memory refers to specific events.
2. (b)   Subjective organization is a consistent grouping in the output of unrelated words.
3. (a)   All we know is that high clustering usually accompanies good recall. We do not know that clustering causes good recall.
4. (c)   Studies such as Stein's show that nonsemantic information is remembered reasonably well.
5. (b)   Organization may be quite helpful in generating information from which an appropriate response may be selected if the response is distinctively encoded.
6. (a)   If snapshotlike images are stored in memory, a hidden object should not be remembered.

True-False Answers Items

1. (True)   Only those things which have been encoded can be retrieved accurately.
2. (False)   The process of organization detects the structure of the material.
3. (False)   Clustering may also occur at retrieval.
4. (False)   A number of studies have shown that nonsemantic information may last as long as does semantic information.
5. (True)   Distinctiveness, regardless of whether the information is semantic or nonsemantic, is a very critical factor for retention.
6. (False)   Imagery effects clearly occur in memory; the disagreement is over how to explain these effects.

Retrieval Processes

6

Answer the following question: What were you doing at 10:00 A.M. on November 24, 1982? At first glance, this may appear to be a difficult question, but we shall give you a clue and let you think about it. November 24 was the Wednesday before Thanksgiving Day. Now can you answer the question? You may remember that since November 24 was the day before Thanksgiving holiday and you had decided to leave school early you were traveling at 10:00 A.M. on that day. Or you may remember that at 10:00 A.M. on Wednesdays during the fall term you were in English literature class. Regardless of the situation, most persons can provide an answer when clues are given and they use a little thought. This simple example illustrates some of the fundamental characteristics of retrieval from memory.

When memory is used to answer questions such as the one just posed, we generally have the sense of narrowing a set of alternatives until we arrive at the answer. Even to begin this process, however, *cues* are necessary to delineate the general set of events from which to sample. Imagine how ridiculous a question such as "What did you do?" is without context. The questioner must provide some cue as to when or where the activity occurred. Given the importance of cues to retrieval, we begin with a discussion of the effect of cues on memory.

What Makes a Cue Effective?

If the retrieval process is critically dependent upon the use of cues, what is an effective cue? The obvious answer is that a good cue is any information which helps us remember. Equally obvious is that this suggestion is not very helpful. If we must wait until the time of a memory test to see what sorts of cues are useful, we have no way of predicting the level of memory performance and, even worse, no way of facilitating memory in ourselves or others. Thus, an idea about the effectiveness of cues becomes essential not only in understanding the retrieval process, but also in improving memory for events. Two such ideas have dominated thinking about cue effectiveness in event memory: *associative strength* and *encoding specificity*.

Associative Strength Theory of Cue Effectiveness

The basic premise of associative strength theory is that a cue is effective if it has occurred frequently with the to-be-remembered event in the past. Such cues are said to be strongly associated with the event. For example, *whistle* frequently occurs with *train,* and *whistle* is a very good cue to help remember *train.* To determine how strongly associated two words are, free association norms are used. Free association techniques were popularized by Freud who, interestingly enough, used free association for roughly the same purpose as does the cognitive psychologist, to study the structure of memory. In free association, a person simply responds with the first word which comes to mind when given the target word. For example: I say *grass.* You say _____ ? Associative strength is determined by the number of persons giving a particular response. The greater the number of persons who give a common response, the higher the associative strength becomes.

A substantial number of memory studies have shown that strongly associated cues produce better memory than do weakly associated cues. In these experiments, subjects are typically shown pairs of words in a study or input session, some of which are strongly associated *(whistle-train)* and some of which are weakly associated *(black-train).* At the time of the memory test, the cue *(whistle or black)* is provided, and the subject must produce the other member of the pair *(train).* Again, the strongly associated cue is more effective than is the weak cue, and this is true even when the cues are not present at input but only in the test.

Associative strength develops as the result of frequent previous pairings of the two events. After many pairings, the occurrence of one event quickly and automatically brings the other to mind. Note that the retrieval process itself is not terribly complicated. Given an appropriately strong cue, the target event is accessed automatically. So the associative strength theory suggests that the number of previous encodings of two events will determine the cue effectivenss of one for the other. This certainly sounds reasonable, so reasonable that it may be surprising that anyone disagrees. Tulving (1968), however, disagreed and proposed his idea of cue effectiveness based upon encoding specificity.

Encoding Specificity Hypothesis of Cue Effectiveness

Tulving does not quarrel with the premise that past experience is very important to current performance. Virtually all psychologists agree with this principle. Tulving's argument, however, is the interesting suggestion that any given event occurs only once. A particular event does not occur several times, allowing frequent pairings with other events, but rather every event has one and only one episode. You can only have one "first bicycle" to remember just as there can only be one "last night's dinner." If this point is true, and at some level it must be, associative strength theory with its emphasis on frequency of past occurrence must be inadequate.

Tulving's alternative is to suggest that effective retrieval cues are those which were present when the event occurred. That is, *a cue will be effective if it was specifically encoded with the target event*—hence the name *encoding specificity.*

Tulving and Thomson (1971) provided evidence for encoding specificity in contrast to associative strength. Subjects were given a list of weakly associated pairs, for example, *black-train,* at input, and then the subjects were divided into two groups at output. One group was given the list of weakly associated cues seen at input. The second group was given strongly associated cues not present at input. The issue is, which group can remember the best? The results of this experiment demonstrated that the cues present at input or encoding are more effective, even though they are weakly associated. Tulving and Thomson suggest that these results provide support for encoding specificity over associative strength.

The primary difference between encoding specificity and associative strength is the role of past co-occurrence of both the cue and the target event. Tulving suggests that a given event occurs only once, and hence cues that occur with that event are the most effective. Yet, there are certainly situations in which the associative strength of the cue is important. When given the cue *salt,* you are likely to think of *pepper;* when given the word *dog,* you are likely to think *cat.* These are strongly associated word pairs which frequently co-occur, but unlike the previous situations, the information retrieved here is not of a specific event but of general knowledge. Tulving (1972) argues that encoding specificity does not apply to the retrieval of general knowledge, and this argument now becomes the basis for the distinction between episodic memory and semantic memory.

Episodic Memory and Semantic Memory Distinction

Episodic memory refers to memory for specific events that happen once at a given time. *Semantic memory* refers to general world knowledge that is not specifically time tagged. "What did you have for dinner last night?" is a question requiring episodic memory. "What do Eskimos eat for dinner?" is a question drawing on general knowledge of the world, or semantic memory. Retrieval from semantic memory is not governed by encoding specificity. For example, the specific events that occurred when a person initially learns that George Washington was the first president of the United States are not necessary to retrieve *George Washington* in answer to the question "Who was the first president of the United States?" The retrieval process in semantic memory is discussed in chapter 7. Here, it is important to understand that the distinction between episodic memory and semantic memory is based on the assumption that encoding specificity applies only to episodic memory.

In one important sense, encoding specificity is similar to the associative strength hypothesis. Both approaches seem to assume that retrieval is a relatively uncomplicated process. Given the appropriate cue, the target information is automatically accessed. Unlike encoding, where information is transformed and changed, retrieval seems to be a simple matter of going directly to the target. But there is not complete agreement on just how simple the retrieval process is. Let us now turn to a more detailed discussion of this issue.

Event Retrieval: How Complex Is It?

Associative strength and encoding specificity are both instances of the general class of *single-process* retrieval theory. Single-process theories all propose that once the important output conditions are met, for example, a strongly associated cue or a cue present at encoding, retrieval occurs automatically. From this perspective, retrieval is not a very complicated psychological process. It is not something that we think about. It just happens. In a sense this is true. Think about trying to remember a forgotten name. Suddenly, the name pops into awareness and is recalled. In another sense, however, easy recall is only part of the story. Before you recalled the name, you struggled a few minutes trying to retrieve it and probably generated, recognized as incorrect, and then rejected several alternatives. Only after some time in this generation process did you finally retrieve the desired response. Some theorists have argued that examples such as this indicate the complexity of the retrieval process. Specifically, retrieval involves *more than* automatic activation of the target information. According to the *two-process* theory, retrieval involves the generation of candidate information which is then subjected to the recognition decision. Let us now briefly describe the two-process view of retrieval.

Generation-Recognition Model of Retrieval

The generation-recognition model suggests that the output process in recall, where information must be reproduced, involves, first, the activation of potential answers and, second, the decision concerning the accuracy of the response. For example, when we are involved in conversation, we may think of things to say, and then reject some as inappropriate or inaccurate.

In recognition, however, the generation stage is unnecessary. A recognition test does not require reproduction but only the decision concerning whether a particular event was or was not present at input. In other words, generation of the original event is not necessary because the event is present on the test. Thus, the two-process view argues that recognition memory and recall memory tests differ in their retrieval demands. Recall is more complex, requiring *both* generation and the recognition decision. Recognition only requires the recognition decision. One-process theories argue that retrieval occurs in the same way in both recognition and recall. Hence, experimental tests of one- versus two-process theories have focused on differences between recall memory and recognition memory.

How Similar Is Retrieval in Recognition and in Recall?

Two-process theory contends that retrieval operates differently in recognition and in recall, whereas single-process theory suggests that retrieval is the same in both processes. How do we decide between these theories? Obviously we look for differences between recognition memory and recall memory, but we shall see that simple differences between the two are not sufficient to decide the issue. For example, recognition has long been known to be easier than recall. Knowledge of this fact is demonstrated by the preference of most persons for multiple-choice examinations as opposed to essay examinations. Multiple-choice examinations are recognition tests and are generally easier, although this need not be the case if the incorrect alternatives are very similar to the correct response.

One interpretation of the greater difficulty of recall is that recognition does not require generation. This is, of course, two-process theory. Single-process theory, however, can also explain the relative ease of recognition in several different ways. One way is to assume that retrieval cues are important in both recognition and recall, and recognition is at an advantage because it always has the best possible cue, the old item itself. The point is that a more subtle means of deciding between these views is necessary.

The research strategy adopted is actually fairly straightforward in conceptualization. If we want to know whether recognition includes a generation process like that in recall, we can try to manipulate some aspect of a recognition test identified as affecting generation in recall. If we get the same effect in recognition as we do in recall, we may assume that generation must have been operating in recognition. For example, the frequency with which words are used in the language is assumed to affect their accessibility, and indeed, high-frequency words are better recalled than are low-frequency words. Examples of high-frequency words are *house* and *people,* and low-frequency words are exemplified by *cider* and *loon.* What happens in recognition? Low-frequency words are usually better recognized. This theory would make sense if it is true that recognition does not require generation but is based on discriminative decision. Low-frequency words are unusual or rare and hence are quite distinctive in a recognition test. Findings such as these are strong support for the two-process theory.

Using the same technique, however, the one-process theorists generated evidence in their favor. As just discussed, retrieval cues are one of the most powerful variables affecting retrieval in recall. If retrieval cues are changed from input to output, recall memory suffers. If *Grape-Jam* is seen at input, changing the test cue to *Traffic-_____* makes it difficult to retrieve *Jam*. By the same token, if a person's name is associated with his face and then at a later meeting the face has changed, say there is now a beard, the name may be more difficult to recall. The difficulty engendered by the change in cues is generally attributed to failure to generate the response.

Do cue changes affect recognition memory? Certainly they do. A change in the physical appearance of a face can affect recall and may also result in complete failure to recognize the face. If a subject sees *Grape-Jam* at input and the recognition test pair is *Traffic-Jam,* recognition of *Jam* is quite low (Hunt & Ellis, 1974; Light & Carter-Sobell, 1970). Since the cue is presumed to influence generation, the detrimental effect of cue changes on recognition suggests that generation may be as important in recognition as recall. These data, examples of which can be seen in figure 6.1, support a single-process view of retrieval.

Further evidence for a single process of retrieval in recognition and recall comes from the paradigm developed by Tulving and Thomson (1973) which produces the phenomenon known as *recognition failure of recallable words.* The subject is given several presentations and several recall tests on a cue-target word pair, for example, *glue-chair.* After a few such trials, recall of *chair* in the presence of the cue *glue* is very good. Without warning, the next test is a recognition test for *chair* in the presence of a new cue, for example, *table.* Recognition of *chair,* which previously was recalled with high probability, is now very poor. How can this happen if recall requires the recognition decision and recognition does not involve generation? The words were recalled, and for the two-process theorists this means that the words were both generated and recognized in recall. But if they were recognized in recall, should they not easily pass the same recognition decision in the recognition test? Why should recognition fail for recallable words? The single-process theorist's answer is clear: recall and recognition both require the generation process and the new cue in recognition disrupts this process. Here we have another example of evidence taken to support a relatively uncomplicated single-process view.

The counterargument (by now one must be expected) to the two-process view is that the cue change in recognition does not disrupt access to the old encoding. Rather, the memory of the old item is different from the new test item, and the recognition decision is to reject the test item as the

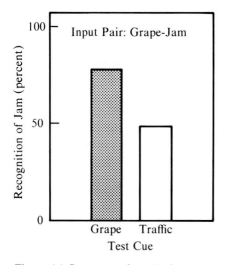

Figure 6.1 Summary of results from a number of studies showing the effect of recognition accuracy of changing a cue from input to test so that the test cue biases a different meaning for the target noun. (From "Recognition Memory and Degree of Semantic Contextual Change" by R. R. Hunt and H. C. Ellis, *Journal of Experimental Psychology,* 1974, *103,* 1153–1159. Copyright 1974 by the American Psychological Association. Reprinted by permission of the publisher and authors.)

one seen (Hunt, 1975, 1976). For example, failure to recognize a friend after he grows a beard is not because you cannot remember what he looked like before the beard, but rather because he looks much different. Similarly, when a subject sees *Grape-Jam* at input and then fails to recognize *Traffic-Jam* at output, it is because the two *Jams* are very different, not because of failure to retrieve the word.

Although this explanation does handle the recognition failure of recallable words without attributing a complicated generation process to recognition, the two-process theorists are now in a rather awkward position. Somehow the copy of the old word in the new cue context is sufficient to access the word; yet the old memory does not match the new test event, and therefore the new event is not recognized. In light of the evidence, the two-process theory may seem unduly complicated and unnecessary. Why not accept the more simple single-process approach?

The reason lies, at least in part, in additional evidence for the two-process view. For example, Rabinowitz, Mandler, and Patterson (1977) showed that the generate-recognize strategy works in recall. Subjects were given a categorized list. One group was instructed at testing to think of as many category members as possible and to decide whether the instance was on the input list. Subjects given these instructions recalled more words than did subjects in the second group who were instructed simply to remember the words. The generate-recognize model seems to work! Furthermore, the generate-recognize model provides a good account of the general superiority of recognition memory over recall memory. It begins to seem as if both sides have considerable support and that a decision between single- and two-process theories of retrieval may be more complicated than the retrieval process itself.

Summary of Single-Process and Two-Process Theories

What, then, are we to make of retrieval of event memories? Before addressing the differences between the two major theories, we should not lose sight of the useful information gained from confrontation between the two ideas. We now know that good event memory depends upon the similarity of cues at input and at output, regardless of whether the test is for recognition or for recall. You can put this powerful piece of information to work by concentrating on developing good cues for material you know you will have to remember. For example, some observers recommend that some study time should be spent in the very room in which the examination will be held. The reasoning is that the room itself can be a useful cue, and this advice can be surprisingly helpful.

Let us briefly return to the nature of the retrieval process. Perhaps there is less difference between the single-process and two-process views of retrieval than initially apparent. If we return to the conceptualization of retrieval as a process of narrowing down the possibilities or of making increasingly fine discriminations, we can see merit in both positions and perhaps find some reconciliation between them. Consider, for example, how to answer the question of what you did in the afternoon two days ago. Usually you initiate the answer by generating fairly general information: "Let's see, two days ago was Tuesday." Then you use the general information to generate more specific information: "On Tuesday I had lunch, and then I went to anthropology class, and I had coffee with friends after class, and we discussed the exam." When generated, such information may lead to finer-grained information about what you did two days ago. This example illustrates what is meant by event retrieval being a *process of narrowing down the possibilities,* and in this particular example, the approach appears similar to the generate-recognize model of event memory. You generate a possibility, consider it, and report it when it is correct and withhold it when it is incorrect.

Sometimes, however, possibilities do not seem to be generated and considered, but rather the event in question is retrieved immediately. Perhaps memory for the event is quite distinctive and cues are so powerful that access is automatic. For example, "Two days ago I took the worst anthropology exam ever" might be an automatic response to the question about what you did two days ago, and response to the question "What is the date of your birth?" might also be automatic. The point is that some events may be so distinctive and the cues so effective that no decision is needed. For more normal day-to-day occurrences, however, this is not likely to be the case. Usually the strategy of narrowing down the events from most general to more specific is employed.

Retrieval and Organization

Finally, we can relate the general process of retrieval to the previous discussion of organization and levels of processing in encoding (Einstein & Hunt, 1980; Hunt & Einstein, 1981). Organization at encoding produces the general information being described in the retrieval process. Organization is the extraction of shared information from among a variety of events. Such information as "all events on Tuesday" and "all events in anthropology class" results from organizational encoding and can be a useful starting point in retrieval. Information specific to each event within the more general organization is also extracted at encoding. This specific or distinctive information is necessary if we are to move from general organization to specific event memory in retrieval. The principle here is simply that what can be retrieved is only what has been stored, and what has been stored can be retrieved only under appropriate circumstances. We can learn more about the interaction between encoding and retrieval as well as about the circumstances appropriate for retrieval by examining retrieval failure.

Overview of Retrieval Failure: Forgetting

Rarely is memory for events noticed until that memory fails. Human memory is so important for our survival that the system is quite efficient, and when it fails, the results are usually frustrating and sometimes serious. Forgetting causes problems ranging in severity from simple inconvenience of a second trip to the store due to forgetting to get some items to potential death due to forgetting to add brake fluid to the braking system of an automobile. Forgetting then becomes a major practical problem for individuals as well as for organizations and industry. As interested as we are in providing solutions to practical problems, we are perhaps more concerned with the basic question of why memory fails.

We first must understand that not all problems we call forgetting are actually due to memory failure. Many times we fail to provide an appropriate answer, not because we forget, but rather because we have never known the information. An examination may be missed because of not paying attention on the days the examination was announced. These instances are not properly forgetting but represent lack of storage or failure to input the event to long-term memory. How some of these storage problems may arise were discussed in the earlier chapters on displacement from the sensory register and short-term memory and capacity limitations on attention. The term *forgetting* is reserved for cases of *failure to access information that is stored.* Why does forgetting occur?

Decay Theory

We discussed two general classes of theories in chapter 4 on short-term memory, decay and interference. Recall that decay theory suggests that information simply weakens or is lost over time if it is not used. You may also recall that decay theory has not been very popular, although at the levels of sensory register and short-term memory it has advocates. Few researchers, however, maintain that long-term memory decays. This aversion to the decay theory is due in part to the fact that natural events are influenced by factors other than the passage of time. For example, if left in a complete vacuum, iron does not rust over any period of time. As a natural phenomenon, memory should therefore not go away due only to the passage of time. Something does happen over time to cause forgetting, but does forgetting result from the complete loss of long-term memory, as implied by the decay theory? Evidence from several sources has long suggested that this is not the case, but rather that long-term memory is permanent. For example, Penfield (1959) suggested that electrical stimulation of certain parts of the brain can activate memories not thought to be available. Patients undergoing neurosurgery are sometimes only given a local anesthetic because the brain has no pain receptors, and once the brain is exposed, very little pain is involved. These patients can talk and report the sensations they are having. Thus, when Penfield stimulated certain parts of the brain, the patients reported memories such as smells and songs from their childhood. This finding is often cited as strong evidence for the permanence on long-term memory, but we should also note the recent criticism of this conclusion by Loftus and Loftus (1980).

Regardless of the ultimate fate of decay theory, we do know that available information sometimes cannot be immediately accessed. How many times do we try and fail to remember something only to remember it later? The fact that the information is remembered later suggests that it was available but something interfered with its access. Let us examine the sources of the interference and the conditions in which it occurs.

Retroactive and Proactive Interference

Two sources of interference to disrupt memory for certain to-be-remembered (target) information are available. *Retroactive interference* is produced by material encountered after the target event is encoded. For example, information acquired in a sociology class may disrupt memory for the information learned in an earlier psychology class. The prefix *retro* means "backward in time," and remembering this fact makes it easy to remember that retroactive interference results from interfering material that occurs after the target material, which thus exerts its interfering effects on information encountered before the interfering event.

Proactive interference is produced by material occurring prior to the target information. In the previous example (psychology class before sociology class) material learned in psychology class might interfere with information acquired later in sociology class. The prefix *pro* means "forward" and therefore remember that proactive interference results from material exerting an interfering effect on material learned later. A schematic representation of situations producing retroactive interference and proactive interference is shown in figure 6.2.

Material that occurs either before or after the event being remembered can make memory difficult. We call one proactive interference and the other retroactive interference, but so far they are just labels for two situations in which forgetting occurs. They do not tell us why some of the events that occur before and after an event cause forgetting. This is the role of *interference theory*.

Interference Theory

During the 1940s and 1950s, when experimental psychology was dominated by the concern with associative learning, the closest approach to the study of memory was called *verbal learning*. All of human learning, including verbal learning, was assumed to be a matter of establishing associations between units known as *stimuli* and *responses*. The degree of learning of an association was described in terms of associative strength, and the primary concern in verbal learning was the fate of associative strength over time. Decrease in associative strength presumably accounted for forgetting. Interference theory developed as the account of changes in associative strength over time (e.g., McGeoch, 1942).

Interference theory proposes two basic mechanisms underlying forgetting, *response competition* and *unlearning*. Response competition occurs when the same cue is associated with two different responses. Suppose that the concept of *behavior* is defined differently in your psychology class than in your sociology class. Assume also that your psychology class meets before the sociology class. If *behavior* is defined in your psychology class,

Retroactive Interference	Proactive Interference
1	Encounter To-Be-Remembered Material	Encounter Interfering Material
2	Encounter Interfering Material	Encounter To-Be-Remembered Material
3	Memory Test for To-Be-Remembered Material	Memory Test for To-Be-Remembered Material

Order in which Events Occur (label on left side, rows 1, 2, 3)

Figure 6.2 Sequence of events in retroactive interference and in proactive interference.

and then in your sociology class the definition for *behavior* is different, the first definition will be in competition with the second definition. The stimulus *behavior* elicits two different responses, the definitions, only one of which is correct. Response competition leads to the second basic mechanism, unlearning.

When the response to the stimulus is incorrect, a likely event in response competition, the incorrect response is not reinforced. That is, we learn that it is wrong, and this lack of reinforcement weakens the associative strength of that response. The problem is that different responses to the same stimulus may actually be appropriate, each in a different context. For example, both the sociological and psychological definitions of *behavior* are appropriate responses to the stimulus *behavior,* but in different contexts. However, when asked for the definition of *behavior* in sociology class and you respond with the definition from psychology class, you will learn that you are wrong. The association between the psychological definition and *behavior* is weakened. You are now likely to forget the psychological definition. Notice that the material you acquired later, the sociological definition, interferes with the earlier event. This is then a case of retroactive interference.

Through the two basic mechanisms of response competition and unlearning, interference theory attempts to explain how retroactive interference and proactive interference cause forgetting. The theory remains the best developed idea about forgetting available, and elaboration of its basic concepts continues to enrich interference theory (Postman & Underwood, 1973). In spite of the refinement of interference theory, alternative accounts of forgetting have begun to emerge from the information-processing framework. The basic premise of one of these ideas is that all forgetting can be analyzed as failure of retrieval cues. Let us briefly examine how this approach explains proactive and retroactive interferences.

Cue-Dependent Forgetting

As discussed previously, many theorists believe that long-term memory is permanent. Once information is stored, it remains. This does not mean, however, that forgetting never occurs. Rather, failure to remember information stored may occur because of inability to gain access to this information. The major reason for access failure is that the cues are inappropriate or ineffective. Forgetting thus becomes a matter of *retrieval failure attributable to poor cues.*

For example, this type of problem was suggested in the discussion of levels of processing and encoding. Nonsemantic orientation leads to poor memory for a word, but not because the nonsemantic information is unavailable in memory. Rather the nonsemantic information is not very useful for reconstructing the semantic unit of a word. Morris, Bransford, and Franks (1977) labeled this problem inappropriate test strategy, but the general difficulty is that the nonsemantic information is inappropriate to retrieve the word. Tulving's encoding specificity principle of retrieval makes exactly the same point. Cues present at input are effective, whereas other cues are less appropriate. Forgetting then occurs because a cue which was not present at input fails to access the stored information.

Tulving's (1974) advocacy of encoding specificity led him to view forgetting as basically a problem with retrieval cues. He and his students argued that both retroactive interference and proactive interference are better understood as cue-dependent forgetting than as unlearning and response competition.

For example, Tulving and Psotka (1971) have shown that retroactive interference can be reduced when appropriate retrieval cues are provided. Retroactive interference was induced by giving subjects a series of categorized lists, each list containing different instances of the same category. The first list might include *dog, horse, cow, shirt, shoes,* and *hat* and the second list *cat, pig, lion, coat, pants,* and *tie.* After five such lists were presented, recall of the earlier lists was much poorer than recall of the later lists, a clear instance of retroactive interference. Furthermore, the decline in performance on earlier lists was due solely to the forgetting of entire categories. Subjects failed to recall a single instance from some categories, while they recalled a substantial number of items from other categories. The later lists seemed to cause complete failure to access some of the categories in earlier lists. In a final memory test, however, the subjects were given the category superordinates, for example, *animal* and *clothes,* as retrieval cues. On the final cued recall test, recall for items from the first list was as good as recall for items from the last list. Providing the cues eliminated retroactive interference. Tulving and Psotka suggest that retroactive interference occurs because the interfering materials result in failure to access the stored information. When the cues are provided, access can be achieved. Clearly, the information is not lost, as implied by either decay or unlearning, but rather is inaccessible due to cue-dependent forgetting.

Although the idea of cue-dependent forgetting is appealing in several respects, many questions remain to be answered. For example, why do subsequent materials interfere with retrieval of entire categories of previous materials? In some respects, Tulving and Psotka's (1971) experiment demonstrates that retrieval cues can be interfered with, but does not tell us a great deal about how this happens. Moreover, all forgetting does not seem to be due to failure to generate the correct event. In many cases, we are able to generate the event information but are confused or indecisive about its correctness. For example, remember times on an examination when you wanted to include the name of a particular research scientist, thought you knew the name but were not sure, and finally omitted it rather than risk being wrong. Here, you retrieved or generated the information, but did not respond due to indecision. Nonetheless, the result is something that can be called forgetting. This type of confusion is a frequent cause of forgetting and is more consistent with the failure of a two-process decision component. Nonetheless, the view of forgetting as cue-dependent retrieval failure promises to clarify certain aspects of forgetting, and after much additional research, it may lead to better understanding of memory failure.

How to Minimize Forgetting

In this section techniques based on the principles of both encoding and retrieval, which minimize the forgetting of events, are discussed. Let us illustrate these principles in the context of study habits that can be developed, but you are warned at the outset that we know of no fancy tricks. On the other hand, developing facility in memory is not particularly complicated; you just need to concentrate on certain basic points.

Indeed, concentration is the first step. What was not stored cannot be remembered, and perhaps the major failure to perform is due to lack of initial storage. In the context of studying, *pay attention* to the lectures. Compulsive note takers may have to return to their notes after class since it may be difficult both to take notes and to think about the lecture. Notes for one day can usually be covered adequately in 10 to 15 minutes, so always try to cover notes on the same day as the class. Adequately covering notes, as well as reading the text, is an important aspect of encoding. As we have seen, encoding involves more than simply allowing the eyeball to pass over words. An important aspect of encoding is to develop *organization* or relationship between discrete parts of an event. This can be done during study by always relating the topic of the day's lecture to the previous class. The same is true of reading assignments where organization is inherent in the text. Most books have various headings and are divided into chapters. Be sure you can relate each subtopic to the next level. These activities are not usually hard to do but do require considerable concentration.

In addition to organization, *elaboration* and *distinctiveness* can be important parts of studying. Relate the material not only to the additional material but also to other known facts. You can decide whether you really understand a concept by trying to state its meaning in your own words. Then try to use the concept with an example of your own. For example, discuss both the meaning of encoding and provide an example of distinctive encoding. Next, increase the distinctiveness of the material by thinking about how it differs from other concepts in the same area. For example, see not only the similarities between *organization* and *distinctiveness,* but also the differences.

In addition to encoding processes, memory can be improved by concentration on certain principles of *retrieval.* Foremost among the principles is the *development* and *use of good cues.* During the course of good studying, persons are likely to develop good cues without intending to do so. The organizational structure of the material once encoded can serve a powerful cueing function. Unfortunately, many persons do not take advantage of the cues at the time of a test. A decent examination question, for example, usually contains cues which should direct attention to the appropriate memory. Too many students, however, spend too little time reading and thinking about a question.

Another important consideration is to *practice retrieval.* Practice in retrieval is better for memory than are additional input trials. One way to incorporate retrieval practice in studying is to pause after each paragraph and without looking at the text repeat the main idea of that paragraph in your own words. This technique not only allows retrieval practice, but also provides a check on how carefully you are reading. Another possibility is to construct your own questions and then answer them. The point again is to practice retrieving information, even if you simply rehearse the material in your free time.

You now see that the practices we suggest are not particularly tricky and certainly are not difficult. They do, however, require time, and studying should be scheduled on a consistent basis. These kinds of techniques cannot be used the night before an examination, if for no other reason than the concentration required will make it difficult to study for long periods of time. On the other hand, we think implementing these techniques in your study habits will improve your performance considerably.

State-Dependent Effects

In this section we turn our attention to the idea of state-dependent effects in memory. Just as memory is dependent upon the effectiveness of retrieval cues, it is also somewhat dependent upon a person's "state" when the information was originally encoded.

State-Dependent Memory

The general notion of state dependency refers to the idea that the "states" or conditions under which an event is learned may be strong and important cues in retrieving particular information. For example, if information is processed while a person has a few drinks, it might be that later recall of the information would be best if the person had a few drinks at the time of recall. This is an instance of alcohol state dependency. There is, in fact, considerable evidence for drug-induced state dependency in memory (Eich, 1980).

    State dependency is a relative concept. In the example just given, if the person can recall the information *only* after a few drinks, and not otherwise, his memory will then completely depend upon restoring the "semi-alcoholic" state present at the time of original learning. Fortunately, memory is usually not this dependent upon perfect and full restoration of the original state. What is usually the case is that memory is only partly dependent on a particular state. A particular state may be the amount of alcohol consumed or the presence of other drugs in the body. Other states may be the emotional mood conditions under which learning takes place.

Emotional Mood States and Memory

One interesting line of recent research is the role of emotional mood states in learning and memory. This research focuses on several kinds of questions. One concerns the effects of emotional mood states on memory and in particular on organizational aspects of memory. Another concerns the phenomenon of the emotional state as a state-dependent factor in memory. Here the issue is whether the prevailing emotional state present during learning provides a retrieval context in recalling a memory.

    Let us consider the issue of emotional mood state dependency first. The research of Bower and colleagues established the notion of mood state dependency (Bower, 1981; Bower, Monteiro, & Gilligan, 1978). In a typical free-recall task, they had subjects learn a list of words in either a happy or sad mood state by the use of hypnotic procedures. At the time of recall, the subjects were tested either in the same mood or in the opposite mood.

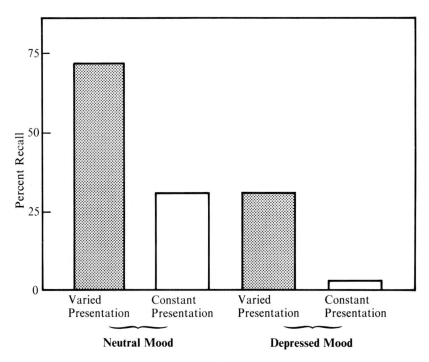

Figure 6.3 Recall of letter sequences as a function of mood state and of constant and varied presentation of items. (From "Emotional Mood States, Strategies, and State-Dependency in Memory" by K. A. Leight and H. C. Ellis, *Journal of Verbal Learning and Verbal Behavior,* 1981, *20,* 251–266.)

The logic of this approach is quite straightforward. If subjects perform better in the same mood than in the changed mood, there is then evidence for a state-dependent effect. The results are strikingly clear. They found that being in the same mood at recall and at learning, whether sad or happy, led to better retention than being in a changed mood.

In a similar vein Leight and Ellis (1981) have shown powerful effects of mood states on organizational processes in memory as well as state-dependent effects. In their study, subjects learned a perceptual grouping task in which a sequence of letters was presented which, when grouped, made up a unit which could be pronounced. In effect, the subjects could discover the structure of the letter sequence and organize it into a more meaningful unit. Thus the task allows organizational processes to operate. The letter sequence either was presented in the same fashion or was varied on each trial. Figure 6.3 shows the basic results. A particularly important finding was that subjects in a depressed mood state showed a remarkably reduced capacity to organize the verbal sequence for recall, whereas those in a neutral mood state performed well.

Recall of the letter sequences was best when subjects were in a neutral mood. But there was an interesting relationship between mood state and varied or constant condition during learning. The neutral mood subjects in the varied condition showed the best recall, whereas the depressed mood subjects in the constant condition showed virtually no recall. Interestingly, the two other groups performed at the same level of recall. These data are also important because they suggest that forcing depressed-mood subjects to process material more actively (the varied condition) helps to improve their recall. Requiring these subjects to be more active apparently acts to compensate for or overcome some of the debilitating effects of a depressed mood.

Finally, in other studies Bower (1981) has shown a *mood congruence effect*. For example, subjects in a happy mood during learning show better memory for happy-theme stories, whereas subjects in a sad mood during learning show better memory for sad-theme stories. There are several possible explanations for the mood congruence effect. One is the selective reminding hypothesis. This assumes, for example, that when one is sad, a sad incident in a story is more likely to remind one of a similar incident in life than a happy incident, and likewise when one is happy, reading about a happy incident will remind one of a happy incident in life. Such reminding can enhance memory for the event being studied.

Summary

In chapter 6 a variety of issues concerned with the output process from memory were raised. One of the obvious facts about memory is that cues are helpful. Indeed, memory cannot be addressed in the absence of some sort of cue. What is less obvious but equally important is what makes a good cue. Associative strength and encoding specificity are two ideas concerning cue effectiveness. More generally, both of these ideas imply an automatic and uncomplicated retrieval process.

A slightly different general idea is that retrieval entails both search and decision stages, which is the more complicated two-process view. The differences between single- and two-process views of retrieval were explored in a number of experiments comparing recognition memory and recall memory tests.

Forgetting, which is the failure of retrieval, was discussed and various theories concerning the process of forgetting were considered, including decay and interference and cue-dependent forgetting.

Practical tips on increasing the probability of retrieval were suggested. Foremost among the suggestions were the development and utilization of effective cues and practice in retrieval.

Finally, a new concept, state-dependent effects on memory, was discussed, and recent research in this area was described.

Multiple-Choice Items

1. Which of the following are the two major theories of cue effectiveness?
   a. levels of processing and associative strength
   b. imagery and encoding specificity
   c. associative strength and encoding specificity
   d. encoding specificity and proactive interference

2. The primary determinant of the associative strength of a cue is
   a. the encoding specificity
   b. the number of times a cue and target are paired
   c. the number of people giving the response to a cue
   d. the length of the retention interval between cue and target

3. The primary determinant of encoding specificity is
   a. the number of times the cue occurs with the target
   b. the associative strength of the cue and target
   c. the amount of time between cue and target
   d. the presence of the cue at encoding of the target

4. Encoding specificity is an example
   a. of the retrieval process
   b. of the generate-recognize model
   c. of a complex retrieval model
   d. of a single-process model

5. The similarity of recognition memory and recall memory is important to the generate-recognize model of retrieval because
   a. they should be the same according to this model
   b. they should be different according to this model
   c. recall should be easier according to this model
   d. all single-process models focus on this issue

6. The view of forgetting which is most compatible with the encoding specificity hypothesis of retrieval is
   a. cue-dependent forgetting
   b. proactive interference
   c. retroactive interference
   d. decay

True-False Items

1. Strongly associated cues normally produce better memory than do weakly associated cues.

2. Encoding specificity does not apply to semantic memory.

3. Recognition memory is normally better than recall memory.

4. The interference theory of forgetting assumes that the forgotten material is available in memory.

5. Proactive interference results from material intervening between the to-be-remembered material and the memory test.

6. The major cause of forgetting is failure to store the materials in the first place.

Discussion Items

1. Describe the experiments used to support the encoding specificity hypothesis over the associative strength hypothesis of retrieval cue effectiveness.

2. Discuss the difference between single-process and generate-recognize models of retrieval, describing the importance of recognition and recall comparisons in this issue.

Answers to Multiple-Choice Items

1. (c) Associative strength and encoding specificity are the two major theories of cue effectiveness.
2. (b) The number of times the cue and the target occur together determines the associative strength.
3. (d) According to encoding specificity, a cue is effective if it is specifically encoded with the target.
4. (d) The only important consideration is the single process of the cue present when the target is encoded.
5. (b) The generate-recognize model suggests that retrieval processes are different in recognition and recall.
6. (a) Failure to remember, according to encoding specificity, is attributable to poor retrieval cues, and this position is the same as cue-dependent forgetting.

Answers to True-False Items

    1.   (True)   All other things equal, a strongly associated cue leads to better memory than does a weakly associated cue.

    2.   (True)   The distinction between semantic memory and episodic memory is based on the assumption that encoding specificity does not apply to semantic memory.

    3.   (True)   Recognition is usually easier than recall.

    4.   (True)   In order for something to interfere with something else, both must be present.

    5.   (False)   Proactive interference results from material which occurs before the to-be-remembered material is experienced.

    6.   (False)   Forgetting refers only to cases in which the material was stored.

Semantic Memory

7

Long-term memory encompasses not only specific past events but also general knowledge of the world. As previously mentioned in the discussion of the distinction between episodic memory and semantic memory, semantic memory refers to general knowledge which cannot be traced to a single event. Rather, general knowledge seems to be the abstraction of common elements from a variety of previous episodes. For example, can you remember the circumstances under which you first learned the meaning of the symbol (Stop) ? Although you have encountered this event numerous times, you probably have few, if any, highly specific memories of the episodes. Nonetheless, you know what to do when confronted by the event, regardless of whether you encounter it driving a Mercedes in New York City or a pickup truck in Dubuque, Iowa. You have the concept or knowledge of this event. Notice that the knowledge you have about even this simple event reaches far beyond just "stop." It includes the action to be taken as well as the consequences of failing to take that action. In short, knowledge of even a simple concept consists of a wide range of information.

This example, of course, represents only a tiny fraction of the vast knowledge that all human beings possess. Psychologists have historically been interested in the acquisition and utilization of knowledge, and recent advancements in ideas and techniques bring renewed activity to this area. In chapter 7 some of the theories and experiments on semantic memory are described. First, however, let us examine the function of knowledge: What can a knowledgeable person do that a less knowledgeable person cannot? The answer to this question can provide a basis for constructing our theories of semantic memory, as well as instruct us as to the interaction between semantic memory and other cognitive processes. The best way to examine the difference between high- and low-knowledge performance is to compare persons who are experts on a topic with persons who are less expert.

Expert Performance

When we speak of high-knowledge individuals, we refer to the highly developed skills these persons have in a particular area, not to their general intelligence. Contrary to the belief of some, most of us are good at something, be it math, automobile repair, golf, or social interaction. Psychologists interested in expert performance have generally studied games (chess and Go, for example) for several reasons. As a matter of convenience, most games have a short duration and can easily be adapted to laboratory situations. More important, games have a clear set of rules and a clear goal state. The goal state is to accomplish a specific action, such as checkmating a king or scoring points, and to do more of this action or do it more quickly than an opponent. It is then possible to present subjects with the partial account of a game in progress, such as a game of chess in which several moves have already been made, and assess various aspects of their knowledge. Furthermore, the unambiguous rules and outcome state of games make identification of experts easier. While other fields such as teaching, auto mechanics, and medicine clearly have experts, identification of these persons takes longer, and the criteria for labeling a person an expert are more complex. The hope is that what is learned about the function of knowledge by studying experts at games will apply in some general way to other domains of knowledge. Let us see what this approach might tell us about semantic memory by examining the work of James Voss at the University of Pittsburgh on knowledge of baseball.

In a series of experiments (Chiesi, Spilich, & Voss, 1979; Spilich, Vesonder, Chiesi, & Voss, 1979), Voss and colleagues reported interesting differences on a variety of measures between people who knew a lot about baseball and people who knew less. Baseball knowledge was assessed by a prior test, and two groups of subjects were identified as high- and low-knowledge groups. Everyone then was given an account of one-half an inning in the middle of a fictitious game. Subsequently, all subjects received a variety of tests on the material, beginning with straightforward memory tests. Not surprisingly, the high-knowledge individuals remembered much more of the passage than did the persons who knew less about baseball. Moreover, the recall of the baseball experts was more ordered and contained more detail relevant to the outcome of the game. High-knowledge persons were likely to have the events in proper sequence and to recall relevant information about the progress of the game. Low-knowledge subjects were more likely to remember less relevant information, like the time of day the game was played.

Finally, the subjects were asked to write what they thought would happen next in the game. For example, suppose the team at bat is behind 5 to 2 in the seventh inning. Runners are on second base and third base with one out. The scheduled batter is the pitcher and the opposing pitcher is left-handed. What is likely to happen next? If you know a good bit about baseball, you can construct a reasonable scenario for ensuing events. If you know little about baseball, your story is likely to be less detailed and accurate. This is exactly what happened in the experiment.

The Function of Knowledge

We suspect that there is very little of surprise in Voss's research, but careful consideration of the experiments shows that they are quite instructive. What sorts of activities does knowledge allow? First, the more that is known about a topic, the better new information related to the topic is remembered. Perhaps memory is so good because the knowledge provides a *framework* for interpreting and organizing the material. Second, the ordering of recall by the high-knowledge group is consistent with the assumption that knowledge aids organization. Third, a much more fundamental role for knowledge is implicated: namely, experiences are interpreted through the existing knowledge base. That is, the meaning of events derives from the information the event activates in semantic memory. The meaning of a particular event seems to be a multidimensional affair. In other words, the meaning of a concept includes perceptual information, conceptual information, and functional information. For example, the meaning of *apple* might include "red, round, fruit, and eat." An important point to note is that the concepts are defined in terms of other concepts, just as words are defined in terms of other words.

This leads to the final important observation from the baseball experiments concerning the function of knowledge. Knowledge, sometimes in conjunction with specific event memory, allows projection into the future. Based upon what is known, plans are laid and schedules made. Just as the high-knowledge subjects in Voss's experiments could project the probable action in the baseball game, so knowledge in other domains allows us to predict what will happen and to plot a course of action. This point is discussed later in relation to academic work and social interactions.

In summary, the functions of the concept of knowledge are to interpret incoming information, to provide the meaning of events, and to allow projection into the future.

The Task of Describing Semantic Memory

Psychologists interested in the study of knowledge have as part of their goal the description of the *structure* of semantic memory. By structure is meant an abstract, theoretical description of the organization of world knowledge. This description must capture the relationships among concepts and in so doing describe the richness inherent in the meaning of concepts.

A prominent view of human cognition is that of a computational system, in which the processes of perception, memory, thinking, and reasoning require calculation to obtain a particular outcome. In order to perceive a boat on the horizon, for example, the perceptual system calculates or computes the information available to arrive at the conclusion "a boat." Any computational system must have a data base from which to perform calculations. The system we know as arithmetic has numbers as its data base. While much formal training in arithmetic concentrates on the processes or rules of calculation, something must also be known about the structure of the data base. For example, even if we rarely think about it, we know that the interval between two adjacent numbers is equal regardless of the size of the numbers. The distance between 99 and 100 is the same as the distance between 0 and 1. As trivial as this fact appears, the description of the structure of the number system is critical to consistently applying computational rules. You know that the difference between 100 and 99 is the same as the difference between 1 and 0 because of the rules of subtraction and because of the structure of the number system.

In a similar fashion, semantic memory serves as the data base for the computational processes of the cognitive system. The content of semantic memory provides the raw data for perception, memory, and thinking, and thus it becomes quite important to know something of the structure and content of semantic memory. Primarily for this reason, the major goal of research in semantic memory has been to describe the structure of knowledge.

Theories of Semantic Memory

The ideas that we discuss concerning semantic memory can be distinguished on two levels. The first concerns the types of general structures proposed for knowledge. Here, two types of structures, network models and feature models are described. The second distinction is the level at which the knowledge is represented. Here, the primary difference is between structures designed to reflect single concepts, best described as words such as *dog, frog,* or *justice,* and more complex structures which reflect higher-order idea units, best described as phrases or sentences such as "The young couple went barefoot in the park." The second idea generally proposes a concept known as the propositional representation.

The differences between these structures will become clear as we discuss the various ideas, and further, certain differences between the retrieval processes proposed by the various theories are described. The discussion begins with consideration of one of the first and simplest ideas about semantic memory, associative network models.

Associative Network Models

When you hear the word *green,* what is the first word that comes to mind? Many persons will say *grass* with no hesitation. Like many other questions, such as "What is your name?" the answer seems to occur automatically. Further, the answer almost feels as if it were linked to the question in the mind. As soon as the question is heard, the answer appears. This situation suggests that the concepts involved are strongly related, perhaps to the extent that one is part of the other's meaning. The theoretical link between concepts has historically been called an *association,* and the associative network model of semantic memory is one in which all of the concepts, all of general knowledge, are interrelated through associations of various strengths. To give you a clear idea of the associative network model, let us begin by discussing one of the first contemporary models of semantic memory, which serves as the basis for more recent associative models.

Teachable Language Comprehender (TLC)

The first major theory of semantic memory was actually designed as a computer program to understand language. This program, proposed by Quillian (1968, 1969), was called the Teachable Language Comprehender (TLC). Quillian's strategy was to develop a memory structure for a computer which would allow the computer to answer questions and if the structure were successful for the computer, to explore whether it had testable implications in human beings for the use of knowledge. So the first challenge was to devise a method of representing knowledge so that even a machine could demonstrate some of the flexibility inherent in human knowledge. For example, questions which seem to be based on inferences rather than on directly known information are easily answered. Does a canary have skin? Assuming that you can answer this question, how do you know? Have you ever had direct experience with canary skin? Have you ever been taught explicitly that canaries have skin? Probably not. The answer to this question is inferred, based on other things known about canaries, and part of the task confronting Quillian was to capture this inferential ability.

The structure proposed by Quillian is actually quite simple. It is a hierarchically organized system in which related concepts are connected by associations. *Hierarchical conceptual organization* means that superordinate concepts are at a higher level and are connected to subordinate concepts. Figure 7.1 provides an example of a limited portion of the structure. Notice that the superordinate *animal* subsumes subordinates *fish* and *bird.* This then represents the knowledge that both mammals and birds are

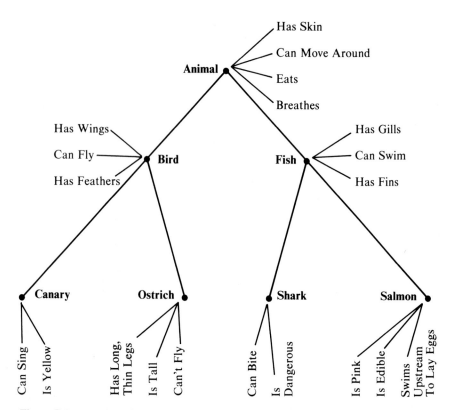

Figure 7.1 A portion of the teachable language comprehender (TLC) model of semantic memory. (From "Retrieval Time from Semantic Memory" by A. M. Collins and M. R. Quillian, *Journal of Verbal Learning and Verbal Behavior*, 1969, *8*, 240–247. Copyright 1969 by Academic Press. Used by permission.)

animals. Similarly, *bird* is superordinate to *canary* and *ostrich* as well as to all of the other facts known about birds. Furthermore, notice that each node or concept has associated with it certain properties characteristic of that concept. Animals have skin and they eat and breathe. Birds have feathers and wings and they fly. Canaries are yellow. At this point, the question of why the properties are not listed at each node might be raised. After all, canaries have feathers and birds breathe. This question brings us to the assumption of *cognitive economy*.

The properties of any concept are stored at the highest possible node. For example, if all animals have skin, then *skin* is not stored with the concept of each animal but is stored with the concept of *animal*. This assumption provides obvious economy of storage in that information is not duplicated unnecessarily within the structure. But if this is the case, how do we answer the question, does a canary have skin?, a question which now takes us to the process of accessing knowledge in the TLC.

The process of retrieving knowledge is quite straightforward. The concept for which knowledge is to be accessed is activated by presentation of a question. The information linked to that concept is also activated by tracing the associative network. For example, the question "Is a canary a bird?" activates the concept *canary* and the association is traced to *bird*. Once the concept *bird* is found in association with *canary*, a yes response can be given to the question. The question "Does a *canary* have skin?" activates the canary node, and the network is traced directly to *animal* where the property "has skin" is found. Since *canary* is a subordinate of *animal*, it is now possible to respond that "Yes, canaries have skin." We can now see that TLC allows us to generate or infer facts not directly stored with a concept. Further, it is evident that knowledge of a concept is represented both by the concept node and by the relationships or associations between nodes. Thus, TLC describes the knowledge of a concept in terms of the representative node and concepts and properties associated with the node.

Tests of TLC The importance of Quillian's computer program for psychology lies in its ability to generate interesting predictions about human performance. One such prediction is quite clear from the model, and the experiments based on this prediction created an explosion of research in semantic memory. The prediction is of a *category size effect:* that is, larger categories require more time for search than do smaller categories. *Animal* is a larger category than *bird;* very simply *animal* includes *bird* as well as a number of other concepts. Within TLC, the superordinate of a large category is farther from an instance in the associative network than is the superordinate of a small category. In other words, in figure 7.1 *canary* is farther removed from the larger category superordinate *animal* than it is from the smaller category superordinate *bird*. From the premise that traversing the network requires time, it should follow that verifying canary as a bird would require less time than verifying canary as an animal. This is known as the category size effect.

Notice that the measure of performance is not accuracy, as in many memory experiments, but rather is reaction time. The reason is fairly obvious: the questions posed to the subject are designed to tap the knowledge base. In order to examine the structure of knowledge, we must ask questions for which a subject knows answers. Because accuracy will be near perfect, another measure of performance is needed. Let us see how reaction time serves as that measure.

In a series of experiments, Collins and Quillian (1969) asked subjects to respond yes or no as quickly as they could to a series of statements such

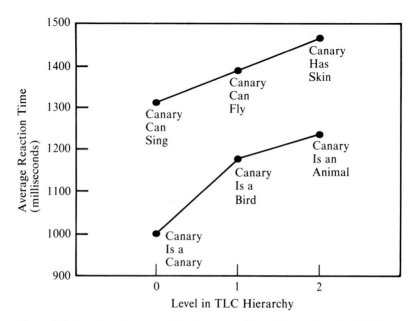

Figure 7.2 Reaction time to verify statements from different levels of TLC hierarchy. (From "Retrieval Time from Semantic Memory" by A. M. Collins and M. R. Quillian, *Journal of Verbal Learning and Verbal Behavior,* 1969, *8,* 240–247. Copyright 1969 by Academic Press. Used by permission.)

as "A canary is a canary," "A canary is a bird," and "A canary is an animal." Based on the TLC model's prediction of a category size effect, reaction time should increase in the order that the statements are listed here. Collins and Quillian's results, which are presented in figure 7.2, are consistent with this prediction. The smaller the category is, the less time is required to verify an instance as a member of the category.

More impressive were the results on sentences stating property relations. For example, the TLC model predicts a regular increase in reaction time to verify the sentences "A canary can sing," "A canary can fly," and "A canary has skin." Again, the information required is stored at different levels of the hierarchy, and on the assumption of cognitive economy, reaction time should be faster to "sings" than to "flies" and faster to "flies" than to "has skin." Figure 7.2 shows that the results of Collins and Quillian's experiment were again consistent with the predictions from TLC.

The initial predictions were quite bold, and the results from this experiment were highly favorable to the model. As is often the case with a promising new approach, however, the work of Collins and Quillian initiated a line of research destined to modify their ideas.

Problems for TLC   The fundamental difficulty with the TLC is in the relationships between various concepts and between concepts and their properties. That is, a strictly hierarchical relationship between concepts is inconsistent with information now available, and the assumption of cognitive economy in the representation of concepts does not seem to be completely accurate.

Conrad (1972) questioned Collins and Quillian's original interpretation of the reaction times to property judgments. Rather than assume that the times to verify "A canary sings" and "A canary has skin" reflect differences in hierarchical storage, Conrad argued that these properties are experienced with different frequency. That is, it is quite common to experience singing and canary together, so that when we think of *canary*, we then think of "singing." But very few of us have any direct experience with canary skin and are unlikely to think "skin" when we think *canary*. To explore these ideas, Conrad collected production frequency norms; she gave subjects a concept such as *canary* and asked them to write all of the facts which came to mind when they thought of *canary*. She was then able to arrange the properties of various concepts in order of how many subjects listed each property. For example, a large number of subjects gave the response "moves" to *animal* but very few responded "has ears." It is important to note, however, that in the hierarchical model of Quillian both properties are listed at the *animal* node and should produce the same reaction time.

By pitting the frequency of responses against their position in the TLC hierarchy, Conrad performed an experiment whose results seriously questioned the strict view of cognitive economy. That is, the speed with which properties are verified is determined by the *frequency* with which they are listed rather than by their location in the hierarchy. Conrad then suggested that the properties are stored directly at the level of the concepts, regardless of the duplication involved.

Although Conrad's data raise serious problems for the cognitive economy of TLC, the idea of direct storage seems a bit implausible. Can it be that "has a backbone" is among the information most of us store for every person we know? This certainly seems unlikely. The problem is that Conrad also seems to be assuming a rigid hierarchical representation, where all concepts are represented in some strictly logical fashion. In fact, these data may be as critical of this type of hierarchical model as they are of the assumption of cognitive economy.

A related, and perhaps more serious, problem for a strict hierarchical network such as TLC is the relationship of various subordinates to a common superordinate. The hierarchical model treats all subordinates of a superordinate as equal; that is, all of the subordinates are directly related to the superordinate. But we know that all subordinates are not equally related to the superordinate. Not all birds are equally good examples of the concept of *bird,* nor are all dogs equally good instances of the knowledge of *dog.* (This point is developed more fully in chapter 10, Concepts and Categories.) Again this fact is known from the production norms described previously. When asked to provide instances of the concept *bird,* persons are most likely to respond with *robin, wren,* and *sparrow* and much less likely to say *ostrich* or *egret,* even though they know these animals are birds. In short, some subordinates seem to be more closely related to the superordinate than do others. This phenomenon is known as the *semantic distance effect.* The failure of early associative network theory to handle this effect adequately provoked revisions in the theory.

Spreading-Activation Model

One recent idea about semantic memory is a direct revision of Quillian's TLC. This model, proposed by Collins and Loftus (1975), is known as the *spread of activation* theory. Collins and Loftus retain the associative network of the earlier Quillian model, but take out the strict hierarchical structure which led to some of the problems described previously. In its place is a more complex structure designed to capture the degree of relationship between various concepts and to deal with the semantic distance effect. Indeed, the major change in structure from TLC is that instances of a superordinate concept are connected to that superordinate by associations of different lengths. As you can see in figure 7.3, *canary* is closer to *bird* than is *ostrich,* and when this model is compared to the original version of TLC represented in figure 7.1, it is evident that the change in associative distance is a major revision.

The various lengths of associations are designed to represent the strength of the relationship between the concepts. *Collie* is closer to *dog* for most persons than is *Afghan* or *basenji.* How do we know? Once again the length or distance between concepts is determined from the production frequency norms. The more persons giving a particular response to a particular concept, say *collie* when given *dog,* the closer the instance will be to the concept. Within associative network models, length of association nicely captures the strength of the relationship because verification or access to semantic memory is assumed to be a matter of traversing the network. This process is assumed to take time, and the farther there is to go, the more time will be required. This fact then predicts the result of faster verification of more strongly related pairs. When we discuss feature set theory, however, we shall see that length or distance is not the only way to represent strength of relationship.

In addition to the structural revision, the spreading-activation model assumes a more complicated retrieval process than does the TLC. Rather

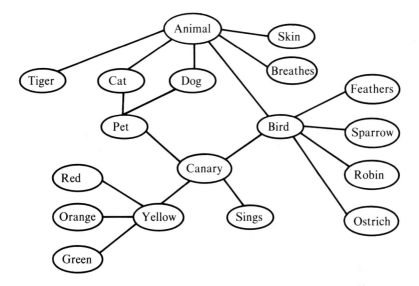

Figure 7.3 Representation of *canary* from the spreading-activation model. Contrast this representation with the *canary* portion of the TLC model in figure 7.1.

than suggest a simple process of moving from one node to another, Collins and Loftus assume that activation of a given concept spreads to related concepts, much the same way that the activation of a tuning fork spreads to other nearby tuning forks. Activation of one node activates the next node, which in turn activates the next node, until the activation spreads through a considerable portion of the network. The strength of the activation decreases as it spreads, so that concepts farther from the originally activated node are less likely to be activated than are closer concepts. This, of course, is sensible because distance represents the semantic relationship among the concepts.

What does all of this mean? A very simple example (it will help to refer to figure 7.3) is to think of the concept *canary*; the *canary* node is now activated. Activation spreads to adjacent nodes with decreasing strength as the nodes become farther removed. In other words, when you think of *canary,* you are also likely to think of *sings* and *yellow.* You are also likely to think of *bird* and *feathers.* You may also think of *pet* and *animal,* but perhaps you may not because these concepts are farther removed from *canary.* You may even think of *green* and *orange* since they are close to the concept *yellow* which was activated. *Skin* is unlikely to occur to you, because activation would have to proceed some distance through several intervening nodes.

The spreading-activation model solves several of the problems in the TLC. In particular, the problem of representing semantic distance is resolved by moving away from the strict hierarchical associative network. The instances of a general concept vary in how close they are to the superordinate, and this structure combined with the process of spreading activation explains why some instances come to mind more readily than do others.

Although the spreading activation model succeeds in dealing with problems for TLC, difficult issues for associative network models such as spreading activation and TLC remain. Particularly troublesome is research showing clear violations of the category size effect. Smith, Shoben, and Rips (1974) reported that people verify sentences such as "A cow is an animal" more rapidly than sentences such as "A cow is a mammal." Likewise, the response to "Scotch is a drink" is more rapid than the response to "Scotch is an alcoholic beverage." In both examples, the first sentences require search of a larger category than do the second sentences; nonetheless, reaction times for the first sentences are faster. This outcome is in clear violation of category size predictions which prescribe faster reaction time for smaller categories. Any associative network theory which argues a logical conceptual structure for knowledge will have difficulty with these data. In such a structure, smaller categories must intervene between instances and the larger category. For example, *mammal* must logically intervene between *cow* and *animal* in the network, and thus, verification of "A cow is a mammal" should always be faster. The data indicating reliable violations of the category size effect thus have had a profound effect upon thinking about semantic memory, producing theories fundamentally different from the associative network models.

Feature Set Theory

Smith, Shoben, and Rips's (1974) research was used as the springboard for their theory of semantic memory which proposes a radically different structure than do the associative network models. Their theory, which is called *feature set theory,* was designed to account for semantic distance effects, category size effects, and violations of the category size effect. To encompass all of these effects, Smith, Shoben, and Rips suggest that we think of knowledge of various concepts as consisting of features. In a sense, the contents of semantic memory would be the attributes of the objects. Rather than propose a node for each concept, knowledge of the concept is represented as a set of features.

The features can be viewed as component parts of the objects, much the same as were the physical features described in chapter 2 on pattern recognition; more precisely, features are values on a dimension. The dimensions may be perceptual, such as shape, size, and color, in which case the features will be particular colors (e.g., red), or shapes (e.g., round), or sizes (e.g., small). Dimensions can also be functional characteristics and abstractions: mode of locomotion, a feature of which might be "flying"; or eating habits, a feature of which might be "worms"; or even abstractions such as honesty and beauty, features of which might be "deceitful" and "gorgeous." Knowledge of any concept then consists of all of the features comprising that concept. This view is considerably different from the assumption that knowledge of a concept is represented by a set of interconnected nodes.

To appreciate the power of the feature set model fully, the distinction between two kinds of features, *defining features* and *characteristic features,* must be considered. Defining features are central to the meaning of a concept; to be called a particular type means that the object has the defining features. To be classified a *bird,* the object must have certain features shared by all of those objects known as *birds.* Perhaps the critical features are feathers, wings, and bipeded; we cannot say for sure what they are, but this is not critically important. What is important is that some set of the features define an object as a member of a particular class, be it *bird, automobile, house plants,* or *college professor.* All objects in the class share the defining features.

The second type of feature is characteristic of the object, but not necessary to its definition. For example, we characteristically associate pipe smoking with college professors, but we also know that pipe smoking is not a defining feature of college professors. Plenty of pipe smokers are not college professors, and plenty of college professors are not pipe smokers. By the same token, we characteristically associate flying with *bird,* but flying cannot be a defining feature of *bird.* Very simply, some of the creatures we know as *birds*— ostriches and chickens, for example— do not fly. So while we may think of "fly" when we think of *bird* (most birds do fly), "fly" is not an attribute that defines an object as a bird.

The meaning of a concept is then represented by the entire bundle of features, both defining and characteristic. When we think of the concept, all of the information contained in these features is activated. If we must call on knowledge to answer a question such as "Is a robin a bird?" the features of both robin and bird are activated, and the decision process begins. The decision is a two-stage process of matching the features of the two concepts. In the first stage, all of the features, both characteristic and defining, are matched. If there are a large number of features in common, the question can quickly be answered yes. If there are very few features in common, the question can quickly be answered no. For example, "Is a robin a bird?" receives a quick yes response and "Is a turnip a bird?" receives a quick no response. Some concepts, however, share an intermediate number of features—"Is an ostrich a bird?"—and then the second phase of the decision process occurs. In the *second phase,* only the *defining features* are matched. The second phase then requires more time in order to produce an answer.

This process of differentially matching characteristic and defining features allows the feature set model to describe the category size effect as well as the anomalies associated with that effect. Furthermore, the model also accounts nicely for semantic distance effects. Understanding how this works begins with the realization that the degree of relationship is determined largely by the total amount of feature overlap. Using this basic premise, let us briefly describe how the model applies to the various empirical findings.

Beginning with the category size effect, persons require more time to verify that a *robin* is an *animal* than that it is a *bird,* the assumption being that *robin* shares more total features with *bird* than with *animal.* The retrieval and comparison processes for *robin* and *bird* can thus be completed in one stage, but the lack of overlap between *robin* and *animal* necessitates the second stage of comparing defining features.

Precisely the same analysis is applied to the semantic distance effect. Persons more quickly verify *robin* as *bird* than *chicken* as *bird,* because *robin* shares more features with *bird* than does *chicken.* To verify *chicken* as *bird* requires matching defining features. Furthermore, the same mechanism is applied to anomalies from the category size effect, cases in which instances are more rapidly verified as members of large than of small categories. *Scotch* is more quickly classified as a *drink* than as an *alcoholic beverage* and *dog* is more readily verified as an *animal* than as a *mammal,* because the instance shares more features with the large category superordinate than with the smaller category superordinate.

Although the feature set model seems to explain semantic distance effects and category size effects, the immediate reaction may be skepticism, because it appears that the explanation is provided after the fact. To counter this criticism, Smith, Shoben, and Rips (1974) suggest that the number of features shared by an instance and its superordinate can be determined by *typicality* ratings. *Typicality* refers to how well a particular instance represents knowledge of the concept, and ratings of typicality are easily obtained by simply asking persons questions like "On a scale of 1 to 10, how typical is *robin* of *bird*?" "How typical is *ostrich* of *bird*?" and so on. We know that two concepts, such as *robin* and *bird,* share defining features when persons classify one as an instance of the other. The typicality ratings then provide an estimate of the number of characteristic features shared by an instance and a superordinate.

According to the feature set theory, the time required to verify an instance as member of a category should be inversely related to its typicality. That is, highly typical instances should be verified quickly because they share a large number of characteristic features with the superordinate. Atypical instances are verified less rapidly because they share fewer characteristic features and require the second phase of the decision process, matching defining features. In a test of this idea, Smith, Shoben, and Rips (1974) found that typicality ratings nicely predicted relative reaction time. Consistent with their idea, typical instances were verified more rapidly than were atypical instances.

Another interesting ability of the feature set model is its account of commonly used linguistic *hedges.* *Hedges* are statements which are qualified in some respect such as *"Technically speaking,* a bat is not a bird." From the standpoint of the feature set model, the idea communicated is that bats and birds share many characteristic features but do not share defining features. Similar knowledge is communicated in such statements as *"Loosely speaking,* a bat is a bird."

As you can see, the feature model differs in both process and structure from associative network models, and in part because of these differences, the feature model nicely explains some of the phenomena which cause problems for the network model. Of course, the feature model also has the advantage of being formulated to account explicitly for some of these problems, particularly the violations of category size effects. Nonetheless, the feature model is also capable of generating interesting predictions, such as the correlation between typicality and reaction time, which have been confirmed. In spite of these successes, the feature model has its troublesome side. Since Smith, Shoben, and Rips's initial proposal, very little development has occurred. This is unfortunate because the model leaves so many questions unanswered. For example, how are the features selected for the match process? Are all features selected? If they are not, what determines which features enter a decision? Much more thinking is required on these and other issues.

Another problem of the feature model is the long-standing criticism of the feature approach to knowledge: specifically, what constitutes a defining feature? Take any concept, *dog* for example, and try to think of one feature which can be removed from an instance so that it no longer is recognizable as a member of the concept. If you see a dog with no tail or no legs, or for that matter no head, is it still clearly a dog? The problem here is that the critical defining features of many concepts are not immediately obvious.

In spite of these difficulties, the feature model is an interesting contrast to the associative network model. Perhaps the most fundamental difference is the way the two types of models capture semantic relationships.

In the network model, the relationship between meaning of concepts is expressed in terms of *distance,* whereas in the feature model the same relationship is expressed *as number of overlapping features.* On the other hand, the two types of models are similar in describing knowledge at the level of the single concept, virtually a description of the knowledge represented by a single word. More recent approaches to the representation of knowledge have recommended higher-level structures.

Propositional Network Theories

Perhaps the most popular current theories of knowledge representation are *propositional network theories.* These theories, and there are a number of variations (Anderson, 1976; Anderson & Bower, 1973; Norman & Rumelhart, 1975), are basically associative network models but have a *basic proposition* represented at each node. A *proposition* is the smallest unit of knowledge which can be asserted. Propositions are also the smallest units about which it makes sense to decide whether they are true or false. In a sense, propositions are "idea units" which represent relationships among events or objects.

The best way to understand what is meant by a proposition is through example. A sentence of any complexity is likely to contain several propositions. For example, the sentence "Sam sells fresh vegetables to Guido, who owns a restaurant" can be divided into at least the following propositions or idea units:

1. Sam sells vegetables to Guido.
2. The vegetables are fresh.
3. Guido owns a restaurant.

Notice that each of these propositions expresses a separate idea, any one of which can be true or false. Propositional theories of semantic memory argue that the basic unit of knowledge is best represented as an individual proposition.

As pointed out in the discussion of the associative network models, knowledge is more than just individual propositions; it also includes the *relationships* among propositions. Taking the knowledge expressed in the sentence in the preceding example, we know the information in each proposition, such as "Sam sells fresh vegetables to Guido" and "Guido owns a restaurant." When the propositions are linked in a network, we know even more. Namely, we know, or at least infer, that Guido serves fresh vegetables in his restaurant. If the two linked propositions were "Sam sells fresh vegetables to Guido" and "Guido owns a canning factory," then this knowledge is in some respects quite different. The propositional network then, like the associative network, describes knowledge in terms of basic propositions and the connections among them.

It is possible to list the propositions, as was just done, and they can also be schematized in a propositional network, much as an associative network model. A schematic representation of the propositional network of the previously used example is presented in figure 7.4. Following custom, the three propositions are represented by ellipses with the subjects and predicates connected to the ellipses. In addition, the information relating the subjects and predicates are connected to each ellipse and labeled relational information. For example, *"vegetables"* is the predicate or object of the subject "Sam" and the relationship between "Sam" and "vegetables" is "sells." Again, this relationship expresses knowledge in the sense that there are a number of activities Sam can do to or with vegetables such as "cook," "grow," "eat," "hate," and so on. But we *know* that Sam sells vegetables, and this particular knowledge is represented by this particular subject-relation-predicate.

From figure 7.4, it can be seen that the information contained at each node has changed, even though an associative structure is maintained. With associative network models, each node represents a concept, but the nodes of a propositional network are the entire proposition. Rather than "Sam," "sells," and "vegetables" being separate nodes, "Sam sells vegetables" is the basic unit of knowledge. This fact reflects the belief of propositional theorists that knowledge is stored in larger units than single concepts. The question then becomes: How do we describe knowledge of single concepts? One answer is to create a propositional network for each concept. You can imagine that the completed product would then be a very complex network indeed, but the complexity may simply mirror the nature of human knowledge.

The complexity of a propositional network may make one doubt the probability of determining whether human beings actually behave in accord with the model. Although there is no extensive evidence as yet, a number of experiments have provided results consistent with the propositional theory. First, the propositional network model easily accounts for all of the reaction time data of the verification experiments. The propositional nodes contain all of the information contained in the nodes and properties of Quillian's TLC and Loftus and Collins's spreading-activation model, and hence the explanation of the reaction time data would be the same in all of these situations. More direct tests of the psychological reality of propositions comes from several sources, particularly from the research of Walter Kintsch.

For example, Kintsch and Glass (reported in Kintsch, 1974) compared memory for sentences consisting of the same number of words but having different numbers of propositions. A sentence such as "The settler built the cabin by hand" expresses one proposition, much as does the previous example "Sam sells vegetables to Guido." An example of the two-proposition sentences in this study is "The horse stumbled and broke a leg."

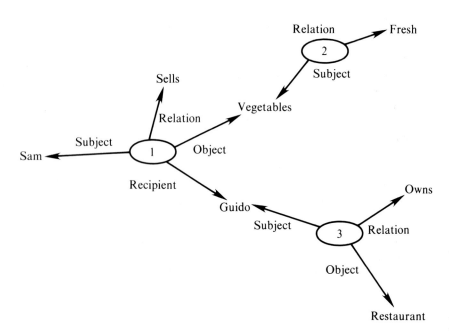

Figure 7.4 Schematic representation of a propositional network.

The propositions are "The horse stumbled" and "The horse broke a leg." Both of these sentences contain four content words, words which are not articles, prepositions, or conjunctions. Subjects showed clear differences in memory for the complete sentences, with much better recall of the one-proposition sentences. Furthermore, partial recall of a sentence was much more likely in the multiple-proposition sentences. Keeping in mind that the number of content words were equated, these data suggest that the number of propositions in a sentence affects the ability to remember the sentence. In particular, it appears that sentences are segmented into semantic units which correspond to propositions. More is said about propositional analysis of comprehension and memory in chapter 8. Data such as these from Kintsch suggest that the analysis of knowledge in propositional units may be quite fruitful.

Summary of Theories of Semantic Memory

Three basic types of ideas about semantic memory which can be distinguished on the basis of theoretical structures were described. Beginning with the historically prestigious TLC model, we discussed associative network theory as it has evolved to the spreading-activation model. Associative network theory proposes a vast system of interconnected nodes, each node representing a basic-level concept. Activation of a particular node or nodes conceptually describes the psychological experience of "knowing" or understanding; the richness of this experience is described or modeled by the spread of activity from the activated nodes to other associated nodes. Thus, when we think of "Santa Claus," we not only know this concept, but also a host of other facts, "presents," "snow," "evergreens," come to mind.

A different way of modeling semantic relationships is proposed by the second type of model. The feature model suggests that the basic concept is represented in terms of its component features or attributes, and the relationship among concepts is determined by the number of overlapping features.

A third type of idea discussed, the propositional model, also prescribes an associative structure for knowledge, but the propositional model differs in an important respect from the associative network model. Propositional models suggest a different structure at the level of the individual node. Nonetheless, the relationships among concepts are described in terms of associative connections, with the degree of semantic relationship directly related to the length of the association.

In summary, the structural differences among the various ideas are designed to account for different kinds of data. We certainly are not prepared at this time to say that one idea is better than another. Human knowledge is an extraordinarily diverse and complex system, and the theories with which we now work can be expected to evolve considerably. Exciting developments will undoubtedly occur in this area as major research efforts uncover new facts to guide theoretical development.

Semantic Memory and Cognitive Processes

This chapter began with a brief discussion of the function of knowledge, and we now return to that issue by examining the role of semantic memory in other processes discussed. The importance of semantic memory becomes clear when we see just how pervasive is the influence of knowledge on simpler processes.

Semantic Memory, Pattern Recognition, and Attention

Semantic memory played the central role in the discussion of pattern recognition, although at the time it was called, simply, long-term memory. Remember it was suggested that the process of pattern recognition is a matter of activating a representation in long-term memory, a process we can now say is the activation of semantic memory. Not only does the process of pattern recognition entail the activation of semantic memory, but also activation of semantic memory can give rise to the recognition response independently of sensory input corresponding to the pattern. This process, which is called *presynthesis* or *top-down processing,* is responsible for filling in gaps in pattern recognition and resolving ambiguity in the sensory information. Semantic memory is then fundamentally involved in the basic perceptual process of interpreting physical energy from the environment.

Semantic memory was also intimately involved in the discussion of attentional processes. If a limited processing capacity is assumed, it is important to direct processing capacity in such a way that continuity in meaning is maintained. One description of how attention operates is that expectations guide the continued allocation of capacity to a particular message. The expectations, as discussed, are basically the activation of the knowledge system by the preceding context, and capacity is then allocated to ensuing information to the extent that it remains consistent with the knowledge of what should follow. In this sense, semantic memory becomes indispensible as a guide to the process of attention.

Semantic Memory and Episodic Memory

Perhaps the relationship between semantic memory and episodic memory is at once more obvious but also more complex. Episodic memory is commonly viewed as the by-product of perceptual activity, or in other words, what is remembered about an event are the patterns that were recognized and allotted processing capacity. Since we have just seen that pattern recognition is the activation of semantic memory, this must mean that episodic memory, as the by-product of pattern recognition, is really the activation of semantic memory. If this is true, is there any point in distinguishing between semantic memory and episodic memory?

We discussed Tulving's answer to this question in the form of the episodic-semantic distinction. Tulving suggested that semantic memory and episodic memory are two different systems in that different principles govern their operation, particularly in retrieval. Events are dated in memory and as such can occur only once, but semantic memory or knowledge is a representation that is not time tagged. Tulving never specifies how, or even whether, episodic memory and semantic memory interact, and a satisfactory understanding of memory requires that this question be addressed. A particularly sensitive issue is how knowledge is acquired if semantic memory and episodic memory are totally different systems. We shall return to this issue momentarily.

More recently, a different view emerged suggesting that no distinction should be made between episodic memory and semantic memory. This approach finds support in several experiments which show that certain experimental manipulations have the same effect upon both semantic memory and episodic memory (Anderson & Ross, 1980; Lewis & Anderson,

1976; McKoon & Ratcliffe, 1979). These results suggest that episodic memory and semantic memory share the same representation and that event (episodic) memory is the activation of some portion of semantic memory. Even this position, however, implies a distinction between semantic memory and episodic memory, at least to the extent that episodic memory is only a portion of the semantic representation. For example, memory of "seeing a bear in a circus" entails only a fraction of the knowledge of bears. Yet this view does differ from Tulving's by stopping short of suggesting that episodic memory and semantic memory obey different principles.

Regardless of whether we take the extreme position that semantic memory and episodic memory are completely different systems or the position that episodic memory is the activation of a small portion of semantic memory, we see that episodic memory results from the activation of semantic memory. A very important question again arises at this point, a question which has yet to be answered. If episodic or event memory is the result of semantic memory activity, how is semantic memory or knowledge acquired? This is actually a very interesting question, as a moment of thought will indicate. Since it is argued that perception and event memory must be interpreted through semantic memory, the semantic system cannot be developed entirely from accumulated episodes. The specific episodes are meaningless until interpreted through the semantic structure; in other words, events cannot be understood or interpreted without knowledge of the events and thus knowledge cannot be derived from the events. Basically the problem is: How can we know something unless we already know something about it?

One solution is to assume that human beings possess some rudimentary or core knowledge at birth which is used to guide the earliest experiences and build the semantic memory structure. Although it may seem strange that a newborn infant would have knowledge, evolutionary considerations suggest that this is perfectly reasonable. Consider, for example, the research of DeCasper and Fifer (1980) on neonates, one-day-old infants. They gave the infants an opportunity to hear voices through headphones when the infants sucked a specially wired nipple. By examining the infants' ability to learn particular patterns of sucking responses, preferences among the voices were determined. The fascinating result of this research is that one-day-old infants strongly prefer their own mothers' voices. Although this outcome may be explained as the result of experience in the womb, it is interesting to note that the infants' second choice is any other woman's voice. That is, the infants prefer any female voice over all male voices, including their fathers'. In terms of survival, this result is quite sensible, because an infant's primary needs are most likely to be met by its mother, and if not by her, then by some other woman. We can certainly call the core information knowledge, and this knowledge can have a profound influence on the child's behavior. So one response to the question of how semantic memory or knowledge develops is to assume that human beings possess some core information at birth, probably through genetic transmission, which then serves as the cornerstone for further development.

A different solution to the issue of how knowledge develops is to assume that knowledge is really *generalized* episodic memory. The basic units of what we call semantic memory are really memories of experienced events. This position, perhaps best represented by Schank and Abelson (1977), is actually another theory of semantic memory. Schank and Abelson propose that knowledge consists of *scripts* which are essentially memories of past episodes. For example, there is a "going to the theater" script which represents knowledge of events likely to happen at the theater. When this knowledge is activated, we understand or know such facts as what a ticket is for, where to sit, and how long to remain seated. This idea represents one approach to the question of knowledge acquisition: namely, knowledge is the accumulation of episodic experience. In this view, there is no distinction between semantic memory and episodic memory.

While the question of knowledge acquisition remains very much at issue, it is perfectly clear that episodic memory as well as the basic perceptual processes is the result of activation of the knowledge system. Indeed, *this premise is one of the defining features of cognitive psychology, that perceptions and memories are, at least in part, products of the knowledge system.* The issue of the interaction between episodic memory and knowledge is pursued in chapter 8, where in the context of the process of comprehension the profound influence of knowledge on episodic memory is described.

Summary

In chapter 7 the area of research known as semantic memory was discussed. Semantic memory refers to what is generally called knowledge, and the discussion began by exploring the research showing what knowledgeable persons or "experts" can do that less knowledgeable persons cannot do. Several theories of semantic memory were then examined and the differences in memory structure proposed by these theories was closely considered. It was stressed that each theory generated interesting research in support of its position, but each theory also has its shortcomings. Finally, consideration of the relationship between semantic memory and other cognitive processes, particularly episodic memory and perception, was begun.

Multiple-Choice Items

1. Which of the following is not a function of the concept of knowledge?
   a. interpret incoming information
   b. limit capacity of the system
   c. provide meaning of events
   d. allow projection into the future

2. In the TLC model, cognitive economy is
   a. the storage of properties at the highest possible node
   b. the second stage of the retrieval process
   c. the shortest distance between two nodes
   d. the duplication of defining and characteristic features

3. The fact that "a robin is a bird" can be verified more rapidly than can "a robin is an animal" is an example
   a. of a propositional model
   b. of a difference in defining features
   c. of the cognitive economy
   d. of the category size effect

4. The difference between the spread of activation theory and TLC is
   a. the assumption about number of nodes
   b. the assumption about defining features
   c. the assumption about hierarchical organization
   d. the assumption about propositions

5. According to Smith, Shoben, and Rips's feature model, "Scotch is a drink" is verified faster than is "Scotch is an alcoholic beverage" because
   a. of differential overlap of characteristic features
   b. of differential overlap of defining features
   c. of differential length of associations
   d. of differential complexity of propositions

6. The basic difference between the propositional network and the associative network model is
   a. the connection between nodes
   b. the retrieval process
   c. the assumption about typicality effects
   d. the type of information at each node

True-False Items

1. Among other factors, an "expert" or high-knowledge person is able to predict what will happen in the future better than is a low-knowledge person.

2. A major implication of cognitive economy is that much of knowledge is not directly acquired but must be inferred.

3. Feature models and associative network models both assume that the similarity of meaning among concepts is represented by distance.

4. The biggest problem with propositional models is accounting for reaction time data generated from simpler models.

5. The more propositions a sentence contains, the harder it is to remember.

6. The reason to make a distinction between semantic memory and episodic memory is because it is known that semantic memory develops from episodic memory.

Discussion Items

1. Why did data on cognitive economy and typicality effects pose such general difficulty for hierarchically organized models?

2. Describe the retrieval process a person would likely use to verify "a robin is a bird" and "an ostrich is a bird" according to the Smith, Shoben, and Rips's feature model.

Answers to Multiple-Choice Items

1. (b) The capacity limitation is fixed and not a function of knowledge.

2. (a) Cognitive economy refers to storage of information at the highest node.

3. (d) The category size effect is faster verification time for smaller categories and "bird" is smaller than "animal."

4. (c) TLC assumes a hierarchical organization and spread of activation does not.

5. (a) Scotch is both "a drink" and "an alcoholic beverage" and thus has defining features of both. The difference in reaction time is due to the number of characteristic features.

6. (d) Associative network models represented simple concepts at each node, whereas propositional models represent propositions at each node.

Answers to True-False Items

1. (True) The research on knowledge of baseball demonstrated that experts are very good at predicting what will happen next.

2. (True) Storing information at the highest possible node implies that we infer that this information applies to subordinate nodes.

3. (False) Feature models assume that similarity of meaning is represented by overlap among features.

4. (False) Propositional models can account for the reaction time data.

5. (True) Kintsch and Glass showed that the more propositions in sentences, even with total number of words equated, the more difficult the sentence was to remember.

6. (False) We do not know that semantic memory develops from episodic memory, and if episodic memory is interpreted through semantic memory, it is hard to see how this could be true.

Comprehension
and Memory

8

In this chapter attention is turned to the process of comprehension and how memory and comprehension are related. Consider the following story:

> Papa, as he was affectionately known to his close family, took his usual morning walk through the sleepy, southern town, dressed in his typical white suit, which somehow always looked rumpled. As October began to settle into the Shennandoah Valley, he increasingly found his thoughts turning to his beloved Mississippi and the old plantation. The chill in the air revived memories of warm, early autumn evenings on the veranda with wife and children. He missed Mississippi, and even more, he missed many of the lost values and traditions of the old south. This mountain town in which he now found himself was so different, the pace of life so incongruously rapid, compared to his earlier days in the deep south. These thoughts continued with him as he turned the block toward his large white clapboard house, where he would spend the rest of the day in essential solitude.

Reading, understanding, and remembering passages such as the preceding paragraph are such routine activities that they may appear trivially simple. But for the cognitive psychologist, an adequate description of these processes is a major challenge. To illustrate the complexity of this challenge, reflect for a moment on your comprehension and memory of the paragraph. Without referring to the passage, what do you remember about it? If your response is typical, it will reveal one of the important characteristics of memory for prose and discourse; namely, material is not normally recalled verbatim. When most of us are asked about a book or a movie, we do not launch into a word-by-word account. Rather, we tend to summarize the material, trying to capture the essential *meaning* or *gist* of what occurred.

One thing that is always included in memory of a passage is the central *theme*. The theme is the general topic or subject of the material. Themes are important because they guide both comprehension and memory for material. For example, based on the information given in the passage, you may develop the theme of "an old, unhappy, southerner forced to leave his former home." This theme then affects your interpretation of the entire passage. Given this theme, you reasonably assume that the last phrase about his returning home to solitude implies lack of opportunity to interact with other persons. You may also assume that the man is rather old-fashioned and unsophisticated. Actually, the passage is a semifictional account of the latter days of William Faulkner, who held a prestigious appointment at the University of Virginia. He, of course, was anything but unsophisticated, and his celebrity status forced him to seek solitude in order to work. Here can be seen the essential function of a theme, to guide the assumptions or inferences made in interpretation of material. In this example, if the passage had been entitled "William Faulkner in Charlottesville, Virginia" your interpretation and memory of the passage would have been different.

The process of inferring information is essential to comprehension in order to connect or organize the various ideas expressed in a passage. The inferences can be as simple as assuming that the "he" mentioned throughout the passage refers to "Papa." Such inferences serve to connect various sentences in the passage and are essential to establishing the coherence of the text. Other types of inferences are less directly tied to the text and consist of information derived from assertions in the text. For example, you probably inferred that the character in the passage was old, but reexamination of the material will show no direct reference to the man's age. As you may have inferred, this simple example illustrates the operation of two apparently opposing processes in comprehension. On the one hand, comprehension is the process of extracting the *general meaning* of a communication and discarding details. Memory is organized around the central theme such that the central idea is abstracted and little else is remembered. The effect of this process is to reduce the amount of information remembered while at the same time to ensure that what the material is about is also remembered. The other process *adds information* to the actual communication. An inference, for example, represents additional information not included in the original assertion. Thus, in one case the information is reduced, while in the other it is increased. There is a real parallel here with the concepts of organization and elaboration, which were discussed earlier. In both cases, abstractions from and additions to the presented material are integral aspects of encoding and memory. Let us now examine these processes as they apply to connected discourse.

Integration and Themes

As just stated, memory of information heard or read is rarely a verbatim account of the information. Rather, the tendency is to summarize the content and integrate the discrete details into higher-order idea units. Integration of details involves combining related information, and this, of course, requires detecting one or more relationships. One of the important cues to detecting relationships is the theme or general idea of the passage or discourse. The guidance provided by the theme facilitates integration of information during comprehension but at the risk of distorting understanding and memory of the material. Just as for the perceptual processes discussed earlier, an increase in cognitive efficiency sometimes comes at the expense of complete accuracy.

Integration and the Loss of Verbatim Information

The phenomenon of integration can be demonstrated in a number of ways, some of which are familiar. The game of whispering a story to a person who in turn whispers it to another person until several persons have heard it can produce amusing results at final recall because of successive integration of the ideas. Indeed, the final version of the story as told to the last person can be dramatically different from the original version.

Controlled observations of the integration effect are possible in the laboratory, as illustrated by a classic experiment of Bransford and Franks (1971). They presented subjects with sentences which were derived from a complex sentence such as "The girl who lives next door broke the large window on the porch." This complex sentence expresses four propositions or ideas: (1) The girl lives next door, (2) The girl broke the window, (3) The window was large, and (4) The window was on the porch. The complex, four-idea sentence itself was not presented for study, but rather various combinations of one-, two-, and three-idea sentences were provided at input. For example, a subject might see the following sentences: "The girl who lives next door broke the window" (two idea units), "The window was on the porch" (one idea unit), and "The girl broke the large window on the porch" (three idea units). When the ideas expressed by these separate sentences are integrated into a single, higher-order idea unit, the representation becomes a complex, four-idea sentence. To explore whether their subjects were actually integrating the input sentences, Bransford and Franks gave a recognition test for the input sentences.

Several types of sentences were available in the recognition test. Some of the sentences were *old;* these sentences were actually presented during study and from this example included "The girl who lives next door broke the window." Some test sentences were *new;* these sentences were not presented at study but could be derived from a complex sentence such as "The

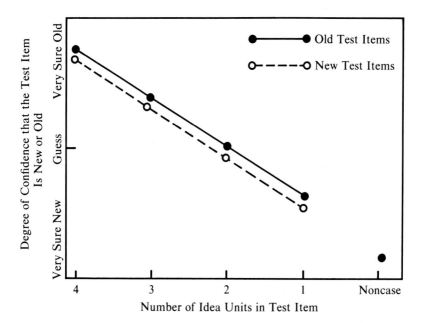

Figure 8.1 Degree of confidence in recognition judgment for *old* and *new* test sentences, depending upon the number of idea units in the sentence. Note that all 4-idea unit test items are new items. (From "The Abstraction of Linguistic Ideas" by J. D. Bransford and J. J. Franks, *Cognitive Psychology*, 1971, *2*, 331–350. Copyright 1971 by Academic Press. Used by permission.)

girl who lives next door broke the large window." Although this sentence sounds familiar, a look back shows that it was not one of the sample input sentences. Finally, a third type of sentence, *noncase*, was included in the recognition test. The *noncase* sentences were quite dissimilar in meaning from the input sentences, for example, "The boy broke a window in the house next door."

The results of Bransford and Franks's study are presented in figure 8.1. As shown in the figure, the outcome of interest was how confident the subjects were that a given test sentence was actually presented during study. Figure 8.1 illustrates three essential points bearing on the integration phenomenon. First, the subjects were incapable of discriminating *old* and *new* sentences. Since the *new* sentences were derived from the complex, four-idea sentences, this result suggests that the recognition judgments were made from memory of the complex sentences. If this assumption is true, integration must have occurred, because the complex sentences were never presented. Consistent with this interpretation is the second major point of the results: namely, as the number of idea units in the *old* and *new* sentences increased, subjects became more confident that all sentences were actually presented. Indeed, the subjects were most confident of the four-idea sentences, the ones which were never actually presented! If the subjects' memory was based on the complex sentences, the test sentences with more idea units would be most like their representation. Finally, the third point is that *noncase* sentences were well recognized as not being among the study sentences. Thus, if the meaning of a test sentence is quite discrepant from the study sentences, subjects can easily reject the sentence.

The conclusion from this experiment is that persons store as a unit different statements related to the same idea. Individual sentences are not maintained in memory, but the *ideas* expressed by the sentences are integrated into a single representation of the general idea expressed by a group of sentences. The implication of this conclusion is that memory for individual sentences is quite poor, but memory for a general idea is good. In other words, integration produces the *gist* of the message, and it is the gist, not the details, which is well remembered.

Themes

Among the major influences on how ideas are integrated is the theme or central idea of a passage or conversation. The theme may occur as the title of a passage or as the lead sentence of a paragraph, or the theme may be abstracted as the recurring, dominant idea of a passage or discussion. Regardless of the form in which it appears, the theme anchors the information in knowledge. Once the central idea is known, the various statements can be organized around that central idea. A good deal of evidence is now available indicating the importance of themes in comprehension and memory.

The theme of a passage is the most likely information to be remembered. This is simply to say that the central idea of a passage is remembered—not a terribly surprising fact. It is also the case, however, that the thematic information is less subject to forgetting over time. In short, memory for a passage will generally begin with the theme of the passage.

Once the theme is retrieved, it can then aid further reconstruction of the material. For example, a friend might say, "Do you remember the conversation we had this morning?" and you respond, "Oh, yes, we were talking about your party last night." From this theme you can then go on to reconstruct some of the details of the conversation. The influence of themes on the reconstruction of passages is illustrated in an experiment by Sulin and Dooling (1974). Subjects in this experiment read the following passage:

> *Carol Harris's Need for Professional Help* Carol Harris was a problem child from birth. She was wild, stubborn, and violent. By the time Carol turned eight, she was still unmanageable. Her parents were very concerned about her mental health. There

was no good institution for her problem in her state. Her parents finally decided to take some action. They hired a private teacher for Carol. (R. A. Sulin and D. J. Dooling, "Intrusions of a Thematic Idea in Retention of Prose," *Journal of Experimental Psychology,* 1974, *103,* 255–262).

A second group of subjects read the same passage except *Helen Keller* was substituted for *Carol Harris.* A week later the subjects were given a recognition test which included the sentence "She was deaf, dumb, and blind." Only 5 percent of the subjects who read the *Carol Harris* passage claimed to have seen this sentence. Of the subjects reading the *Helen Keller* passage, over 50 percent of the subjects thought they had seen the sentence. These kinds of data encourage the generalization that the theme is the focus of the memory representation and much of what is remembered is reconstructed from the theme.

The importance of themes to both comprehension and memory has been illustrated dramatically by Bransford and Johnson (1973). Consider the following passage:

The procedure is quite simple. First, you arrange things into different groups. Of course, one pile may be sufficient, depending upon how much there is to do. If you have to go somewhere else due to lack of facilities, that is the next step; otherwise, you are pretty well set. It is important not to overdo things. That is, it is better to do too few things at once than too many. At first the whole procedure will seem complicated. Soon, however, it will become just another facet of life. After the procedure is completed, one arranges the materials into different groups again. Then they can be put into their appropriate places. Eventually they will be used once more, and the whole cycle will have to be repeated. (J. D. Bransford and M. K. Johnson, "Considerations of Some Problems of Comprehension," in *Visual Information Processing,* edited by W. G. Chase. New York: Academic Press, 1973.)

Although you can understand the individual sentences in this passage, the relationship among the sentences is unclear, and consequently integration of idea units is virtually impossible. This is because the passage is written such that the theme is quite obscure, and thus the passage is difficult to understand. Subjects in the Bransford and Johnson experiment had a very difficult time remembering this passage. However, if the title "Washing Clothes" is supplied, the passage becomes both more comprehensible and memorable.

Themes are central to comprehension and serve as the focus for organizing memory for discourse. Good use of this observation can be made in class by always extracting and understanding the theme of each subsection of the material. In brief, the first thing to do when trying to understand a lecture or reading assignment is to know what it is about. Actively construct a hierarchy of themes, relating each topic to its superordinate. For example, the general topic of memory was discussed, with the subordinate topic encoding processes and its subtopics organization and individual item processing. By setting up such a hierarchy of themes and understanding the relationship among them, you are in a much better position to appreciate details such as individual experiments and their implications. Indeed, as simple as this activity sounds, it is at the heart of what is called understanding, and if you will be aware of its importance, you can easily increase both comprehension and memory for all kinds of materials.

Presuppositions and Inferences

When a communication is understood, the directly asserted information is usually elaborated such that what is understood goes far beyond what was said. For example, to understand most statements requires that other factors are *assumed* or *presupposed* to be true. The old joke "Have you stopped beating your wife?" is amusing because any answer presupposes that the person once beat his wife. Although the presupposition is not expressed explicitly, memory for some event is likely to include presupposed information. Furthermore, each assertion or statement implies further information, and given those implications, inferences which subsequently may be remembered are made. With both presuppositions and inferences *more* is remembered than was actually said.

Presuppositions

Many statements can be understood only if other things are presupposed to be true. For example, when a professor says, "Congratulations, Smith, you have made the highest grade again," the professor is asserting that Smith made the highest grade this time, and the presupposition is that Smith had made the highest grade in the past. A presupposition must be made in order for an assertion to be understood fully. Either or both can be remembered and either or both may be true or false. Smith may or may not have made the highest grade this time, and Smith may or may not have made the highest grade in the past. Professors have been known to make these kinds of mistakes. In other situations, false presuppositions can have more serious consequences.

Consider the effect of eyewitness testimony upon a jury. If the jury must make a presupposition to comprehend the testimony of a witness, that presupposition may be remembered and later influence the decision. Thus, a clever attorney may try to discredit a witness by asking, "Do you still drink heavily?" The witness must deny not only the assertion, but also the presupposition. An indication of the subtlety and power of presupposition on eyewitness accounts has been illustrated nicely by Loftus's research. For example, Loftus and Palmer (1974) showed subjects a film of an automobile accident and then questioned them about what they had seen. One of the questions was "About how fast were the cars going when they *(hit, smashed)* each other?" Some of the subjects saw the verb *hit* and others saw the verb *smashed*. The subjects who were asked in the context of *hit* gave much lower estimates of the speed than those asked about *smashing* cars. Furthermore, the subjects who saw *smashed* remembered seeing broken glass in the scene; those who saw *hit* generally did not. No broken glass was actually depicted in the movie. The subjects in this experiment were influenced by presuppositions invoked by the verbs *hit* and *smashed*. *Smashed* presupposes a more violent collision, a fact which influences both estimate of speed and amount of damage. This presupposition then dramatically but subtly influences memory for the actual event. The fact that verbal labels can influence perception and memory has been established in many studies (e.g., Ellis, 1968; Ellis, 1973; Ellis & Daniel, 1971; Daniel, 1972). However, Loftus's work shows the additional role of presuppositions in memory.

Inferences

Understanding a statement usually leads to certain conclusions or implications. If you say, "Jim does not own one single shirt with an alligator on it," I may infer from this statement that it is important to you that a person own such a shirt and then go on to attribute to you a number of personality characteristics common to people who have such beliefs. Clearly, I have then gone far beyond your simple and rather straightforward statement. In fact, my inference may be totally wrong. You actually may have been expressing admiration for Jim, in which case a completely different set of inferences would be appropriate. In either case, this simple example illustrates the prevalence of inference in comprehension and subsequent memory. Virtually every statement anyone utters or writes leads the listener or reader to certain inferences.

Notice the distinction between an inference and a presupposition. A presupposition is knowledge activated by an assertion in order to understand it. An inference is knowledge that is activated once the assertion is understood. Certain types of inferences, known as *logical inferences,* must follow from what was said. Logical inferences are, in a sense, demanded by the assertion. For example, the assertion that "John's actions forced Mr.

Pettigrew to fire him" logically implies that John was fired. Unlike a presupposition, you do not have to think "John was fired" in order to understand the assertion, but the assertion does demand the inference because it would make little sense to conclude the assertion with "but Mr. Pettigrew did not fire John."

As an example of the effect of logical inference, consider the following experiment by Bransford, Barclay, and Franks (1972). Subjects saw sentences such as "Three turtles rested on a floating log and a fish swam beneath it." Subjects were then given recognition memory tests for new, logically implied sentences such as "Three turtles rested on a floating log and a fish swam beneath them." A large number of the subjects consistently claimed that they had seen the new sentences, which suggests that the logical inferences had been constructed and stored when the original sentences were presented.

Not all inferences, however, are logically demanded. Some, perhaps the majority, of the inferences are invited by the assertion. This second type of inference is known as *pragmatic inference*. A pragmatic inference does not have to follow from an assertion, but rather is reasonable based on world knowledge. For example, to say that "Bill and Mary were looking at engagement rings" in no way demands the inference that Bill and Mary are to be engaged; however, that inference is certainly reasonable given what is known about the world. A large number of experiments have been reported which demonstrate that pragmatic inferences are remembered as part of the original event.

As an example of these studies, Johnson, Bransford, and Solomon (1973) presented subjects with sentences such as "John was trying to fix the birdhouse. He was pounding the nail when his father came out to watch him and to help him do the work." This passage clearly implies, although it does not logically demand, that John was using a hammer. Subjects later falsely recognized the sentence. "John was using a hammer to fix the birdhouse when his father came out to watch him and help him do the work." As with the logical inference, the pragmatic inference is remembered as if it had actually occurred.

Recognition of the prevalence and power of inferential processing is extremely important in understanding communication. Much of what is communicated is in fact left unsaid. Speakers rely on listeners to draw appropriate inferences and listeners generally trust the inferences drawn from speakers' statements. The ability to communicate without explicitly saying everything we are trying to convey enormously enhances efficiency in communication. As with other cognitive processes, increased efficiency comes at the cost of increased error. Again, the error and the efficiency result from the diametrically opposed processes of abstraction and integration on the one hand and elaboration through inference on the other hand.

The Locus of Constructive Processes

A question of recent interest is, Do inferences actually occur at encoding or at retrieval? For example, you know that a friend has an examination in a particular class and you later see the person leaving the class in an obvious state of pleasure. Do you immediately infer that the examination went well and remember the inference, or do you later remember what you actually saw and based on that memory infer that the examination went well? Beginning with Bartlett's (1932) early work, retrieval has been assumed to be reconstructive; that is, inference is assumed to occur during retrieval. More recent research suggests that constructive processes also occur during encoding.

Constructive Processes at Encoding

In the previously mentioned work of Bransford and Johnson, paragraphs very difficult to comprehend in the absence of a title or theme were presented either with or without the title. Further, the title was given either during the study period or at the time of the memory test. Persons were better able to remember the paragraph when the title was given during the study period than at the time of the memory test. Since the title facilitates making inferences which render the paragraph more comprehensible and memorable, this result suggests that inferences occur during the study phase itself.

Another line of evidence for constructive processes at input comes from the work of Kintsch and students (Kintsch, 1974). Consider an experiment by Baggett (1975) which is representative of this research. Subjects saw a series of picture frames which told a story, much like a newspaper cartoon. One story showed a rather long-haired man entering a barbershop, then sitting in a barber chair, and finally leaving the barbershop. The sequence is depicted in figure 8.2. In a subsequent recognition test, subjects also saw a frame depicting the actual haircut, which had not been presented originally. Persons were reasonably good at remembering that this frame was not present at input *if* they were given the test immediately after study. But if the test occurred a week after the initial presentation, most persons claimed that they had seen the haircutting picture. Baggett suggests that when they are tested immediately, subjects are able to discriminate the old pictures from a plausible inference scene because they still have some of the surface information about the pictures in memory. After a week, however, the surface information decays, and the discrimination between what actually occurred and the inferences drawn from what occurred can no longer reliably be made. This interpretation, then, emphasizes the storage of inferences during input or encoding. Similar results and interpretations from stories presented verbally were also described by Kintsch (1974).

Test

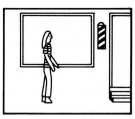
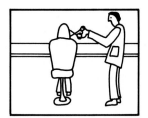

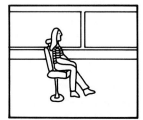

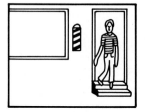

Figure 8.2 Sequence of pictures used by Baggett to examine inferences. Note that the test picture is not present in the study sequence, but can be inferred to have occurred between the third and fourth frames. (From "Memory for Explicit and Implicit Information in Picture Stories" by P. Baggett, *Journal of Verbal Learning and Verbal Behavior*, 1975, *14*, 538–548. Copyright 1975 by Academic Press. Used by permission.)

Reconstructive Processes at Retrieval

Equally clear, however, is that inferences and presuppositions can be induced at retrieval. In recounting an event, memory for what actually happened may lead to enrichment of the account with plausible inferences. For

Chapter 8

example, we may remember that Bill and Mary were seen looking at engagement rings and, on the basis of this memory, tell someone that they are to be married. In this case, information is reconstructed from what was remembered about the actual event. Inferences which occur during this type of reconstructive retrieval begin with memory for a specific aspect of the actual event.

Other cases in which inference clearly occurs at output are the situations represented by the Loftus and Palmer (1974) experiment discussed earlier. In some instances, the way in which memory is probed leads to responses which are inconsistent with the original event. For example, Loftus and Palmer were able to influence memory for speed of the automobiles by changing the verb in their question from *hit* to *smash*. Actually, it is not so clear that the question distorted the subjects' "memory of the speed"; the subjects may not have stored such information directly. For example, McEwan and Yuille (1981) have shown that subjects are not influenced by presuppositions if they have clear memory for an event. If subjects can remember only that an accident occurred and are forced to answer the question, their estimate of speed is really a guess which is heavily influenced by the presuppositions demanded by the verb. The point here is that some aspect of an event which was not clearly attended and stored may subsequently be reported incorrectly, and the magnitude and direction of the inaccuracy can be influenced by the questions asked of memory.

It would seem, then, that inferences and presuppositions occur during both input and output. Memory is constructive in that events are elaborated with inferences and presuppositions in order to comprehend. Memory is also reconstructive in that inferences are added to what is retrieved about the original event. This conclusion suggests that real-world memory is always potentially suspect, is at the mercy of the comprehension process, and is likely to be distorted. Such a conclusion appears different from the impression gained from the previous discussion of studies based on lists of words. Are the differences between these two situations so great that the concepts derived from list studies cannot be applied to memory based on comprehension of higher-order discourse? Let us examine this issue.

Concepts from Discourse and List Memory

The most striking difference between research using connected discourse and research using list of discrete items, such as words, is the level of verbatim memory in the two tasks. As would be expected from experiences in retelling stories, the research on memory of stories or passages shows clearly that the account is not usually recalled verbatim, but rather major themes are selected, related ideas are integrated, and the actual event is elaborated with inferences and presuppositions. Is this not considerably different from studies in which persons appear either to remember a word or not remember it? The answer is yes and no.

The complexity of connected discourse, either prose or conversation, far exceeds that of a simple word list. Hence, studies of comprehension and memory for connected discourse allow important observations and insights into the complex psychological processes brought to bear in interpreting normally encountered information. For example, list studies have never produced the dramatic evidence for elaboration and addition of self-generated information that was evident from the outset in studies of connected discourse. On the other hand, concepts derived from studies of list memory have been at the heart of the analysis of prose memory.

The general view of comprehension as an active process of transforming the surface material into a meaningful psychological representation is in principle the same as the encoding of single words into their conceptual representation. In both cases, the information is actively transformed and retained in an abstract, semantic code. Furthermore, in both cases the abstract semantic code is assumed to be elaborated upon and organized in accord with the existing knowledge structure. The work from levels of processing on elaboration of individual words leads to the same sort of idea about memory as does the work on inferences in prose memory. The organization of word lists and abstraction of a superordinate category is similar conceptually to the integration of idea units and the abstraction of themes. In summary, it is reassuring to understand that theoretical descriptions of memory for words and for connected discourse converge on the same basic ideas about human memory.

To illustrate this point, let us briefly examine one of the prominent theories of comprehension and memory.

A Theory of Comprehension and Memory

First, it should be realized that all of the theories of semantic memory discussed in chapter 7 are designed to explain comprehension. Although any of the theories can explain at least some aspect of the comprehension process, the ideas which seem most applicable to connected discourse are those which rely on a knowledge representation larger than a single word, namely, the propositional theories. Propositional theory is particularly useful because the knowledge extracted and remembered from connected discourse encompasses units larger than individual words. We shall outline a general overview of one such theory which was explicitly designed to describe memory performance following comprehension.

The general idea, proposed by Kintsch and van Dijk (1978), is that comprehension begins with the extraction of propositions from the textual material. These propositions follow the rudimentary organization of the text, but further organizational processes are imposed, as part of comprehension. For example, related propositions are grouped, although much of the grouping occurs through organization of the text itself. Further, the propositions are organized around the goals of the reader.

The goals may simply be to understand and interpret the material, as, for example, in reading a novel for entertainment. Here the rules about stories guide organization of the propositions; good stories begin with a setting, proceed through a series of events, and end with a resolution. Propositions can be organized around these segments such that ultimate comprehension and memory for the story is highly ordered. With other types of materials, the purposes or goals may be different, as in reading an academic text. You may have a specific goal, such as finding evidence for feature theories of pattern recognition, or a general goal of understanding and remembering the material on comprehension and memory. In the latter case, the text structure should help you organize materials, in that section headings provide a theme around which to group ensuing propositions.

Additions to and deletions from the material occur in accord with the purposes and goals of the reader. For example, when the search is for a specific bit of information that cannot be found, an inference to fill the gap may be made. The text may provide information which is unnecessary for the purpose, and those propositions are deleted from memory. Suppose you are interested in determining the inflation rate in Germany following World War I, and the material you read mentions that a loaf of bread cost two bags of money. Although this is not yet specific information about the inflation rate, you are able to make a clear inference. The material might also mention that the physical size of the money was quite large, but since size has nothing to do with your purpose, you delete this proposition.

The view emerging from Kintsch and van Dijk's theory is of an active process of comprehension in which propositional representations are extracted and organized around themes. The organization may involve integration of separate propositions and almost certainly will include inferences. Although theories of comprehension and memory are in their infancy and will undoubtly undergo dramatic revision, the ideas of Kintsch and van Dijk provide a useful description of the processes involved including integration, thematic organization, and inference.

Miscommunication in Advertising

Surely all of us occasionally say things in such way that the listener is in a position of inferring information which may not be entirely accurate. Interestingly, we do not consider this a case of blatant lying, but simply claim that the listener is misled. To establish whether a speaker was indeed dishonest, the speaker's intentions must be discovered, a very hard thing to do if the actual assertion is in fact accurate. Consequently, it is easy to mislead either when sufficient information to evaluate an assertion is intentionally withheld or when vigilance about drawing inferences is not observed. Good advertising copy provides an interesting case in point.

Among our favorites is a currently running television commercial for a pain reliever. The script asserts "This product contains more of the pain reliever that doctors recommend. You can't buy a more effective pain reliever without a prescription." The last sentence encourages the inference that this product is the most effective pain reliever to be bought without a prescription, but this clearly is not what the sentence asserts. Further, the pain reliever that doctors recommend most is aspirin, and beyond some maximum dosage, which can be obtained from two or three tablets of any brand, additional aspirin has little effect. By not mentioning that the pain reliever in question is aspirin, the advertisement sets us up to infer that the product contains some esoteric drug and lots of it. Successfully competing in the aspirin business is difficult, since all of the brands are very much alike, and thus any competitive edge provided by advertising is helpful, including misleading information. Are we really susceptible to such techniques?

Harris (1977) reported an experiment which indicates that persons are quite susceptible to the inferences created by advertising assertions. Harris used the following text from a Listerine commercial:

"Wouldn't it be great," asks the mother, "if you could make him cold proof? Well, you can't. Nothing can do that. [Boy sneezes.] But there is something that you can do that may help. Have him gargle with Listerine Antiseptic. Listerine can't promise to keep him cold free, but it may help him fight off colds. During the cold-catching season, have him gargle twice a day with full-strength Listerine. Watch his diet, see he gets plenty of sleep, and there's a good chance he'll have fewer colds, milder colds this year."

Harris substituted "Gargoil" for "Listerine" in the text, but otherwise the advertisement was heard verbatim. Although the advertisement never asserts that "Gargoil" prevents colds, every subject in the experiment responded yes to the question "Does gargling with Gargoil prevent colds?" Does this commercial perpetuate a falsehood? The Federal Trade Commission says it does and is currently suing the makers of Listerine for making false claims.[1]

Regardless of the source of the information, the point of this discussion is that the elaborative nature of comprehension can be and is used to

1. Harris, R. J. Comprehension of pragmatic implications in advertising. *Journal of Applied Psychology,* 1977, *62,* 603–608.

imply potentially inaccurate information. Based on what you now know about comprehension and memory, you are in the position of protecting yourself against this possibility by directly questioning assertions and carefully analyzing your own inferences.

Summary

Comprehension is a very active process of organizing and elaborating the material that is heard and read. Memory is then a product of the organization and elaboration. As with simple pattern recognition, much of what is remembered was not contained in the original message, but is inferred from knowledge of the world. The processes which elaborate the original event seem to occur at both input and output and can be viewed as analogous to the same types of processes operating in studies of list memory.

Most theories of comprehension rest on the propositional representation of knowledge and assume that text is analyzed and remembered in propositional form. Finally, an understanding of comprehension and memory can enable you to communicate more precisely as well as to understand precisely what is said and what is left unsaid.

Multiple-Choice Items

1. When material is integrated in comprehension, memory for that material is likely to be
   a. verbatim
   b. highly detailed
   c. gist
   d. inference

2. Which of the following did *not* occur as a result of Bransford and Franks's experiment?
   a. old sentences were better remembered than new
   b. new sentences were frequently called *old*
   c. *noncase* sentences were frequently called *new*
   d. sentences never presented were recognized as *old*

3. Themes do all of the following except
   a. guide organization of text
   b. influence the type of inferences drawn
   c. facilitate comprehension
   d. prohibit presuppositions from occurring

4. If I say, "The doctor was able to save the child" and you then think "The child was cured," you are
   a. establishing a theme
   b. drawing a logical inference
   c. drawing a pragmatic inference
   d. making a presupposition

5. Inferences seem to occur
   a. at neither input or output
   b. at both input and output
   c. only at input
   d. only at output

6. According to the Kintsch and van Dijk model of comprehension, what is remembered is
   a. primarily due to retrieval processes
   b. not really influenced by the structure of the text
   c. influenced by the purpose for reading the material
   d. not influenced by the theme

True-False Items

1. Without inference, we would have to say a lot more to communicate with others.

2. Bransford and Franks's study showed that persons are very good at remembering the wording of a sentence.

3. If I say, "Tom is smarter than Bob, and Bob is smarter than Sam" and you then think, "Tom is smarter than Sam," you have made a logical inference.

4. Research has clearly shown that eyewitness testimony is quite reliable and accurate.

5. Persons do not make inferences with visual stimuli as they do with verbal materials.

6. The discussion suggests that the processes involved in memory for lists of words are drastically different from the processes involved in memory for connected discourse.

Discussion Items

1. Describe Bransford and Franks's experiment and results, explicitly discussing the points which provide evidence for integration.

2. Discuss the relationship between themes and inferences. What effects do each have on comprehension and on memory?

3. Discuss how inferences can be made from advertisements on television.

Answers to Multiple-Choice Items

1. (c) Integration is the process of discarding detailed surface information and remembering a semantic unit or gist.
2. (a) The *new* sentences were called *old* with just as much confidence as the *old* sentences were called *old*.
3. (d) There is no reason to assume that themes preclude presuppositions.
4. (c) What you thought was an inference drawn from what I said, and it is not a logically required inference, but rather is based on what you know about doctors and sick children.
5. (b) Inferences can be drawn at input during comprehension and can be based also upon what is retrieved at output.
6. (c) Purposes and goals have a lot to do with what is remembered from the text.

Answers to True-False Items

1. (True) Much of what is communicated is implied, not directly stated.
2. (False) Bransford and Franks found that people cannot discriminate between *new* and *old* sentences on the basis of wording.
3. (True) Logic dictates the inference that is drawn in this case.
4. (False) Research has shown that eyewitness testimony is quite subject to distortion about the actual event.
5. (False) Baggett's study using pictures showed a clear tendency to make inferences.
6. (False) While discourse is more complex and may involve somewhat more complicated processing, many of the same processes seem to be operating in the two situations.

Language

9

The one kind of activity that appears to distinguish most clearly human beings from other organisms is their facility with language. Although it can be demonstrated in controlled laboratory situations that lower animals can think, remember, learn concepts, and solve problems, language is frequently said to be a distinguishing human feature. Recent investigations of language behavior in chimpanzees suggest, however, that the human species may not be the sole possessor of language. Even these animals have been shown capable of using language at a simple level. But we shall see that the issue of language in animals depends upon what features of human languages can be said to be truly shared by animals.

Language is our principal means of communication with other persons. Yet we frequently take this complex ability for granted. Perhaps this is because, as adults, we have little memory of the long process of language acquisition. For many of us language is a natural and simple process until, as adults, we attempt to learn a second language. This is not to say that learning a foreign language is the same as learning a first language. Indeed, early language learning appears relatively effortless as compared to learning a foreign language as a college student.

One theory of the relation between language and thought is that language is "the tool of thought." Jean Piaget, a distinguished Swiss psychologist, made an interesting analogy in pointing out that language is to thought as mathematics is to physics. Just as mathematics is used as the language of physics, ordinary language bears a similar relationship to thought.

Language is composed of words combined according to certain rules. Words themselves represent symbols which are composed of basic vowel and consonant sounds. These sounds are called *phonemes,* and a phoneme represents the basic unit of language. At a more general level, ordinary language represents the major system available to the human being for communication. Signs can also be used to communicate. For example, deaf persons communicate with sign language, small children count by raising their fingers, mathematical formulas convey information, and signs can convey emotional feelings. All are symbols in the sense that they convey meaning. They provide some kind of information which in turn allows some kind of response by other human beings.

In chapter 9 we examine some of the basic features of language. In particular, we discuss the functions of language, the structure of language, the processes in language, and a range of selected issues in language.

Functions of Language

Language serves several identifiable functions which are all related to the fundamental process of communication. Perhaps most important is that language conveys meaning and is part of almost all kinds of social interaction. Language conveys intentions, motives, feelings, and beliefs. Language is used to issue requests and commands such as "Get me a glass of water." Language is also used to teach and to convey information. Indeed, a vast range of knowledge and beliefs can be conveyed via language, which makes it a highly flexible and hence useful system.

Language is useful because it can represent ideas and events that are not tied to the here and now. You can communicate about the past as well as convey plans for the future. You can describe abstract ideas such as beauty and justice as well as concrete objects of everyday experience. Thus language is *symbolic,* in that speech sounds and utterances stand for or represent various objects, ideas, and events.

In any spoken communication system there consists a speaker, a listener, and a system for communication such as the English language. Communication begins with speakers who decide to convey information. They select a medium of communication such as the English language and produce sentences. Listeners receive the signals (speech sounds) being presented and represent them in memory. There are three elements of human communication which operate in this speaker-listener situation: they have been identified as speech acts (Searle, 1969, 1975), propositional content, and thematic structure. We will examine these elements in the following section, and the description follows the analysis outlined by Clark and Clark (1977).

Speech Acts

Speakers normally intend to have some influence on their listeners and must get them to recognize their intentions. For example, a person who says "Let me buy you a beer" is conveying the desire to buy another person a beer and also probably to have a conversation. Such statements are called *speech acts.* Speech act theory holds that all utterances can be classified as to the type of speech act they represent. For example, speech acts may transmit information, convey thanks, give a warning, or issue a command. Typical examples of speech acts include the following: "I insist that you turn down the volume on the stereo" (a command), "What are your plans for Saturday night?" (a question), and "I know that Professor Jones is the best instructor in the psychology department" (an assertion). In these examples, we see the acts of ordering, questioning, and telling, which are common speech acts.

Propositional Content

The second element of communication concerns the *propositional content* of a sentence. In communication, speakers want to convey certain ideas and to do this they must be sure that they are understood. Thus the content around a speech act is very important. As a general rule the propositional content of a sentence is used to describe certain states or events, it can also describe certain facts about the states or events, or it can be part of other propositions. For example, the sentence "The bright student received an A in calculus" expresses two separate propositions, "The student is bright" and "The student received an A in calculus." Combined into a single sentence the propositions convey what the speaker intends to convey.

Thematic Structure

Finally, the third component in communication is *thematic structure.* To communicate effectively, good speakers pay careful attention to their listeners. Good speakers have to judge what listeners do and do not know, keep track of where they are leading their listeners, and regularly examine any assumptions about the listeners' knowledge of the topic being discussed. In short, the speaker must be able to make reasonably accurate judgments of the listener's current level of understanding.

All of these features are present in good teachers, entertaining and effective storytellers, and interesting conversationalists. Unfortunately, all of us at one time have probably experienced a talk, lecture, or presentation in which the speaker droned on without any apparent interest in our level of understanding. Sometimes we are victims of eager monologists who are so anxious to relay their views of the world that they forget to check our understanding of what's being said. Similarly, there is the occasional teacher who lectures "in a trance," following a rigid format and without pausing to check on audience comprehension. Indeed, this inability to be sensitive to the listener is a major problem in communication.

One function of thematic consideration is to convey both given (understood) and new information. Good speakers attempt to tailor their sentences to fit what they think their listeners already know. For example, the sentence "It was your *son* who scored the touchdown" assumes that the listeners (parents) know that a touchdown was scored, but not that their son scored the touchdown. Thus the given information in the sentence is that a touchdown was made, and the new information is that their son made the touchdown. The emphasis or stress in the sentence is on *son,* not on the fact that a touchdown was made.

Sometimes a speaker emphasizes a particular phrase in a sentence by placing it at the beginning. In this fashion the speaker focuses attention on the particular context in which the event occurred. For example, "At her cocktail party Mrs. Jones was very gracious" makes it clear that Mrs. Jones was gracious in a particular context. The reader is thus implicitly cautioned that Mrs. Jones may or may not be gracious in other settings, without this specifically being mentioned.

To summarize, the functions of language are seen in speech acts, propositional content, and thematic structure. Speakers signal their intent by the choice of a speech act which includes telling, asking, or commanding someone. The propositional content of a sentence is the particular information that is conveyed. And the thematic structure involves making judgments about the listener's knowledge, often by stressing new information in the context of known or given information. Now we turn our attention to certain structural properties of language.

Structure of Language

The structure of language can be divided into three basic parts: phonology, syntax or grammar, and semantics. The first of these, *phonology,* concerns the rules for pronunciation of speech sounds. The second aspect of language, *syntax,* deals with the way words combine to form sentences. And *semantics* focuses on the meaning of words and sentences. In this section we examine certain aspects of the structure of language.

Basic Units of Language: Phonemes and Morphemes

All languages are made of basic sounds called *phonemes.* Adult human beings can produce approximately 100 phonemes, and the English language is made up of about 45 phonemes. Languages vary in the number of phonemes, ranging from as few as 15 to as many as 85. One reason why it is difficult for many Americans to learn foreign languages is that different phonemes are used. For instance, Germanic and Slavic languages contain phonemes never used in the English language.

Phonemes are in turn composed of about twelve *distinctive features.* The linguist Roman Jakobson (Jakobson and Halle, 1956) constructed a classification of distinctive features by which phonemes differ. For example, a given phoneme (speech sound) may be sounded nasally or orally.

Another feature is the explosive or tense character of some sounds as seen when /p/ or /f/ (phonemes for the letters *p* and *f*) are pronounced.

A *phoneme* can be defined as any single change in the sound of a word that also makes a difference in meaning: *pin* versus *bin,* for example. Furthermore, contrasts that make a meaningful difference in one language may not make a difference in another language. English speakers do not, for example, distinguish between the aspirated and unaspirated forms of /p/: *pin* (aspirated /p/) versus *spin* (unaspirated /p/). To demonstrate that the /p/ in *pin* is aspirated, hold a match in front of your mouth while saying the word and note that the flame flickers. However, this does not happen when *spin* is said.

Another unit of language is the *morpheme,* which is the smallest meaningful unit in a language. Morphemes usually consist of combinations of two or more phonemes and roughly correspond to the most elementary words. The words *good, put,* and *go* are single morphemes. *Goodness, putting,* and *going* consist of two morphemes. Thus, single morphemes may be root words of a language; they may also consist of prefixes or suffixes.

At about two years of age the young child begins to combine two words to form the most rudimentary kind of sentence. The combination of words into sentences is referred to as *syntax.* A young child will frequently use sentences like "Want cookie," "Where ball?" and "Drink Mommy" which clearly convey meaning. These sentences are quite systematic, are usually understood by the parent, and are similar to adult English sentences with the unessential words omitted (cf., Brown, 1973).

Higher Levels of Linguistic Analysis

We have just considered the most basic analyses possible of language. The study of the speech sounds which make up a language is called *phonology,* and the study of how these sounds combine to produce morphemes is called *morphology.* However, psychologists are frequently interested in a more global analysis of language than is provided by phonology and morphology. Psychological investigations of language typically adopt words, phrases, sentences, or prose as the most fundamental unit of analysis, rather than more elementary speech sounds.

There are several levels at which these higher-order analyses can be made. First, one could analyze the *lexical content* of a sentence or of some other unit of language production. When a lexical analysis is performed, the question is simply: What words are used in this sample of language? This was the basic approach of Thorndike and Lorge who tabulated the frequency with which different English words occurred in large samples of printed material. For example, these investigators reported the average frequency of occurrence per million words of text for each of a large number of common words such as *kitchen* (over 100 times per million) and rare words such as *rostrum* (only 1 time per million). Information gained from lexical analyses of language such as that by Thorndike and Lorge has proved to be very useful in predicting the ease with which different words can be learned in laboratory situations.

At another level of linguistic analysis, the *syntactic content* of language text may be investigated. In the study of syntax, interest is focused on the arrangement or ordering of words to form phrases and sentences. The question asked in this type of analysis is: How is this phrase (or sentence) structured? Psychologists and linguists interested in syntactic theory have attempted to specify rules that will generate an infinite number of grammatically correct sentences and no incorrect sentences. The set of rules indicating how the elements of the language may be combined to make intelligible sentences is referred to as a *grammar*. Although a large number of different grammars have been proposed, linguists have not been able to write down the extremely complex system of rules which generates all the syntactically correct sentences of the English language, or of any other natural language. At present, there is little agreement about the necessary features of an adequate grammar. However, an important part of many of the proposed grammars is the rules for phrase structure, which we consider in the next section.

Perhaps the most important level of analysis of language is the one which considers the *semantic content* or meaning of a passage. This perspective on language results in the asking of questions such as: What does the passage communicate? What is the meaning of this particular sentence? Unfortunately, psychologists and linguists know less about the rules for determining the meanings of words and combinations of words than they do about the rules of syntax or morphology. The critical role of semantics, however, has been clearly demonstrated in a number of psychological investigations. For example, when subjects listen to passages of connected discourse, their recognition memory for sentences after a short delay is much more sensitive to changes in semantic (e.g., subject-object reversal) than to changes in syntactic content (e.g., switching from active to passive voice) (Sachs, 1967). Current views of semantics and comprehension in general view the listener (or reader) as an *active participant* who formulates hypotheses about subsequent input based on context (both verbal and situational), knowledge of constraints in the language, and knowledge of the world. This is in contrast to the more passive view of the comprehender as someone who waits for the input before acting upon it.

Although theories of semantics cannot here be considered in detail, it is appropriate to point out the dramatic differences in approaches to theorizing in this area. On one hand, associationistic theories have been proposed in which meaning is viewed simply as a conditioned response. Thus the responses made to a word are thought to be modifications of the unconditioned response once made to the object referred to by that word. In contrast to this approach, more recent theories have suggested possible structures of the semantic memory necessary for the use of language. This newer approach has considered the human being as an information-processing system rather than as an association learner and has resulted in a number of computer programs which attempt to model human ability to deal with semantics. Certain of these computer programs provide persuasive demonstrations of their understanding of portions of the English language. For example, computer programs have been written which can respond in ordinary English to questions concerning the properties of objects or events which the computer has stored in its memory after being presented with a series of sentences describing those objects or events. These issues were discussed in some detail in chapters 7 and 8. The collaboration among computer scientists, psychologists, and linguists seems to offer one of the most promising approaches to the study of how human beings acquire knowledge of semantics.

Phrase Structure in Sentences

In order to understand language in the adult, it is necessary to examine the structure of sentences. At one level of analysis a sentence can be regarded simply as a string of phonemes. The single phoneme, however, is not a particularly useful way of analyzing sentences since this would be looking at a sentence as a series of isolated speech sounds. At another level, a sentence can be regarded as a series of morphemes, which are groupings of phonemes. From this viewpoint, however, the sentence is viewed as a string of words. Linguists have found it more useful to describe a sentence in terms of *phrases,* which are groupings of words.

Analysis of a sentence into its various phrases describes the *phrase structure* of a sentence. A sentence is viewed as composed of two basic phrases, a *noun phrase* and a *verb phrase,* which are in turn composed of subcomponents. Figure 9.1 shows the phrase structure of a simple sentence "The boy rode the bicycle." The noun phrase is composed of a *determiner* and a *noun,* and the verb phrase is composed of a *verb* and *noun phrase;* the latter noun phrase is also composed of a determiner and a noun. The relationship between the two phrases is portrayed in the tree diagram of figure 9.1. Very brief pauses in speech are sometimes defined by phrase marking. For example, we are most likely to say "The boy . . . rode . . . the bicycle," pausing ever so briefly after *boy* and *rode.* We are not likely to say "The . . . boy rode . . . the bicycle," grouping *boy* and *rode,* or "The . . . boy rode the . . . bicycle," grouping *boy, rode,* and *the.* While in normal speech a speaker may search and grope for a particular word, and thus alter the pauses, the listener still tends to understand the message.

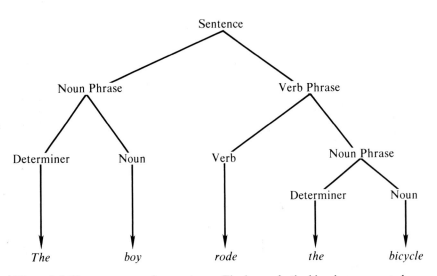

Figure 9.1 Phrase structure in a sentence, The boy rode the bicycle, represented by a tree diagram. (From *Fundamentals of Human Learning, Memory, and Cognition,* 2nd ed., by H. C. Ellis. Dubuque, Iowa: Wm. C. Brown Company, 1978.)

Surface Structure and Deep Structure in Sentences

Linguists distinguish between surface structure and deep structure of sentences. The *surface structure* is the organization that describes the sequences of phrases in a sentence as it is actually spoken (or read) and reflects simply the relationship among the parts of the sentence. In contrast, *deep structure* pertains to sentence meaning or underlying structure, that is, to the specification of the logical relations between the words in the sentence.

Consider the sentences "John threw the ball" and "The ball was thrown by John." Both sentences convey the same meaning despite the fact that they sound different. Hence their deep structure is the same. But consider the sentence "The lamb is ready to eat" which can have two meanings. The lamb may serve as food to be eaten, or as an animal, the lamb is prepared to eat food. Thus, the deep structure can vary with the same sentence, depending on what meaning the speaker wishes to convey. Consider the following sentences, "Visiting relatives can be a nuisance," "Bill shot the man with a gun," and "The corrupt police can't stop drinking" and evaluate their meanings.

These illustrations indicate the necessity of distinguishing between surface and deep structures. The deep structure of a sentence conveys the basic or underlying information in the sentence. When certain theoretical rules of grammar are applied, it is possible to link the surface structure of

Language 181

a sentence to its deep structure. Rules for the specification of this linkage process, called *transformational rules,* have been developed by Noam Chomsky (Chomsky, 1965, 1975) and other linguists.

Transformational rules have clear implications about what features of sentences human beings do store in memory. If the sentence is very simple, so that its deep structure approximates its surface structure, then features of the surface structure may be stored. As sentences become more complex, what is thought to be stored is some underlying base structure or *schema,* plus one or more "footnotes" that serve as rules necessary to regenerate the sentence in its original surface form. This is simply to say that what is stored is some coded representation of the complex sentence.

This brief description only begins to sketch some of the complexities of language. What is clear is that young children have an enormously complex task in learning to speak, read, and use language in a meaningful fashion. The fact that human beings can acquire and use language emerges as a remarkable achievement.

Transformational Grammar

As was noted, phrases appear to be the way in which information is naturally grouped for thinking and memory. Information tends to be remembered in chunks, and chunking is one type of organizational process. Some linguists such as Chomsky point out that the phrase structure analysis of language is nevertheless incomplete and that the complete analysis of language must have a transformational component. By making a distinction between the underlying structure of a sentence and the surface form of the sentence, transformational grammar provides a way to represent relationships among sentences which on the surface take quite different forms. Transformations are based upon rules which apply to sentences, and the transformation allows the same idea to be expressed in, say, either an active or a passive sentence. For example, "The dog chased the cat" and "The cat was chased by the dog" have quite different phrase structures as sentences, but both share a common underlying or deep structure.

The surface structure of a sentence is produced by the application of various transformational rules to the deep structure. For instance, the first sentence, "The dog chased the cat," is an active-declarative transformation of the deep structure, and the second sentence, "The cat was chased by the dog," is a passive-declarative transformation. A variety of different surface structures may be produced by the same deep structure. The basic idea of any sentence is to express a relationship between a subject, a verb, and an object; the idea is called a *base marker* from which many different sentences can be generated. The base marker having to do with the dog chasing the cat can be transformed into various forms (such as "The cat was chased by the dog" and "Did the dog chase the cat?"). While the surface structures may be different, they all relate to a common base marker.

Processes in Language

In this section we will examine some basic processes in language. The focus is on three processes: production of language, speech perception and comrehension, and language development.

Production of Language

The beginning of any dialogue is, of course, the production of speech by one of the participants. But before uttering any sentence the speaker must do some planning, and this involves the intent of the speaker to produce a specific effect on the listener. Thus speaking is very much an *instrumental act*, which is to say that speakers talk in order to produce an effect of some kind.

The process of speaking is basically concerned with planning and execution. But just how is speech planned and executed? Clark and Clark (1977) described a rough outline of this process which involves five steps. The first step for speakers is to decide on the kind of discourse to be initiated, which is the issue of *discourse plans*. Do they want to engage in a conversation, or describe an event, or give instructions, or regale a friend with a humorous story? Each type of discourse has a particular structure, and speakers must plan their utterances to fit that structure. For example, if you are telling a joke, you first describe the setting or context, then describe the sequence of events, and end with the punch line. If you fail to follow this structure, you obviously will not be an effective joke teller. For example, if you give away the joke by accidentally telling the punch line before the appropriate time, you will defeat your purpose. Similarly, instructions and conversations have an orderly structure.

Planning discourse is planning at the global level. The second stage involves *planning of sentences*, the components of discourse. Once the nature of the discourse is decided, specific sentences that will accomplish the objective must then be selected. The speech act, the propositional content, and the thematic structure need to be determined. The order in which sentences are produced and the type of information to be conveyed must be thought about. For example, suppose you are describing your new house. You might first describe the location: "We're ten miles outside of town near the mountains—in South Sandia Heights." Next, you might describe the overall type of house: "It's a two-story contemporary house made of redwood, stucco, and stone." Then you might proceed to describe the floor plan and arrangement of rooms and finally give specifics of each room. Notice that there is a structure present which involves going from global or general information to progressively more specific details.

The third phase deals with *constituent plans* of the sentence. Once a sentence is decided on, its components must then be planned. The appropriate words, phrases, and so forth, must be picked out and put in the right order. These first three phases describe three levels of planning. At the most general level, planning is directed toward the type of discourse. At the next level, planning concerns the type of sentence to be uttered, and finally planning deals with specific components of the sentence.

An interesting feature of slips of the tongue is that they point out regularities in the planning stages of productions. For example, slips are seldom "illegal" combinations of sounds for the language; morphemes tend to slip as entire units (Clark & Clark, 1977). Some classic slips are known as "bloopers" in the world of radio and television. Some bloopers are fairly obvious. For example, an announcer for the "Friendly Homemaker Program" said, "And now we present our homely friendmaker." Another example is a remark of the commentator covering a visit of the king and queen of England, "When they arrive, you will hear a twenty-one son galute." And from the commercial world comes this classic, "And Dad will love Wonder Bread's delicious flavor, too. Remember it's Wonder Bread for the breast in bed."

The fourth phase deals with what is called the *articulatory program*. This concerns the plans for the execution of speech which is a coordinated sequence of muscular contractions in and about the mouth. And the final phase is *articulation* itself. This is the actual output of speech. Interested readers are referred to Clark and Clark (1977) for a detailed discussion of planning and execution of speech.

Speech Perception

The comprehension of speech begins with the perception of raw speech sounds. Comprehension starts where speech production ends. Speakers produce a stream of sounds that arrive at the listeners' ears. And listeners are able to analyze sound patterns and to comprehend them. Speech perception is not, however, the simple identification of sounds. It involves the complex processes of encoding and comprehension discussed in earlier chapters. In other words, interpretative processes, meaning, contextual influences, and the like, play important roles in speech perception. Thus the transformation from raw speech sounds to propositions in memory is a complex process. The physical signal that reaches the ear consists of rapid vibrations of air. While the sounds of speech correlate with particular component frequencies, there is no direct one-to-one correspondence between the sounds of speech and the perceptions of listeners.

Recognition of words is very much dependent on context, expectations, and knowledge. For example, a hungry child can interpret the question "Have you washed your hands for dinner?" as a call to come directly to dinner. The role of context can also be easily seen in incomplete sentences where context allows words to be inferred quite easily. For example, the sentence "The young girl was awakened by her frightening d . . . " allows listeners to infer readily *dream*. There is no need to think about what the word might be; it just seems to pop out automatically. A similar context effect was studied in the laboratory by Warren (Warren & Obusek, 1971) using phonemes. Subjects were read sentences such as "The state governors met with their respective legislatures convening in the capital city." The first *s* in *legislatures* was masked with a coughing sound; that is, the subjects couldn't hear the first *s*. The experimenter then asked the subjects to tell where the cough occurred and they could not because they had in effect "restored" the *s* sound. They perceived the *s* as if it were still present in the word, a phenomenon called *phonemic restoration*.

Many persons have the impression that the words they hear are distinct, separate combinations of sounds. But this impression is not correct. Cole (1979, 1980) and other speech researchers have demonstrated that words usually run together as sound patterns. This is seen by use of a spectograph which is an electronic device for measuring the variations in energy expended when a person talks. Moreover, it is often the case that a single word cannot be recognized correctly when it is taken out of its sentence context. This was shown some years ago by Pollack and Pickett (1963) who played different segments of a normal conversation for subjects. But when the subjects heard just one word from the conversation it was often incomprehensible. Without the context of the meaningful sentence the single word could not be understood.

More generally, an important feature of speech perception is that speech is not comprehended simply on the basis of the sounds per se. Rather, speech is comprehended on the basis of many additional factors which include intentions, context, and expectations, from which an interpretation of what the speaker says is constructed.

Language Development

Language development follows a fairly orderly course. The beginning of language is evidenced in babbling, which is an elementary type of vocalization. Children do produce sounds earlier than six months of age, but babbling, which is the repetition of speech sounds, is most clearly evident beginning around six months. By the time children are seven or eight months of age, most parents can correctly identify different cries by an infant as indicating hunger cries, request cries, or cries of surprise (Ricks, 1975). Between six and nine months of age, infants are able to produce all of the basic speech sounds (phonemes) that make up a language.

The emission of speech sounds, even at this early age, can be controlled to some extent by an adult. For example, the rate at which infants emit speech sounds can be increased by having an adult repeat the sounds after the infant. These responses, called *echoic responses*, can be trained or shaped in the sense of increasing their rate just like other instrumental responses. Language learning is not, however, the simple result of reinforcement of particular speech sounds and sequences. Language involves learning to use complex rules of grammar.

One of the striking features of language acquisition is that children of various cultures learn their unique languages in similar ways. For example, children of different cultures acquire speech sounds at about the same time. Later on, they develop syntactic patterns at about the same time. These regularities in language development suggest that some features of language learning are *universal* (Slobin, 1973).

Making speech sounds is only the first step in acquiring language. The sounds must come to represent objects, symbols, and events in the child's environment. This is simply to say that the sounds must acquire *meaning* for the child. Moreover, children must learn to associate particular sound symbols with particular aspects of their environment. Children are familiar with many aspects of their environment before they learn to speak. Their parents are familiar stimuli; toys, pets, siblings, and household objects are also familiar stimuli. At this early stage of language development, their task is one of learning to associate particular environmental stimuli with particular responses. For example, they must learn to associate the sight of mother with the sound of *mama*. Similarly, the sight, feel, and taste of a cookie must become associated with the sound of *cookie*. Only when such associations are acquired can the speech sound come to represent or symbolize a specific object or event for the child. Thus, the development of meaning begins with the acquisition of associations between objects and events, on the one hand, and speech sounds, on the other hand.

One popular view of the acquisition of word meanings is that children learn semantic features and then attempt to apply an original word that includes the features to objects that share features in common. For example, a child may learn the word *ball* and then overgeneralize it to other round objects such as moon, grapefruit, and the like.

The association of speech sounds to environmental stimuli is, of course, only a part of language development. Once children acquire a rudimentary vocabulary, they must then begin to form sentences. At first young children form quite simple sentences, usually consisting of two or three words, such as "Want drink." Even as the vocabulary expands, short sentences continue to be used. The very first words that children produce often combine saying a word with a gesture such as "bye-bye" accompanied by a hand wave. Similarly, the speech act of asserting something is often accompanied by a pointing gesture, such as saying "Mama" and pointing toward the mother (Greenfield & Smith, 1976).

Gradually the child begins to construct more complex sentences that take on the characteristics of adult language. This is an enormously complex task (Brown, 1973). Children must learn to construct increasingly complex sentences, most of which they have never heard. Thus any type of imitation theory of language learning seems quite inadequate. Another possibility is that children might learn language by way of reinforcement principles. According to this view, children learn new utterances by being encouraged by their parents or other adults. But there is little support for the reinforcement view. Indeed, Brown reports that there is almost no evidence that parents make approval contingent upon the grammaticality of what their children say. In addition, there is an almost infinite number of possibilities in constructing sentences, so that we cannot regard the process of sentence construction as resulting from reinforcement of grammatically correct sentences.

What the child learns are sets of *grammatical rules* for constructing sentences. Usually the child is unable to verbalize the rules. Indeed, many adults who speak grammatically acceptable English are unable to specify the rules they use. But these rules allow us to generate an almost infinite number of different sentences. One of the best pieces of evidence for learning syntactic rules is the phenomenon of overgeneralization (syntactic). For example, children learn to say *went* correctly, apparently by rote, then learn the rule of forming the past tense by adding *ed,* and then incorrectly say *goed.* They later learn the exception to the rule and go back to saying *went.*

Some Issues in Language

In this section a few issues in language are examined. Included are the topics of language and thought, language in animals, cultural differences in language, and language and the brain.

Language and Thought

Language and thought are related events. The ability of children to handle concepts is related to their language development. Indeed, children who can verbalize relationships such as "nearer than" or "larger than" are better able to deal with problems involving relationships among stimuli than children who cannot yet verbalize such relationships.

Nevertheless, language does not seem to be *essential* for complex mental processes, despite the fact that language facilitates problem solving. For instance, deaf children, who are deficient in language, are able to handle many concepts. Thus, although language is a facilitating factor in thought, it does not appear to be essential in a critical sense for the development of cognitive capacities. As noted, this is the case because deaf children can develop other modes of communication by acquiring symbol systems other than conventional language.

The most explicit attempt to relate language and thought is seen in the *linguistic relativity hypothesis* developed by Whorf (1956). Whorf's hypothesis contends that the structure of one's language leads one to conceive of the world in particular ways, ways that differ from a person using a different language. This is simply to say that a person's language imposes a particular view of the world. Presumably, cognitive processes are in some way inevitably affected by the structure of language. The notion of *linguistic relativity* is emphasized because thought is presumed to be relative to the particular language used.

Vocabulary differences provide one instance of how language is presumably related to thought. For instance, Eskimos have several different words for labeling snow, depending upon its characteristics, whereas only one is widely used in English. Skiers, of course, do distinguish between several kinds of snow. Some cultures have many words for the various colors; other cultures have only a few. For Whorf, the range of words or labels available influences the range of cognitive activities in which human beings may engage. Persons having a number of different descriptive labels that they can apply to a range of events are presumably able to think about these events in more different ways than are persons having only a few labels.

There are two versions of Whorf's hypothesis. The *strong version* emphasizes that language *invariably* influences thought, whereas the *weak version* emphasizes that language affects thought when the particular task directly depends upon properties of the language system. There is little support for the strong version of the hypothesis. For example, if the strong version of the Whorf hypothesis is true, we would expect that persons who have many different words for different colors (parts of the visual spectrum) would perceive more distinctions among colors than persons who have only a few words. But this is not the case. Rosch (1973) compared the performance of the Dani, a primitive people of New Guinea, who use only two words for colors, with English-speaking subjects who use many different color terms. Despite differences in color terms, the two groups appear to perceive colors in much the same way. In short, just because a language lacks a range of terms for various stimuli, it does not mean that the user of the language necessarily ignores the various features of the stimuli.

On the other hand, the evidence consistent with the weaker version of Whorf's hypothesis comes from research on the effects of verbal labels on perception and recognition memory of visual patterns. In his summary of this research, Ellis (1973) noted that verbal labeling of visual patterns can affect the ease with which they are subsequently perceived and remembered. For example, if different visual patterns are all labeled with the

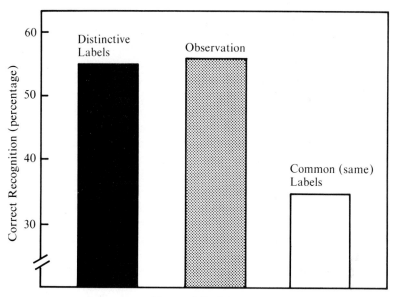

Figure 9.2 Shape recognition following practice in labeling and observation of shapes. (From "Stimulus Encoding Processes in Human Learning and Memory" by H. C. Ellis, in G. H. Bower, Ed., *The Psychology of Learning and Motivation,* Vol. 7. New York: Academic Press, 1973.)

same term, the patterns then become more difficult to recognize. Conversely, if the patterns are given different and meaningful verbal labels, they become more recognizable compared with control tests.

An example of the typical results of Ellis's studies in which subjects label visual (or tactual) shapes with verbal labels and then are tested for recognition of the shapes is shown in figure 9.2. The figure shows that subjects who are instructed to label shapes with unique, *distinctive* labels do better in subsequently recognizing the shapes than do subjects who attach *common* verbal labels. Subjects who simply observe the shapes, but are allowed to covertly label them, do as well as those who give them distinctive labels. Ellis contends that the common verbal labels lead the subject to attend to the more common or similar features of the pattern. Hence the subjects achieve a *less* distinctive encoding for each pattern and thus have greater difficulty in recognizing the patterns.

Not all studies have shown that observation of shapes leads to as good recognition as does uniquely labeling them. Ellis (1968, 1973) also reports that if the labels are *representative* of the shapes then labeling itself leads to superior recognition.

Language in Animals

Many people have raised this question: Do animals have language? The answer depends upon how one defines language. Animals clearly communicate with each other, and in this sense animals can be said to have language. But communication is not synonymous with language, although it is part of language. Language is composed of symbols which stand for other concepts. The word *dog* stands for the object dog; the word *joy* stands for an emotional experience. Words are used in accordance with complex rules of grammar, and the intent is to convey meaning.

Psychologists have made a number of attempts to teach language to chimpanzees. Early attempts by language researchers were largely unsuccessful, with only limited evidence for language being learned. In one of the most famous studies the Kelloggs raised their son with a chimpanzee named Gua. The chimpanzee learned to understand a number of commands, but never produced a single word. In a similar study a chimpanzee raised by the Hayeses learned to speak only three identifiable words, *mama, papa,* and *cup,* and only after great difficulty and extended training. As a result of these failures, many psychologists conclude that chimpanzees lack the vocal chord structures necessary for humanlike speech and that such efforts are doomed to failure.

The vocal inability of chimpanzees was recognized in more recent attempts to teach chimpanzees language by Gardner and Gardner (1969, 1975) and Premack (1971) who took a different approach to the problem. Their approach was to teach chimpanzees a *nonverbal* version of language. The Gardners attempted to teach their subject, Washoe, the sign language used by the deaf, which consists of making signs for different words. Using her hands, Washoe eventually learned over one-hundred-fifty signs. Of even greater importance was that Washoe learned to string signs together to make up primitive sentences. The fact that Washoe was able to produce simple strings is suggestive of a very primitive form of language. Premack's approach was to teach another chimpanzee, Sarah, a form of sign language using colored plastic chips displayed on a board, where each chip stood for a word. For example, a red square stood for *banana.* Sarah learned to "write" by placing chips on a magnetized board and with practice learned to construct simple sentences. But does this mean that Sarah uses language like human beings do? Probably not. Indeed, the language that is learned may be restricted to skills in word substitution, that is, transforming a phrase like "Mary eat banana" to "Mary wash banana."

More recently Terrace and colleagues continued this research in animal language with a chimp named Nim Chimpsky (Terrace, 1979). Nim was raised in a very rich social environment something like that of a young child. For example, he was bottle fed, praised, and given affection. Like

Washoe, Nim was taught the American Sign Language and gradually learned a total of one-hundred-twenty-five signs. But after almost four years of research, Terrace came to doubt that Nim was learning language in the same sense that a child does. For instance, when a human child learns a language, the average length and complexity of the utterances increase, whereas the average length of Nim's utterances showed little growth. Moreover, Nim gave no indication of an expanding grasp of syntax.

Do these studies allow the conclusion that chimpanzees possess language? What we can say is that chimpanzees do show the ability to produce simple sentences, which is *one* criterion of language. But they have not shown other features characteristic of human language. For example, when these animals produce strings of three or four signs, the strings are repetitive rather than sentencelike, according to Terrace and colleagues (Terrace, Pettito, & Bever, 1976). Some linguists contend that the uniquely human aspect of language is its *self-reflexive* quality, that is, the ability to refer to oneself. Meanwhile, the chimpanzee studies of language suggest that there are clear limits on the primate's ability to use symbolic communication systems. We anticipate that the debate on this question will continue.

Cultural Differences in Language

One of the fascinating issues in language is the question of how individual differences in language are to be explained. More specifically, one issue is the development of cultural, regional, and ethnic differences in language. Well-known regional variations in the dialect of English in the United States include dialects associated with the South, New England, New York City, Texas, and the Midwest. The Midwestern dialect is frequently referred to as standard, and this accent is sometimes preferred for radio and television broadcasting. Some natives of the Outer Banks of North Carolina and Appalachia speak with a sixteenth-century English accent (similar to a cockney accent). It is not clear how all these variations are maintained other than the general conclusion that we each learn the language patterns typical to our particular culture.

Many black Americans speak a dialect different from standard American English as spoken by Midwesterners and television announcers. Black American dialect is different in several ways from standard American English including slight differences in sound and important differences in grammar. For example, the expressions "I do," "I did," and "I have done" are the accepted forms of the verb *to do* in standard English; however, a black child might say "I do," "I done," and "I have did." While these forms depart from standard English, some linguists have recently recognized that such forms are grammatical.

Until quite recently the use of nonstandard English by blacks has been assumed by some white educators to be a reflection of the cultural deprivation of blacks. Some have felt that the use of nonstandard English may be the principal basis for blacks scoring lower than whites on the average on standard intelligence tests and for school performance of blacks to reflect slower progress than whites. While there may be a relation between language and scholastic performance, recent evidence argues that nonstandard English is logical, orderly, and grammatical. It has been proposed that if whites were required, for example, to take an IQ test based on black culture and language, they would also show poorer performance.

This issue can be placed in another perspective. Is nonstandard black English like any other dialect, or is it a less optimal form of language that may possibly limit the intellectual functioning of those who use it? Although we do not have a full and complete answer to this and similar questions, the recent arguments of some linguists lead us increasingly to the position of regarding black English as a dialect in its own right, having its own rules and its own sense of time.

Language and the Brain

The human brain is divided into two hemispheres which are not functionally equivalent. Each hemisphere receives information from the senses, but the two hemispheres generally receive separate information. Information from the visual environment is usually divided, with information from the right visual field being projected to the left hemisphere and information from the left visual field being projected to the right hemisphere. Nevertheless, information which reaches each half of the brain is usually coordinated or integrated in some fashion.

The fact that the human brain is asymmetrical is especially important for language. For most human adults, the left cerebral hemisphere controls the functions of language which include production of both spoken and written language and comprehension of verbal information. In contrast, the right cerebral hemisphere is frequently unable to produce language or to comprehend abstract words. In turn, the right hemisphere is concerned with perceptual processes such as picture recognition and comprehension and learning of visual forms.

The knowledge of this dual functioning of the brain stems from what is called the *split-brain* experiment. A split brain usually results from surgery which severs the corpus callosum, fibers connecting the two hemispheres, in order to alleviate symptoms of certain rare forms of epilepsy. Since the normal interaction between the two hemispheres is eliminated by this operation, it is possible to observe the function of each largely independent hemisphere. Important differences in how the two hemispheres are involved in language behaviors have been discovered. For example, when a split-brain patient held an object in the right hand, allowing sensory information to be sent to the left cerebral hemisphere, the patient was able to name and describe the object. In contrast, when the patient held the object in the left hand, allowing sensory information to go primarily to the right hemisphere, he was unable to describe the object verbally although he could match the object to an identical one in a recognition task. Similarly, when a split-brain patient was shown a picture of an object so that sensory information went to the right hemisphere, he was unable to label the object in the picture; however, he was able to pick out the object in a recognition test when it was presented with others (Gazzaniga, 1970, 1977).

A number of systematic studies have begun to reveal the functioning of the two hemispheres. This separation of language and perceptual functions is the beginning of an important line of work.

Summary

In chapter 9 some of the main features of language were described. As was seen, language is the principal means of human communication. The three functions of language discussed are speech acts, propositional content, and thematic structure. Speech acts involve ordering, questioning, and telling others; propositional content refers to the actual content surrounding a speech act; and thematic structure involves keeping track of what listeners understand.

The basic units of language are phonemes. In order to understand adult language the structure of sentences must be examined. Sentences possess both a surface structure and a deep structure which can be related by transformational grammar.

The important processes of language production, speech perception, and language development were examined. Language production involves five phases: discourse plans, sentence plans, constituent plans, articulatory programs, and articulation. Speech perception begins with the production of speech sounds and ends with their interpretation in memory. Speech perception is not a matter of one-to-one correspondence between the sounds of speech and the perceptions of listeners. Rather, speech perception is heavily dependent upon content, intentions, and knowledge. Language development is a progressive and orderly process in which children learn general rules of language so that they can communicate.

Language and thought are related processes; however, the evidence does not support a strong version of the Whorf hypothesis. Animals such as chimpanzees can be taught certain features of language, but do not appear to possess all the complex features of human language. Language is heavily dependent upon the left cerebral hemisphere, whereas perception is predominantly dependent on the right cerebral hemisphere.

Multiple-Choice Items

1. A sentence can serve several functions including a request for information, a command, a description, and so forth. These functions refer
   a. to speech acts
   b. to grammar
   c. to syntax
   d. to semantics

2. The function of language which most clearly involves the role of the listener is
   a. propositional content
   b. thematic structure
   c. speech acts
   d. phonemes

3. The phrase structure of sentences emphasizes the way human beings
   a. associate single words
   b. group information for thinking
   c. transform information from deep structure to surface structure
   d. derive meaning

4. The production of language is basically concerned with _____ ?
   a. phonemes
   b. emotions
   c. planning
   d. conditioning

5. The idea that language leads us to perceive and think about the world in particular ways is called the
   a. distinctive-feature hypothesis
   b. cultural hypothesis
   c. transformational hypothesis
   d. linguistic relativity hypothesis

6. The fact that children produce sentences which they have never in fact heard is taken as support of which conception of language?
   a. grammatical rules are learned
   b. imitation
   c. reinforcement-learning theory
   d. linguistic relativity

True-False Items

1. The consideration of thematic structure by a speaker involves making judgments about the listener's current state of knowledge.

2. Language development is largely a matter of simple imitation.

3. Black English is a less grammatical form of English.

4. Split-brain studies suggest the same locus for language and perceptual functions.

5. Language production is viewed as a five-stage affair beginning with the planning of a sentence.

6. Phonemic restoration refers to the tendency of a listener to "fill in" a missing phoneme while hearing sentences.

Discussion Items

1. Outline several major features of language development.

2. What is the role of context and expectations in the interpretation of speech?

3. Suppose that you had language for only four colors of the visual spectrum, say, red, yellow, green, and blue. Speculate as to how this might affect the way you think about colored objects in the environment.

4. Summarize the basic issues and findings regarding language in chimpanzees.

5. If it is assumed that various dialects of English are all grammatical, are there advantages to learning standard English? Discuss.

Answers to Multiple-Choice Items

1. (a) All utterances or sentences can be classified as to the type of speech act they represent.
2. (b) Good speakers pay careful attention to their listeners, judging their level of knowledge and comprehension. This process takes into account thematic structure.

3. (b) Phrases appear to be the way in which information is naturally grouped for thinking as well as for memory. Pauses in speech allow for the effective grouping or chunking of phrases in memory.

4. (c) Prior to speaking, the speaker decides what kind of discourse to initiate, which involves planning. This is followed by planning at the sentence level and then at the constituent level of the sentence.

5. (d) The idea that language influences perceptual and cognitive processes is called the linguistic relativity hypothesis, developed by Whorf.

6. (a) The production of novel sentences is thought to occur as the result of using the rules of grammar.

Answers to True-False Items

1. (True) Consideration of thematic structure by speakers means that they are aware of the listeners and make fairly accurate judgments of their level of understanding.

2. (False) Imitation appears to be at best only a small part of language learning. Learning a language is very much a matter of learning the set of rules which govern the use of language.

3. (False) Many linguists now regard black English as a dialect whose grammatical form is quite lawful.

4. (False) Split-brain studies do suggest a separate locus for language and perceptual functions.

5. (False) Language production is viewed as a five-stage affair; however, it begins with overall discourse plans and is followed by sentence plans.

6. (True) Phonemic restoration is the process of "filling in" a missing phoneme in a word when a sentence is heard.

Concepts and Categories

10

Concepts provide us with a certain kind of stability in interacting with the environment. Concepts allow us to rise above the specific details of the environment and to treat events that have common properties as members of a class. For example, in forming the concept of *dog,* young children learn to classify a variety of specific instances as members of a set. They learn that the label *dog* may be applied to specific instances, but more important they learn that *dog* refers to a *class of instances* which have certain properties or features in common.

If children apply the concept of *dog only* to a specific dog, such as their own, they have not really developed the concept of *dog.* It is only when they can apply the term to a number of specific instances in a reasonably accurate fashion that we say they have acquired the concept. Moreover, it is important not only that they apply the term appropriately in the presence of instances, but also that they recognize other events or objects that are properly not part of the concept. Thus, for example, they must properly exclude instances such as cats, rabbits, and other animals. Thus, the formation of concepts refers to *both* the *selection* of appropriate instances and the *rejection* or exclusion of inappropriate instances.

The development and refinement of some concepts take place over an extended time period. Moreover, the forming of many concepts involves progressing from some gross, diffuse state to a highly refined condition in which fine-grain distinctions can be made. Thus, students may have only general concepts about some things and very precise concepts about others. In addition, they may be in the process of refining some of their more vague concepts. In the course of formal learning, students' concepts of abstractions such as "justice," "freedom," and "integrity" constantly grow and change as they are exposed to new experiences and knowledge. Similar is the situation in which understanding of a particular concept sharpens and expands with additional experience, advanced training, or new knowledge.

A great deal of teaching is directed toward the development of concepts because they are necessary for more complex behaviors such as learning of principles, problem solving, and symbolic activities such as thinking.

One of the principal objectives of formal education is the teaching of basic concepts that enable individuals to function in society in conjunction with teaching also the notion that concepts can be revised, altered, and amended on the basis of new knowledge and experience. The ability to handle concepts as they currently exist and to deal with them in a flexible and changing fashion is a joint objective of school learning.

Types of Concepts

Psychologists have used a wide variety of stimulus objects in the study of how concepts are formed and how things are classified. These stimuli range from natural objects in the environment such as trees, plants, and so forth, to useful objects such as furniture and automobiles, to artificial stimuli constructed in the laboratory. In much laboratory research on concept formation during the period 1955–1970, artificial concepts were typically used. These concepts possess a certain convenience because their precise features are specified. A stimulus is usually either a member of the concept or not a member.

Logical Concepts

Logical or artificial concepts are used in tasks in which subjects are presented varied stimulus patterns not normally experienced in their everyday environment. The stimuli are constructed so as to vary systematically along certain dimensions. Typically, the laboratory researcher constructs visual patterns varying in size, shape, or color. Thus the stimuli consist of such things as red squares, green circles, blue triangles, and so forth. The concept to be learned is arbitrarily selected, such as large green objects. This category includes, then, all stimuli that are large and green regardless of their shape. Stimuli which cannot be placed in this category are not instances of the concept. Stimuli consisting of both positive instances (exemplars) and negative instances (nonexemplars) are presented. They vary in several *dimensions,* one or more of which are relevant to the concept, whereas others are irrelevant. Each dimension may take on two or more *values.* For example, we may have shape, size, and color as dimensions, with two values for each dimension: circle and square for shape, large and small for size, and red and green for color. This arrangement produces eight stimuli, as shown in figure 10.1.

The particular concept to be learned is arbitrarily determined by the experimenter. If the concept to be learned is *square,* then the green and red instances enclosed by the dotted line are positive instances of that concept. A similar arrangement can be made for the size concept. Moreover,

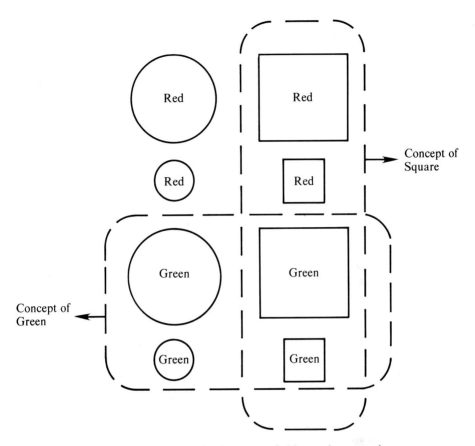

Figure 10.1 Schematic diagram showing instances of objects relevant to the concept *square* and to the concept *green*. (From *Fundamentals of Human Learning, Memory, and Cognition,* 2nd ed., by H. C. Ellis. Dubuque, Iowa: Wm. C. Brown Company, 1978.)

various combinations could be used such as *small red* and *large green* objects, which designate a more complex kind of concept.

We can increase the number of instances dramatically simply by increasing the number of attributes. If the three dimensions (shape, size, and color) are each represented by three attributes, we have twenty-seven instances rather than eight. Figure 10.2 shows this set of instances. Note that the attributes for *shape* are square, triangle, and circle; for *size* they are small, medium, and large. *Color* is represented by three different shadings.

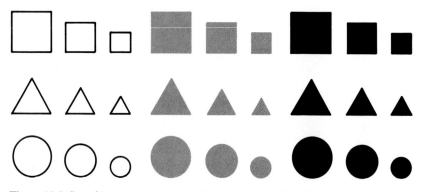

Figure 10.2 Set of instances generated from three stimulus dimensions each represented by three attribute values.

Natural Concepts

As noted, a great deal of laboratory research has been done using logical concepts. They are defined on the basis of certain relevant dimensions which are combined according to a rule. Once the concept is figured out, all new exemplars presented can be categorized correctly. Thus, the concepts are tightly defined and the instances are unambiguous instances of exemplars or nonexemplars of the concept, which is to say that logical concepts are *deterministic*.

In recent years objections have been raised to the use of these concepts. Rosch (1973a, 1975) expressed concern over their appropriateness and argued for the use of *natural concepts. Artificial* (logical) concepts are not representative of the kinds of concepts encountered in the everyday world. The world is not so neatly divided into instances and noninstances, so Rosch notes. Indeed, the majority of concepts in everyday world experience do not fall into neatly defined categories. Many concepts have fuzzy boundaries with some uncertainty. For example: Is a tomato classified a fruit or a vegetable? Many *natural* concepts fit the situation of having fuzzy boundaries. And some examples of natural concepts are considered to be better examples than others. For instance, a chair is a very typical example of the concept of *furniture,* whereas a beanbag is a less representative example.

Color concepts are an interesting example of natural concepts. The color spectrum is divided into a fairly similar manner in different cultures. Try visualizing a perfect blue, or red, or yellow. Persons tend to agree on what colors best represent each. But consider a color halfway between blue and green. When asked to identify it, some persons call it blue, others call it green, and a few are unsure of the color.

The point in noting the distinctions between logical and natural concepts is to emphasize that natural concepts are not defined in terms of clear, distinguishing attributes and precise rules. These concepts or categories are characterized by possessing certain features, some of which are more typical than others. We call these *prototypical concepts*. For example, *chair* is considered a very good (representative) example of furniture, whereas a *chest of drawers* is regarded as being a less typical or representative example. More generally, a prototype refers to the best representative of a category.

Natural concepts are also sometimes *probabilistic*. They possess some uncertainty. For such concepts the relationship between the attributes and the concept is less than perfect. For example, high grades in high school do not automatically mean high grades in college. There is, of course, some probability that high grades in high school predict similar performance in college, but the correlation is far from perfect. We do not know all the relevant variables that predict college success, and we thus must deal with a probabilistic situation.

Varieties of Categories

We can further distinguish a variety of ways in which human beings categorize objects and information. How are categories defined? On what basis are stimuli grouped and organized? Probably the most general way categories are defined is by the sharing of common attributes. Things may be categorized on a variety of bases such as similar function or use and similar appearance.

Categories and Verbal Context

The way an object is classified very much depends on how it is perceived and encoded. This fact was demonstrated in experiments by Labov (1973) who showed how the verbal context associated with an object can influence the way subjects classify the object. In these experiments Labov used cuplike objects, examples of which are shown in figure 10.3. All these drawings resemble cups, although some are a bit unusual. The cups along the left side of the figure (cups 5 through 9) show increasing elongation. The cups across the top (1 through 4) show an increase in the ratio of width to depth; as they become wider they begin to look more like bowls. Other differences are obvious. Cups 10 through 12 are cylindrical, cups 13 through 15 are conical, and cups 16 and 17 have stems. In Labov's experiments these drawings were presented one at a time, and subjects were simply asked to name them. This defined a *neutral* instructional condition. In other conditions subjects were asked to name the objects under different instructional sets. For example, subjects were asked to imagine the object sitting

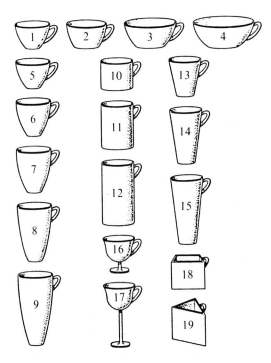

Figure 10.3 Series of cuplike objects for classification. (From "The Boundaries of Words and Their Meanings" by W. Labov, in C. J. N. Bailey and R. W. Shuy, Eds., *New Ways of Analyzing Variations in English*. Washington, D.C.: Georgetown University Press, 1973.)

on a dinner table or filled with mashed potatoes or that someone was drinking coffee from it. After the various instructions, subjects were asked to identify the objects, one at a time, using a label or phrase.

The results are presented in figure 10.4, which shows the percentage of subjects giving a particular name as a function of width of the object and instructional set. The figure shows two important points. First, the frequency of "cup" responses decreases while the frequency of "bowl" responses increases as the width of the objects increases. The change is gradual, indicating that the boundary between cup and bowl is fuzzy. This, of course, is not particularly surprising. The second point is that the frequency distributions of the *cup* label and the *bowl* label are influenced markedly by the verbal instructions or context. For example, an object is more likely to be called a bowl if it is thought of as filled with mashed potatoes as compared to the neutral context. These results show convincingly that a category is defined *both* by the *perceptual features* of the object (width) and by the prevailing *verbal-instructional context* under which the judgments are made.

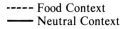

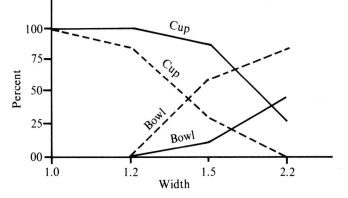

Figure 10.4 Percent of different name types applied to objects as the width increases and as a function of the verbal set. (From "The Boundaries of Words and Their Meanings" by W. Labov, in C. J. N. Bailey and R. W. Shuy, Eds., *New Ways of Analyzing Variations in English*. Washington, D.C.: Georgetown University Press, 1973.)

The importance of verbal context in classifying objects is related to similar effects in human memory. Not only does verbal context affect how objects are classified and, hence, encoded, but also verbal context affects the discriminability and recognizability of objects (a fact long known). In a series of experiments, Ellis (1968, 1973) showed that the way visual shapes are verbally labeled affects memory for the shapes. Using random shapes, subjects were instructed to label them with verbal labels representative of the shapes. For example, a shape that looked something like a mountain was labeled "a mountain." Other subjects labeled the shapes with words having no relationship to the shape or with nonsense words. Under a variety of situations subjects' memory for the shapes was superior under the representative label condition, indicating that the label can influence how a shape is encoded and remembered. The effects of verbal context are important and operate in memory as well as in classification tasks.

Perceptual Categories

It is obvious that human beings have color concepts and that they learn to categorize colors in a reasonably consistent way. Are some colors better examples of color categories than are others? For example, are some reds more representative of the category *red* than others? Rosch argued that there are some colors that are best examples of a particular color category, just as there are some forms that best represent a particular form category. These best examples, as noted earlier, are called *prototypes*.

How are prototypes developed? In the case of color Rosch hypothesized that prototypicality might be based on certain properties of the nervous system. A best blue might be best, among all the blues, because the visual system is more sensitive to that particular blue. One can then speculate that, if this is the case, persons from different cultures might respond to the same color prototypes. Rosch was able to test this possibility by doing a series of color experiments with the Dani, a fairly primitive people in New Guinea. The Dani have no color-naming system as such; they differentiate colors only as dark and light. Since they have the same nervous system as persons of Western cultures, Rosch argued that they should respond to the same prototypical values of color.

In one experiment, she found that the Dani subjects learned to associate names with color chips more rapidly when the colors were prototypical. For example, subjects learned to respond to a pure green more rapidly than to a color peripheral to the category such as yellow-green, even though they did not initially possess names for the colors. When the color chips were arranged in groups of three, say blue-green, pure green, and yellow-green, subjects learned the prototype more rapidly if it was made central in the category than when one of the other chips was made central. Similar findings were reported in studies of form categories. That is, there are prototypical squares and triangles as well as prototypical colors. The importance of Rosch's studies is that they establish the point that color concepts are internally structured, with some colors being more representative of a color category than others.

Semantic Categories

We have seen that perceptual categories such as color are organized such that prototypes for various colors exist. Does the same hold true for *semantic* categories? Semantic categories have no apparent perceptual basis as do color and form. So a different approach is required to answer this question and it was developed by Rosch (1975). She simply asked subjects to rate words which were members of categories, such as furniture and vehicles, as to how representative they were of the category. The results were strikingly clear; semantic-category prototypes do exist. For example, subjects agreed that *chair* is very representative of the category furniture whereas *desk* or *chest of drawers* is less representative. A *rocking chair* is regarded as intermediate in representativeness. Subjects also show a high degree of agreement in this task. Examples of norms for two categories, furniture and vehicles, are shown in table 10.1.

Table 10.1
Norms for Goodness-of-Example Rating for Two Semantic Categories

Member	Goodness of Example Rank	Member	Goodness of Example Rank
Furniture		*Vehicle*	
Chair	1.5	Automobile	1
Sofa	1.5	Station wagon	2
Couch	3.5	Truck	3
Table	3.5	Car	4
Easy chair	5	Bus	5.5
Dresser	6.5	Taxi	5.5
Rocking chair	6.5	Jeep	7
Coffee table	8	Ambulance	8
Rocker	9	Motorcycle	9
Love seat	10	Streetcar	10
Chest of drawers	11	Van	11
Desk	12	Honda	12
Bed	13	Cable car	13

From "Cognitive Representations of Semantic Categories," by E. Rosch, *Journal of Experimental Psychology: General*, 1975, *104*, 192–233. Copyright 1975 by the American Psychological Association. Reprinted by permission.

Rosch also showed that the time required for a subject to judge whether an item belongs to a given semantic category depends on the degree of category membership. Subjects were presented with statements of the form "A doll is a toy." In some cases the example was a good one, that is, very representative of the category, and in other cases the example was a poor one. Where the statement was *true*, subjects took longer to respond yes when the example was a poor member of the category.

Prototypes and Defining Attributes

An interesting issue concerns the kind of mental representation or memory code a person has for categories. Put simply, what kind of mental representation occurs when you think of a category, such as tree or fish? Two general kinds of views have been proposed. One theory says that you think of a list of *defining attributes* or features. For example, fish swim and have gills. You could list the defining features of fish and then determine whether the particular example in question meets the criteria of possessing the defining features.

A second view contends that we think of the *prototype,* that is, the best example of a category. For example, a prototypical fish might be about the size of a trout (12 to 15 inches), have scales and fins, swim in an ocean, a lake or a river, and so forth. We have a general or abstract conception of fish which somehow is typical or representative of the variety of examples with which we are familiar. When given a particular example, we compare it to this abstract prototype of the category. If it is sufficiently similar to the prototype, we then judge it to be an instance of the category.

Attempts to differentiate these two views have been somewhat complex. One way of investigating this issue is to use a matching task in which subjects are required to determine whether two simultaneously presented words are the "same" or "different." The "same" judgment can mean physical identity, such as orange and orange, or categorical identity, such as apple or orange. When subjects are presented with a category label *before* seeing the two words (a procedure called *priming*) the effect of priming on how subjects make same-different judgments can be determined. This procedure is used to infer the kind of mental representation subjects have.

Here is the reasoning behind the procedure: If as a result of priming a person's representation of a category is like the list of attributes, then *same* responses to any pair of words should be faster, regardless of their degree of category membership. But if a person's representation of a category is more like that of the prototype, then reaction to the word pairs more typical of the prototype should be faster. The results were that priming facilitated the category matches, but that facilitation was greater for the good (more representative) examples of the category. These results, Rosch argues, favor the prototype interpretation over that of the defining attribute view.

Additional evidence in support of the prototype view comes from an experiment by Rosch and Mervis (1975). They examined the question of whether all members of a given category have features in common. Their experiment required two separate groups of subjects. One group was given a list of twenty instances each from six familiar categories (furniture, vehicles, fruit, weapons, vegetables, and clothing). They were asked to rate how typical or representative each instance was of its respective category. The second group of subjects was also given the same twenty instances and asked to identify the attributes (features) of each instance.

With these two sets of data, Rosch and Mervis then selected the five most typical and the five least typical instances of each category, and for these instances counted how many attributes were common to the most typical and least typical members. The results were strikingly clear. The most typical category members had several common attributes, ranging from three to thirty-six attributes, whereas the least typical category members had few or no common attributes, ranging from only zero to two.

These results are also consistent with the view that category concepts are represented as the prototype. A category is thus seen to have a common set of attributes.

Basic-Level Categories

The final issue in this section concerns the organization of categories. Rosch proposes that categories distinguish themselves best at what she calls the *basic level.* The basic level is the level at which a category has the clearest perceptual attributes *and* is most readily distinguished from other categories. A basic-level category is at the most general level and yet still corresponds to real-world objects. For example, consider the hierarchical sequence of categories: *evergreen, pine tree,* and *ponderosa pine tree. Evergreen* is the most inclusive or general of this category. An *evergreen* refers to a great variety of trees, shrubs, and so forth, that remain green year-round. But there are many different kinds of evergreens. A *pine tree* is a much clearer, distinctive category. *Pine trees* have needles, shed some but not all needles in the fall, and usually grow straight. In contrast, a *ponderosa pine,* while distinctive, is similar to other pines such as yellow pine, black pine, and so forth.

The basic-level category is thus seen as an intermediate category. It is sufficiently distinctive to be easily distinguished from other categories, and yet it has sufficient number of features so as to be fairly concrete rather than abstract. Rosch argues that basic-level categories are the ones that human beings can most easily use and the ones that allow good, concrete images.

Concept Formation

Thus far certain of the properties of concepts and categories were discussed. But little was said about how concepts are formed. Briefly noted in the section on logical concepts were the methods for studying concept formation and we return to this issue now.

In laboratory research using logical concepts, two basic procedures have been used. The first employs the *reception paradigm* in which the stimuli are presented in some random or predetermined order by the experimenter and the subject classifies each stimulus as it is presented. Following classification the subject is given informative feedback, that is, is told whether the classification is correct. Usually only one stimulus is presented at a time; thus subjects are required to depend on their memory of the events over a series of trials.

The second procedure is called the *selection paradigm.* As the name suggests, subjects select the stimuli, one at a time, from a set of stimuli placed before them. The subject is presented the entire set of stimuli at the onset of the experiment and selects each stimulus, trial after trial, on which feedback is desired. An obvious advantage of the selection paradigm is that the experimenter can observe how the subject goes about solving the problem.

Attributes and Rules

The laboratory-constructed or artificial concepts have two important features: attributes and rules. We have already noted that these concepts have attributes, which are the characteristics of the stimuli relevant to the concept. Simple concepts may involve only a single attribute, such as *color*. Or they may have two attributes such as *sweet* and *sour*, which are essential aspects of the Chinese dish sweet-and-sour pork.

Attributes may be combined in several different ways to define a conceptual rule. In the preceding example, the Chinese dish consists of sweet *and* sour pork, that is, *both* the attributes of sweetness and sourness along with pork must be present. In this case we have an instance of a conjunction (joint presence) rule.

Other concepts may employ a disjunctive rule where the combination is *either/or*. For example, the concept of a *person* may refer either to a man or to a woman. The concept includes, of course, persons of all ages. There are several rules for combining attributes of which conjunctive or disjunctive rules are instances. Thus, in describing a concept we must refer to its attributes and how the attributes are combined (rules).

A simple conceptual rule defines a concept simply by *attribution*. If the object possesses the simple attribute which defines the concept, the object is then an example of the rule. For example, if the correct attribute is redness, then all objects regardless of size or shape which are red are classified as instances of the concept. Thus a positive instance of the concept is any instance which shares the relevant attribute. A more complex concept is the *conjunctive rule* in which the concept is defined by the joint presence of two features. In the example in table 10.2 the concept is illustrated by an object which is both red and square.

Another type of conceptual rule is the *disjunctive rule*. If it is assumed that the correct attributes are still red and square, then any object which is red *and/or* square is an instance of the concept. The important feature of the disjunctive rule is the and/or relationship. We can distinguish between conjunctive and disjunctive rules by using real-life examples. A green car is an object which is *both* green and car; hence, a green car is a conjunctive concept. An eligible voter might legally be defined as anyone who is a resident and/or a property owner; hence, an eligible voter is an instance of a disjunctive concept. Finally, conditional and biconditional rules are used in studies of concept learning. A *conditional rule* is one in which

Table 10.2

Certain Major Conceptual Rules

Rule Name	Verbal Description of Concept
Attribution	All red objects are examples of the concept
Conjunction	All objects which are both red *and* square are examples of the concept
Inclusive disjunctive	All objects which are red or square or both are examples of the concept
Conditional	If an object is red, then it must be square to be an example of the concept
Biconditional	Red objects are examples of the concept if and only if they are squares; a red nonsquare or a nonred square is not an example

From *Fundamentals of Human Learning, Memory, and Cognition,* 2nd ed. by Henry C. Ellis. Dubuque, Iowa: Wm. C. Brown Company, 1978. Adapted by permission.

what counts as a correct (relevant) attribute depends upon the presence of another attribute. If an object is red, then the object must be square to be an instance of the concept. If the object is *not* red, it is automatically assumed to be an instance of the concept regardless of the shape of the object. The *biconditional rule* is illustrated by the example of red objects if and only if there are squares. Similarly, in real life the behavior of turning on the air conditioner if and only if the weather is hot is an instance of the rule.

Strategies in Attribute Identification

From this discussion you can infer that the formation of concepts involves at least two processes. First, the subject must determine which features or attributes are relevant. For example, the subject must determine if the relevant attribute is size, shape, or color. This process is called *attribute identification.*

In going about this process, subjects are known to adopt strategies in an effort to focus on the relevant attribute. Suppose that a subject is presented with a set of stimuli varying in size, shape, and color, each with three values, for a set of twenty-seven stimuli. How can the subject go about selecting the relevant attribute most efficiently? The manner by which subjects go about selecting attributes is not a random or haphazard process, at least for most subjects. Rather, human beings frequently show a systematic approach to attacking this problem which is called a strategy. Strategies were first clearly described in classic studies by Bruner, Goodnow, and Austin (1956).

One type of strategy is called *conservative focusing.* Consider the case in which a subject has just been told that a large red square is a positive instance of the to-be-discovered concept. Conservative focusing requires that the subject's initial hypothesis include all three attributes of the stimulus in the hypothesis. The subject might then select a large red triangle as the next stimulus. If he is told he is correct, he then knows the shape is an irrelevant dimension. He might then select a small red square; if he is again correct, he knows that size is irrelevant, but that color is the relevant feature. Thus the important aspect of conservative focusing is that only one feature is changed at a time until the concept is identified. In general, human beings do better with conservative focusing than with any other type of strategy.

A more risky strategy is *focus gambling.* With focus gambling a person takes a chance and varies two or more attributes at a time in trying out hypotheses. If this strategy is successful, learning can then take place quickly. Using the stimuli in the example just given, the subject first selects a large red square, and if the strategy of focus gambling is followed, the subject might then select a small red triangle, changing both size and shape. If, in fact, blue is the relevant feature, the subject would have then learned the concept in one trial. On the other hand, if the subject fails in the gamble, learning is then slower.

Rule Learning

The second process in concept formation is *rule learning.* This requires that subjects learn how the particular attributes are combined, which is a rule. The process of rule learning has been studied most extensively by Bourne (1970, 1974) and his students. In an early investigation, Bourne (1970) examined the effects of rule complexity on concept learning. Subjects were informed of the relevant attributes prior to the experiment. Thus their only task was to learn the particular conceptual rule for classifying the stimuli. Conceptual tasks consisting of four different rules—conjunctive, disjunctive, conditional, and biconditional—were used. The ease of learning these four tasks is plotted in figure 10.5. The figure shows that on the first problem the biconditional and conditional rules were most difficult for the subjects. But by the sixth consecutive problem, performance was essentially perfect for all rules.

Having established the order of difficulty of conceptual rules, Bourne proceeded to conduct a number of rule-learning studies. For example, Bourne (1970) showed that practice in learning one set of rules results in faster learning when subjects are shifted to a new rule. The point of this experiment is that interrule transfer effects occur.

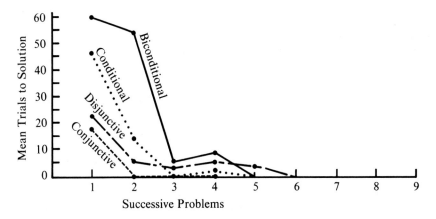

Figure 10.5 Learning-to-learn concepts defined by four basic concept rules. (From "Knowing and Using Concepts" by L. E. Bourne, Jr., *Psychological Review*, 1970, *77*, 546–556. Copyright 1970 by the American Psychological Association. Reprinted by permission of the publisher and the author.)

Task Factors in Concept Formation

In this section three task factors which influence the way human beings form concepts are examined briefly. These are positive instances versus negative instances, relevant and irrelevant attributes, and feedback.

Do human beings learn faster from positive instances than from negative instances? In general, the answer is that we learn faster from positive instances. But this is not the whole picture. One reason human beings prefer positive instances is that they are much more likely to encounter positive instances in everyday life. Positive instances also usually convey more information. Rarely are concepts in everyday life formed by negative instances alone. One close approximation is medical diagnosis, where a physician may judge a disease category by the absence of certain symptoms and by negative laboratory tests. Different diseases may have similar symptoms, and thus the only way they may be clearly distinguished is by the absence of other symptoms.

The number of relevant and irrelevant attributes also affects the ease of concept learning. As the number of relevant redundant attributes increases, concept learning becomes more rapid. Relevant redundant attributes refer to the number of overlapping features; if every square is blue and every circle is red, then shape and color are redundant. Thus it is possible to obtain a solution based on either shape or color. In contrast, increasing the number of irrelevant features increases the difficulty. This is quite understandable because increasing the number of irrelevant attributes makes it more difficult to discover the relevant attributes.

Finally, feedback is a very important factor in learning concepts. Feedback is important because it provides information as to the correctness or incorrectness of an hypothesis. Merely being told "right" or "wrong" on each trial is insufficient unless the subject attends to and picks up the appropriate information in the example. The effects of feedbck can be intuitively appreciated if they are thought about in the context of an ordinary conceptual game such as twenty questions. In this game players are allowed to ask twenty questions in order to solve a problem and can ask only categorical questions (that is, questions that can be answered by yes or no). Players ask one question at a time and try to zero in on the correct concept. They answer each question with yes or no. The more time players have to think about the information gained from the answers to the questions, the more readily they are likely to solve the problem. Indeed, for this reason the twenty questions game is sometimes played at a particular pace so as to control the rate at which information is conveyed.

Theories of Concept Formation

A variety of approaches have attempted to account for the process of concept formation. Three main types of theories can be distinguished: association theory, hypothesis-testing theory, and information-processing theory. The oldest of these approaches is association theory.

Association Theory

Association theory adopts the basic assumption that learning is a matter of forming stimulus-response associations. Stimulus-response associations are connections between stimulus events in the environment and responses a subject makes. Associations are strengthened when these two events are repeatedly presented together, and reinforcement will strengthen the association. Using these notions, early theorists attempted to explain concept formation (e.g., Bourne & Restle, 1959). A conceptual task is seen as consisting of a series of instances in which each instance (or example) consists of both irrelevant and relevant attributes. A person responds on each trial and is sometimes correct and sometimes incorrect. Each response to a positive instance of the concept is reinforced by feedback. The theory contends that associative strength between the relevant dimension and correct response is gradually built up to some point at which a person can be said to have acquired the concept. In turn, any strength of the irrelevant dimension is gradually weakened because it is not consistently reinforced. Thus, concept formation is similar to discrimination learning in that discrimination between relevant and irrelevant cues is gradually developed.

With this approach a concept is viewed as a learned association between a class of stimuli having some common element and an overt response. The associative strength is, however, between the common element and the response. For example, when the concept of *green* is learned, associative strength between the property of "greenness" in the various stimulus objects presented develops, and the response "green" is made to these various objects.

When a person responds to a new stimulus object that contains the relevant feature or cue, that person is said to generalize. Thus, once a concept has been acquired, it may be applied in new situations. This occurs if the new situation contains the relevant features, because of the built-in associative strength between the features and the response. Thus, to refer to the previous example, new objects that are green will tend to evoke the correct response by virtue of the generalization process.

Later modifications of association theory introduced the concept of *mediation*. Mediational theories assume that concepts are formed because of mediating responses to the stimulus instances. For example, tacos, steak and cheese are members of the concept *food,* not because of their physical characteristics, but because they produce a common mediating response. The importance of mediational views of concept formation is that an intervening step is introduced between stimuli and responses. Instead of a direct association between the relevant attributes of stimuli and overt responses, the important association is the mediating response connecting stimuli and responses.

Hypothesis-Testing Theories

Hypothesis-testing theories of concept formation emphasize that human beings construct and try out various hypotheses. This means that human beings actively select and test possible solutions to a task. The emphasis on hypotheses testing stems from the classic studies of Bruner, Goodnow, and Austin (1956). Bruner and colleagues discovered that persons make hypotheses and adopt strategies when they try to discover a concept. This cognitive view of concept formation is difficult to cast into associationistic terms. Moreover, the hypothesis-testing, strategy-making view came to displace the earlier associationistic view. Two of these strategies, conservative focusing and focus gambling, were described earlier and will not be repeated here.

A variety of hypothesis-testing theories have been developed. It is beyond the scope of chapter 10 to review them in detail except to note their general characteristics. Most of the early theorizing was done by Restle (1962), Bower and Trabasso (1964), and Trabasso and Bower (1968). Interested readers will find a detailed description in Bourne, Dominowski, and Loftus (1979). The general approach of hypothesis-testing theory is to develop a theory with a set of explicit assumptions about how human beings discover concepts. The basic idea is that a person formulates an hypothesis, remembers it, tests it, and revises it on the basis of new information.

In general, the following kinds of assumptions have been made in hypothesis-testing theories. The first is that subjects' hypotheses control their overt behavior. What a person does in the conceptual task is a function of the momentary hypothesis being considered. The second general assumption is that a person samples from a set or pool of available hypotheses. For example, the subject might hypothesize that "all large stimuli are correct," that "all large and green stimuli are correct," or that "all large circles are correct." The subject may test only one hypothesis at a time, staying with it if it is confirmed or shifting to a new one if it is not. The third assumption is that learning occurs in an all-or-none fashion. This means that after the trial at which the correct hypothesis is first sampled, a person will make no more errors. The fourth assumption is that of sampling-with-replacement. If an hypothesis is sampled and rejected, it is then returned to the hypothesis pool and can be sampled later. This, of course, implies the assumption of no memory for the hypothesis. Neither the assumption of sampling-with-replacement (no memory) nor the notion of testing only one hypothesis at the time has held up in experimental tests. Modifications and new developments in hypothesis-testing theories continue. In general, the approach has been to make formal assumptions about hypotheses, to test assumptions in experiments, and then to revise them when necessary. This enterprise continues in the work of Levine (1975).

Information-Processing Theories

Finally, theories have been developed which emphasize the information-processing character of concept learning. These theories derive from computer analogies and view concept learning in terms of a sequence of decisions made by the learner. The general idea is of an analogy between human beings and high-speed computers. Both are seen as accepting external information or stimuli, as processing the information in a variety of ways, and as producing some terminal (final) response. Information-processing theories assume hypothesis testing by the learner in which hypotheses are first generated and then tested.

One approach used in the development of information-processing theories is computer simulation. A computer program which is designed to simulate conceptual behavior is written so that it attempts to describe the decisions that make up conceptual behavior. The computer then solves the problems of the same type given to human subjects, and the two performances are compared. If the performance of the computer simulation is similar to the performance of the human subject, the theorist may then begin to suspect that the decisions in the program may be like those of the human subject.

One of the earliest attempts to produce an information-processing model for the learning of concepts was by Hunt (1962). In general, a model must deal with three phases. The first phase is perception, which means the identification of features. The second phase concerns the identification of positive instances of the concept to be learned. And the third phase concerns the development of a decision tree. A decision tree describes a plan for the sequence of steps one goes through in making decisions. For example, a subject asks, "Is the concept a circle or a square?" and then proceeds to the next question, "Is it red or blue?"

Practical Principles

It is appropriate to turn to some practical principles and to see how you can usefully apply the principles. In this section four practical points are discussed: (1) thinking of new examples, (2) using both positive and negative instances, (3) using a variety of examples, and (4) highlighting relevant features.

A moment's reflection may lead to the recognition that much of classroom instruction involves going from concepts to examples and from examples back to concepts. Frequently, instructors introduce a concept by briefly defining it and then proceed to illustrate the concept by giving one or two examples. After a few illustrations they proceed to refine and clarify the concept, developing it to the level required by its inherent complexity. Many textbooks also reveal this characteristic. In order that a concept be fully grasped and understood, *it is important that you think of additional examples beyond those presented by an instructor.* The instructor typically has time to present only one or two examples, perhaps a few more at best, and depends upon these examples to provide sufficient information for the essential features of the concept to be abstracted. Unfortunately, you may fail to understand the concept from only one or two examples, or at best you may achieve only a general idea of the concept. The instructor, however, may expect you to achieve a much more detailed and elaborate concept, one that cannot be obtained unless you continue to think of additional examples to aid in refining and enriching the concept.

Obviously, examples must be pertinent to the concept. If you are in doubt about the adequacy of your examples and hence about your full grasp of the concept, you must check by talking with other students or by continued reading in other sources, or by asking the instructor about the adequacy of your ideas. Generating new examples not only helps to sharpen and refine the particular concept, but also provides practice in retrieval of information, a process important for memory. Test questions frequently ask the student to produce new examples or illustrations as distinct from those given in a lecture. Thus, thinking of new examples not only sharpens, refines, and enriches the concept, but also provides practice in the important process of information retrieval.

The sharpness and precision of a concept develops as both positive and negative instances of a concept are processed. In learning a particular concept you must discriminate between instances of the concept and those instances which fail to fit the category. If you see only positive instances of the concept, you then have no opportunity to compare.

Consider teaching a young child the concept of *dog* in which all the examples are positive instances. Assume that the child is shown pictures of a collie, fox terrier, miniature poodle, and German shepherd. The child learns to say "dog" to each picture. But what are the relevant attributes of the concept? What features of these examples control the child's response? Obviously, we cannot be entirely sure in this situation. Moreover, if we show the child a picture of a cat or rabbit, we cannot be sure of the response unless we have additional information about the child's experience with these animals. Indeed, the child may well regard a picture of a cat as another instance of *dog*. It is for this reason that inclusion of carefully selected negative instances is helpful in developing a concept.

In order for a sharply delineated concept to be developed, negative instances must contain, toward a latter stage of training, irrelevant attributes that are likely to be found in the positive instances. Both dogs and cats are four-legged animals, so the property of "four-leggedness" is an irrelevant feature. Cats are frequently smaller than dogs, but obviously not always. Hence size is not a reliable feature. Nor is the presence of tails, paws, or coats of fur. It is clear that differences between cats and dogs are based on the presence and absence of several features in combination. Features like head shape and presence or absence of claws help to distinguish the two. Even with head shape there may be difficulty when a child is first shown a picture of a Pekingese. The more general point is that if concepts are taught only by the use of positive examples or if only positive examples are used for learning concepts, subjects may fail to respond to the *essential* features of a concept and respond instead to a superficial or unessential feature.

The use of a *variety* of examples is also important. The preceding discussion implicitly emphasized the importance of a variety of examples in learning concepts. When only one example is used, learners may easily attend to a nonessential feature of the concept and erroneously assume that they have learned the concept.

How many examples should be used? No simple answer can, of course, be given, because concepts vary in difficulty and complexity. Perhaps the best answer is that examples should be selected so that they encompass the *range* of the concept. Practical limitations will prevent consideration of all possibilities, but by sampling examples along a specific range, you are likely to include highly pertinent ones.

Finally, the highlighting of relevant features in order to make them distinctive is important. From the viewpoint of teaching, a major task is to highlight or emphasize the relevant features of concepts. One objective is to make the relevant aspect or essential parts of a concept more distinctive than the nonessential features. You can highlight the essential features of a concept by verbalizing these features to yourself. This effort can involve trying to define the concept in your own words, as distinct from memorizing a formal definition of the concept.

Relevant features of concepts can be made more distinctive by the *simultaneous presentation* of both positive and negative examples. This simply means that when a particular concept is taught, a positive instance as well as a negative instance should be presented to learners at the same time, allowing them to compare the instances. For example, when the concept *lake* is taught, show pictures of a lake, a stream, a river, and an ocean at the same time. Leaving all the pictures in view minimizes the burden on memory and makes discrimination between the relevant and irrelevant features easier. This superiority of simultaneous over successive presentation of stimulus examples holds for simple discrimination learning as well as for concept learning.

Summary

Chapter 10 described some of the major characteristics of concepts and categories. We examined two major types of concepts, logical and natural concepts. We further saw that many concepts are prototypical and probabilistic.

Categories can be described in a variety of ways. Categories can be defined by perceptual features and appearance. Categories are also based on semantic properties. The mental representation of a category has been described in terms of defining attributes and in terms of prototypes, with evidence better supporting a prototype view. How objects can be categorized also depends on the prevailing verbal context. Categories appear to be most easily used at the basic level.

Concept formation involves learning about attributes and rules. Human beings adopt a variety of strategies in concept formation including conservative focusing and focus gambling. Some important task factors in concept formation include use of positive and negative instances, number of relevant and irrelevant features, and feedback. Hypothesis-testing and information-processing approaches have dominated the area in recent years. Finally, several practical suggestions for effective concept formation were noted.

Multiple-Choice Items

1. When a person has learned to classify a number of items such as apples, bananas, oranges, and so forth, as a member of the category *fruit,* we can say that a(n) _____ has been formed.
   a. hypothesis
   b. theme
   c. retrieval
   d. concept

2. Logical or artificial concepts are usually (but not necessarily) unambiguous, with all exemplars being either members of the concept or not members of the concept. In this case, the concepts are
   a. deterministic
   b. probabilistic
   c. uncertain
   d. fuzzy

3. Labov's study, which required subjects to judge pictures of objects that looked like cups or bowls, showed the importance of _____ in judgmental tasks.
   a. features
   b. verbal context
   c. color
   d. size

4. The best or most representative example of a category is called
   a. a relevant dimension
   b. a salient cue
   c. a prototype
   d. a category

5. The strategy of focus gambling is one in which a person
   a. changes only one attribute at a time
   b. assumes that the first hypothesis is correct
   c. is limited to only three hypotheses
   d. varies two or more attributes at a time

6. Laboratory-constructed concepts have two basic characteristics which are
   a. attributes and features
   b. features and rules
   c. rules and attributes
   d. rules and exemplars

True-False Items

1. A deterministic concept is one in which an instance can be classified as either a member of the concept or not a member.

2. A streetcar is likely to be prototypical example of a vehicle.

3. Labov's study showed the importance of verbal labels in classifying objects.

4. A basic-level category does not correspond to or relate to real-world objects.

5. In the conservative focusing strategy, a subject changes only one feature at a time in testing concepts.

6. Of the four types of rules studied, Bourne found the biconditional rule the most difficult to learn.

Discussion Items

1. Distinguish between artificial and natural concepts.

2. What makes a concept prototypical?

3. What are the various bases by which objects and events can be categorized?

4. What are the essential features of attribute and rule learning?

5. Briefly note the essential features of three types of theories of concept formation.

Answers to Multiple-Choice Items

1. (d)   The ability to classify objects properly is a major aspect of concept formation.
2. (a)   A concept in which all the exemplars can be classified as a member or not a member of a concept is a deterministic concept.
3. (b)   Labov's study showed that the verbal context or label assigned to the object influenced the way it was judged.
4. (c)   A prototype is the best or most representative example.
5. (d)   Focus gambling involves varying two or more attributes at a time.
6. (c)   Rules and attributes are the two basic characteristics of laboratory-constructed concepts.

Answers to True-False Items

1. (True)   Deterministic means that an instance is either a member of the category or not a member.
2. (False)   A streetcar is not very representative of vehicles.
3. (True)   Labov's study showed that the label influenced the kind of judgment subjects made.
4. (False)   A basic-level category is general, yet is tied to or related to real-world objects.
5. (True)   This is the characteristic feature of conservative focusing.
6. (True)   The biconditional was the most difficult to learn, followed by the conditional, disjunctive, and conjunctive.

Problem Solving

11

Human beings face and solve problems everyday. Problems vary in complexity from the simple problem of locating a car in a large parking lot, to the more complex one of deciding on priorities in paying bills, to the very complex one of planning one's life work. Some problems are solved with little effort. For example, it is easy to decide which television channel to select for watching the evening news. But other problems require considerable effort and may never be completely resolved. For example, weighing the pro-and-cons of a midlife career change may preoccupy a person for an extended period of time. And the same problem may vary in complexity from person to person. In buying a new house, for example, one person may be able to decide quickly after inspection of two or three choices, whereas another may agonize over alternatives for months.

Psychologists have preferred to concentrate their research efforts on problems of roughly intermediate difficulty. With this type of problem the solution is not immediately obvious (and thus trivial), and the task and solution options are fairly well-defined. Interest is focused on how a person arrives at a solution to a problem. Problem-solving tasks are usually structured so that many response alternatives are possible, although only one solution may be correct. Some tasks are artificial, but many are borrowed from everyday life. Tasks can include such situations as chess problems, anagrams, verbal problems, mathematical problems, cryptarithmetic problems, analogy problems, logical problems, and puzzles such as the famous Rubik's cube.

Representative Problems: Importance of Mental Representation

The following examples are typical of problem-solving situations used in the laboratory. They are all characterized by presenting subjects with an initial state, including assumptions and constraints, and asking the subjects how they would go about achieving a specific goal state. The first is the bird-train problem. Critically important to the solution of the problem is

221

how it is interpreted. Obviously, if it is misinterpreted, there is little chance of solving it.

> Two train stations are fifty miles apart. At 2 P.M. one Saturday afternoon two trains start toward each other, one from each station. Just as the trains pull out of the stations, a bird springs into the air in front of the first train and flies to the front of the second train. When the bird reaches the second train, it turns back and flies toward the first train. The bird continues to do this until the trains meet. If both trains travel at the rate of twenty-five miles per hour, and the bird flies at one hundred miles per hour, how many miles will the bird have flown before the trains meet? (M. I. Posner, *Cognition: An Introduction.* Glenview, Ill.: Scott, Foresman, 1973.)

Posner points out that if this problem is interpreted in terms of the bird's flight pattern, the solution might be very difficult to achieve. For example, one method is to calculate how far the bird flies on its first trip, add that amount to how far it flies on its second trip, and so on. But if a less obvious or less direct representation of the problem—how much time does the bird spend in flight?—is selected, the problem then becomes solvable. Since the two trains are 50 miles apart and travel at 25 miles per hour, it will take only one hour for the two trains to converge. And since the bird flies at 100 miles per hour, it will cover 100 miles during that hour.

Consider another example of how the mental representation of a problem can affect the ease of its solution. This problem is the Buddhist monk problem and originated with the psychologist Karl Duncker.

> One morning, exactly at sunrise, a Buddhist monk began to climb a tall mountain. A narrow path, no more than a foot or two wide, spiraled around the mountain to a glittering temple at the summit. The monk ascended at varying rates of speed, stopping many times along the way to rest and eat dried fruit he carried with him. He reached the temple shortly before sunset. After several days of fasting and meditation, he began his journey back along the same path, starting at sunrise and again walking at variable speeds with many pauses along the way. His average speed descending was, of course, greater than his average climbing speed. Show that there is a spot along the path that the monk will occupy on both trips at precisely the same time of day. (Karl Duncker, "On Problem Solving," *Psychological Monographs,* No. 270, *58,* 1945.)

Again, how this problem is represented determines its ease of solution. A mathematical-type solution, as in the bird-train problem just discussed, might be tried, but would not produce the accurate solution. Further thought might produce the decision that there is *no* such spot, or that it is most unlikely that the monk would find himself at the same spot on two different days. This decision is also incorrect. However, when a mental picture of the monk climbing to the temple and then descending is visualized, the solution becomes clear. Plotting the monk's travels in the mind will easily show that the two paths must meet at some point. That is, the monk must climb from the bottom of the mountain to the top and then return, and this activity occurs each trip within the time period of one day. No matter how fast or how slow the monk goes, there must be a meeting point, given the manner in which the problem is structured. If you have trouble with this, consider this solution: It can be easily solved if you think of one monk starting up the mountain at the same time another monk is starting down. They must cross one spot at the same time.

Finally, consider one more problem. This is the Christmas tree problem described by Hayes (1981). The problem is this: Arrange ten Christmas trees in five straight rows of four trees each. When I (HCE) first encountered this problem, I found it very difficult. I drew several arrangements of trees, none of which provided the solution. Only after I realized that the trees must be arranged in more than one row was I able to solve the problem. The solution is, of course, obvious once it is seen. The problem is solved when the trees (represented as dots) are arranged in a star pattern. Prove this by arranging ten dots so that when they are connected a five-pointed star is formed.

With these examples in mind, we now describe some of the features of problem-solving activity.

Stages in Problem Solving

Typically there are several stages in the process of solving problems. Sometimes progress through these stages is done in a matter of minutes. Other situations may require days, weeks, or longer periods for solution. Psychologists have described several stages in problem solving, but all can be reduced to a basic few: (1) understanding the problem, (2) generating hypotheses about solutions and selecting among the alternative hypotheses, and (3) testing and evaluating the solutions. Although a person logically goes through the three stages in the order mentioned, *understanding, generating,* and *evaluating,* much problem-solving activity involves recycling through the stages. For example, when a solution is found to be worthless, a person may return to the first stage in an attempt to better understand the problem.

Understanding the Problem

Before a problem can be solved, it must first be understood. Unless you have a clear, accurate picture of the problem you will most likely fail to reach an accurate solution. Individuals vary in the amount of time spent in trying to understand the problem. Regardless of the nature of the problem, the key to a successful solution lies in how the problem is *represented*, that is, how a person comes to interpret the problem. And in interpreting the problem a variety of factors may need to be identified including what is known or given about the problem, criteria for solution, constraints placed on solutions, and various solution options.

Return for the moment to the Buddhist monk problem. It was shown that a visual representation of a problem will allow it to be solved. In that case, visual representation of the monk climbing and descending within the same time frame clearly showed that there was one place on the path which the monk would occupy on both days.

Another example of a problem whose successful solution depends on the appropriate representation is presented in figure 11.1. This is the nine-dot problem. The problem is to draw four straight lines through all of the nine dots without lifting the pencil. The problem can prove difficult when subjects have an inadequate representation of it. Subjects frequently assume, incorrectly, that the solution requires that all lines intersect at one of the dots. This tends to prevent them from seeing the solution, which requires that the lines be extended past the dots. As a general rule, if you are not making good progress in solving a problem, back up and take another look at it. You may discover that you misinterpreted the problem in the first place and that a second look will correct the situation.

Generating Solutions

The next stage in solving a problem involves generating one or more solutions. Human beings generate possible solutions to a problem in several ways. At one extreme the attempt at a solution is haphazard and unsystematic, and at another level the approach is organized and systematic (cf. Cohen, 1971; Newell & Simon, 1972; Simon, 1978). As a general rule, persons attempt to solve problems by using some kind of *strategy*, which represents the systematic attack of a problem.

Algorithms and Heuristics

Psychologists distinguish between two general kinds of strategies, algorithms and heuristics. An *algorithm* is a set of rules or procedures which ensures the solution. A *heuristic* strategy, by contrast, is a rule of thumb or approximation which may or may not ensure the solution. A simple example makes the distinction clear. Suppose you are trying to locate the address of a friend, J. Smith, in the telephone book of a large, unfamiliar city. Inspection of the directory shows that there are forty-one persons named Smith having the initial *J*. One solution is to simply phone, one by

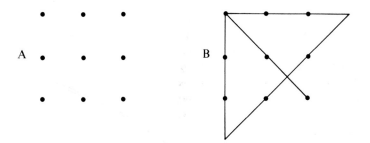

Figure 11.1 Example of a problem whose solution depends on appropriate representation. *A*, The nine-dot problem. *B*, The solution to the nine-dot problem.

one, all the J. Smiths in the directory until you find your friend. This strategy is guaranteed to work (assuming your friend is listed and is at home when you call). The strategy, however, is quite cumbersome and time-consuming. By contrast, if you assume that your friend lives in one section of the city, say the northeast area, you can phone only the J. Smiths listed in that area first. This general rule of thumb or heuristic has a reasonably good chance of working, but it cannot guarantee that you will locate your friend. It is a short cut method that is worth trying but is not perfect.

Why would a person use a heuristic rule of thumb when an algorithm is guaranteed to solve the problem? Many problems simply do not have an algorithm, and even when it exists, an algorithm may be cumbersome or time-consuming. In the example just given, making forty-one phone calls would be time-consuming and also expensive.

Generate-Test Method One type of heuristic is the *generate-test method* (Newell & Simon, 1972). As a process it is similar to the generation-recognition models of retrieval described in chapter 6. The basic idea is a two-step process in which, first, a possible solution is generated and then tested to see whether it works. This is something like the old trial-and-error process in which solutions are tried and discarded until one that works is discovered. But there are problems with this type of heuristic. One problem is that there may be a large number of alternative solutions to consider. This is simply to say that the *problem space* may be very large. Consider this question: What is the best place in town to eat? If there are a hundred restaurants, then it is not practical to test all the alternatives. Moreover, it is not really practical to test the alternatives if you are a visitor in town and plan to dine out only once.

Means-Ends Analysis Another heuristic that is useful is called *means-ends analysis*. In studying problem solving, Newell and Simon (1972) observed that subjects frequently attempted to change (by various means) from one state of knowledge about a problem to another (an end). As a general rule, the effort of subjects can be described as the attempt to change from the initial problem state to a desired solution or end state. This process requires that they determine the *ends* they wish to achieve and the *means* by which they will reach these ends. For complex problems the desired end cannot be accomplished in one stroke. Subjects must establish subgoals which gradually lead toward the final desired goal.

To study problem-solving behavior Newell and Simon used several problems including "cryptarithmetic problems." These problems are puzzles in which it is necessary to substitute digits for letters to solve a problem. Each letter in a problem represents a unique digit. A typical problem is as follows:

$$\begin{array}{ll} \begin{array}{r} \text{D O N A L D} \\ + \text{ G E R A L D} \\ \hline \text{R O B E R T} \end{array} & \quad \text{D} = 5 \end{array}$$

The problem is correctly solved when the digits are substituted for the letters in an arithmetically correct sum. The difficulty is in finding a complete solution in which all specific digits can be substituted for the letters. All this cannot be accomplished at once, so the problem must be broken into steps. How this works can be seen by examining a few steps.

Step 1

$$\begin{array}{ll} \begin{array}{r} \text{D O N A L D} \\ + \text{ G E R A L D} \\ \hline \text{R O B E R T} \end{array} & \quad \text{D} = 5 \end{array}$$

Now substitute 5 for D, to give

Step 2

$$\begin{array}{r} \text{5 O N A L 5} \\ + \text{ G E R A L 5} \\ \hline \text{R O B E R T} \end{array}$$

Since D = 5 and T = D + D, then T must be equal to 1∅ (the slashed zero distinguishes it from the letter O) and carry 1.

Step 3

$$\begin{array}{r} 1 \\ \hline \text{5 O N A L 5} \\ + \text{ G E R A L 5} \\ \hline \text{R O B E R ∅} \end{array}$$

What next? Note that $R = 2L + 1$. Since two times any number is always an even number, the carried 1 means that R must be an odd number. But as also can be seen from the first column, $R = 5 + G$, R must be at least 5, because G must be at least $\emptyset$. Since $R = 2L + 1$, R must be 5, 7, or 9, and L must be 2, 3, or 4. Since each letter has its own unique number, and D is 5, then R must be 7 or 9 and L 3 or 4. Try $R = 7$, $L = 3$ which gives

Step 4

```
    5 O N A 3 5
+   G E 7 A 3 5
    _____
    7 O B E 7 ∅
```

From this start it should be possible to carry the problem to the complete solution. Again, the important point is to note that means-end analysis involves the setting of successive subgoals that eventually allow the final goal to be reached.

Working Backward As you can see, means-end analysis is a step-by-step process in which the process is in a forward direction toward the solution. It is also possible to *work backward* toward the solution. This amounts to seeing what the solution ought to look like and then working backward from the solution to the current problem state. Consider an example used by Ellis, Bennett, Daniel, and Rickert in which the problem is stated: "How can I spend the spring vacation in Mazatlan?" (Mazatlan is a popular beach resort on the west coast of Mexico.) They note:

> Working backward from the goal, it will be noted that an essential step is to get to Mazatlan. Thus, some means of transportation will be required. Transportation costs money, so the next step backward is to determine how to accumulate the needed funds. Eventually, the working-backward strategy may lead you to forego a planned ski trip so as to have money to purchase transportation to go to Mazatlan to enjoy your spring break. (H. Ellis, et al., *Psychology of Learning and Memory.* Monterey, Calif.: Brooks/Cole, 1979.)

Note that in either case, working backward or forward, a large, complex problem is divided into a set of subgoals. Each subgoal is then solved one at a time while the complete solution is gradually worked toward.

Evaluating Solutions

The final stage in problem solving is to evaluate the proposed solution. Some kind of judgment regarding the effectiveness of the solution being considered must be made. As long as the criteria are clear, this is a relatively easy step. For example, in the cryptarithmetic problem just discussed, a solution is correct if the addition works. When a vacation to Mazatlan is planned, the important thing is to be able to obtain sufficient funds. Of course, "sufficient" must be carefully defined since it depends on how elaborate the vacation is to be. For instance, do you plan to camp on the beach, stay in an inexpensive small hotel, or stay in one of the luxury resorts on the north beach? Therefore an effective solution will depend upon the willingness and ability to spell out the criteria clearly.

Evaluating solutions can be much more complex when the criteria are vague or unspecified. Under these circumstances it is desirable to identify the important features of a solution as clearly as possible.

Incubation in Problem Solving

Problem solving typically involves the three stages just described. Some psychologists have pointed out, however, that an additional process sometimes occurs. When all the possible hypotheses are thought of and tried and none is a suitable solution, a person may temporarily withdraw from the problem and engage in other activities. The French mathematician Henri Poincaré (1929) described this process during the period that led to one of his important discoveries. During a period in which he was trying unsuccessfully to solve a certain mathematical question, he temporarily abandoned his work to take a beach vacation. One morning during a walk, the solution to the mathematical question came to him almost spontaneously as he was thinking about other things. Poincaré's example raises the question of the occurrence of unconscious mental activities during the period in which a person turns away from the immediate problem. This rest period is called the *incubation stage* in which problem-solving activity continues, but without conscious attention to the problem. Most of the evidence about incubation comes from introspective reports of mathematicians, artists, scientists, and other persons who report the sudden solution to a problem after a period of preoccupation with unrelated issues.

Why an incubation period seems to help in the effective solution of problems may be for several reasons. First, it may be simply a matter of rest which allows fatigue to dissipate. It might also be that incubation allows for forgetting of inappropriate sets and approaches to the problem and thus permits new approaches to be more easily perceived. Also, additional practice may occur during incubation, even though many persons report that they do not practice. For whatever reason or reasons, incubation appears sufficiently useful that it is recommended when you are stalled in the effort to solve a problem.

It should be cautioned, however, that most of the evidence for incubation is anecdotal. While we may regard incubation as "the pause that refreshes," Wickelgren (1974) has noted that there is very little experimental evidence to consistently support the concept. Our recommendation, which is reasonable, is nevertheless based on anecdotal reports rather than on laboratory evidence.

An Illustration of the Stages in Problem Solving

As we have seen, human beings typically go through three stages in solving problems, and each of these stages was looked at. Now let us illustrate these stages in an everyday setting.

Suppose that you are trying to select a major area in your college career. Your problem is that you cannot decide on an appropriate major, and you therefore flounder around taking general courses in the hope that a solution will appear. How will you select an appropriate major? How will you solve this problem? The first step is simply to recognize that the problem exists. You decide that you must select a major, and normally you must do this no later than the beginning of the junior year in college. In order to interpret this problem, you must collect information about yourself; you need information about your abilities, aptitudes, interests, and goals. You need to decide what kinds of things you like as well as the kinds of things you dislike. You might also wish to be informed about the realities of the job market and the predicted future needs in various job areas. With this basic information you proceed to the next stage, which is to generate hypotheses. You may have decided that the health sciences represent one of your major areas of interest and ability, and that an undergraduate major with emphasis on premedical studies is appropriate for entering a professional program such as medicine or dentistry or a graduate program such as clinical psychology. If more than one alternative is plausible (such as a premedical course versus a pharmacy course or a premedical course versus a course in medical technology), you must then decide among the plausible alternatives. Once you choose a particular plan, you must test the reasonableness of your choice. In other words, you must evaluate your choice, which may take several semesters. You will pursue your program of, say, a premedical course as long as you do excellent academic work. However, a few instances of poor grades in biology and chemistry should lead you to reevaluate your decision and to consider other alternatives.

This example illustrates the stages of problem solving in choosing a career goal, a problem which is usually not solved quickly and which indeed many persons may take years to solve. The same sequence of stages generally occurs even for problems which can be solved in a shorter time. For instance, to solve problems such as where to live, where to obtain an undergraduate education, and what topic is suitable for a term paper, persons tend to go through the three stages of problem solving, although decisions about where to live are usually reached more quickly than decisions about choosing an undergraduate major.

Processes in Problem Solving

In the discussion thus far we have already referred to a number of processes in problem solving. We have emphasized the importance of problem representation, noting that the way a problem is represented will influence the ease in achieving an effective solution. Indeed, appropriate representation of the problem is critical to a successful outcome, although it does not guarantee one. We also discussed some of the problem-solving strategies that a person can develop. In this section we shall examine some additional processes in problem solving.

Persistence of Set

When a person repeats a mental activity, there is some tendency for it to persist in a new situation. But the persistence of an old strategy or mode of attack in a new situation may be inappropriate. This type of process was extensively studied by Luchins (1942) in what is called "the water jar problem" and provides a clear demonstration of the *persistence of set* in problem solving. The task requires a person to determine how to fill a jar of water in order to obtain a specified amount. All problems follow this general form: "You will be given three empty containers, A, B, and C, and your task is to describe how to obtain a specific quantity of water, Y."

Table 11.1 illustrates a typical problem sequence. Problem 1 is an illustrative problem. Here the solution is to fill jar A, then remove 9 quarts from it by filling jar B three times. Problems 2 through 6 are training problems in which the solution is always to fill jar B first, and then from that jar fill jar A once and jar C twice, which leaves the exact quantity specified. All problems, therefore, have the general solution of the form Y (the quantity specified) = B − A − 2C. Problems 7 and 8 can also be solved this way. However, for Problem 7, there is a much simpler and direct solution in which jar A is filled first, then poured into jar C once, leaving the exact amount required for Problem 7. For Problem 8, the amounts in A and C are added. Problem 9 requires a simple solution. Go through the sequence of problems in table 11.1 and actually solve the problems so that you experience the task.

If human beings receive no instructions about the change in Problems 7 and 8, they tend to persist in solving these problems like problem sequences 2 through 6. It is as if the repeated use of one successful strategy makes it difficult to discover alternative approaches. This simply illustrates the more general principle, namely, that most human beings have a strong tendency toward *persistence of set. Once you have learned a rule that works, you may tend to continue applying that rule even when a simpler solution is possible.* Old strategies continue to be used even when they are less efficient if we *fail to perceive* that the situation has changed.

Table 11.1

An Example of the Water Jar Problem

Problem		Size of Jars (in quarts)			Quarts of Water Desired
		A	B	C	Y
Example →	1	29	3	—	20
Training Problems →	2	21	127	3	100
	3	14	163	25	99
	4	18	43	10	5
	5	9	42	6	21
	6	20	59	4	31
Test Problems →	7	23	49	3	20
	8	15	39	3	18
	9	28	76	3	25

From *Fundamentals of Human Learning, Memory, and Cognition*, Ed. 2, by Henry C. Ellis. Dubuque, Iowa: Wm. C. Brown Company Publishers, 1978.

Another example of persistence of set can be seen in anagram problems. The anagram has been a popular task in studies of problem solving and reasoning (Dominowski, 1972, 1977). The anagram is a scrambled series of letters such as *BOLREMP* which when rearranged makes a word such as *PROBLEM*. The subject may be asked to form only one word or may be given an anagram which allows several possible solutions and asked to produce as many words as possible. Usually the first procedure is used. Either the number of correct solutions achieved in a fixed time period or the time to obtain a solution is measured.

Anagram problems can be used in a fashion directly analogous to the water jar problem. Subjects can be given a series of anagrams such as the following:

Training Problems	**APMR**
	OSYB
	AEVH
	OTAG
	AFIW
Test Problems	**LCAM**
	OFRT

The first five anagrams can be solved by the formula 4–1–3–2, where 1–2–3–4 is the presented order of the letters. For example, unscrambling

OTAG yields *GOAT*. During training subjects learn a particular rule, although it may not be verbalized. During the next part of the sequence, the subjects are given test anagrams which require a new rule for solution. The problems are presented in a continuous series so that subjects do not know, of course, that the rule has changed. Under this circumstance, subjects have a strong tendency to persist in trying to use the old rule, taking longer to discover the new rule than do control subjects who did not undergo the initial training.

Many instances of the persistence of set can be seen in everyday life. For example, you may continue to try to solve mathematics problems using a rule no longer appropriate to the situation. The mathematics problem may require a combination of two rules or principles, whereas you may be using only one of the rules. Similarly, inexperienced chess players may continue to make the same types of moves even when the moves are no longer strategic or efficient. Only when they can "break their set" will they have the opportunity to consider a new mode of attack.

Functional Fixedness

Another kind of interference in effective problem-solving strategy occurs in tests of functional fixedness. *Functional fixedness* refers to the tendency to think of objects as functioning in one certain way and to ignore other less obvious ways in which they might be used.

A typical problem is one developed by Duncker (1945). The subject is given a set of objects and asked to arrange them as a stand capable, say, of supporting a vase of flowers. Some of the objects are appropriate to solving the problem, while others are inappropriate or irrelevant. The point of such a task is to require one to use a familiar object in a novel fashion. In this example, the objects consist of a rectangular piece of plywood which has a wooden bar wired to it, pliers, and two L-shaped metal brackets. The first step is to use the pliers to loosen the wire and detach the wooden bar. The wooden bar can be used as a support for the plywood board, but this in itself is not sufficient. Use of the L-shaped metal brackets appears reasonable to many subjects, but the brackets will not support the board. In order to solve the problem, the subject must use the pliers in an unusual way as legs for the plywood stand. This is accomplished by opening the pliers and placing them under the stand. The weight of the stand keeps the pliers steady at one end, while the wooden bar supports the stand at the other end.

As emphasized, the principal interest in this kind of task is to see whether a subject uses a familiar object in a novel and unusual way to solve a problem. The ability of human beings to solve this kind of problem is hampered to the extent that they tend to think of the pliers in terms of typical function. One must be able to break an established set in order to deal with this type of problem.

Another demonstration of functional fixedness introduced by Duncker involves the candle problem. A subject is presented a box of tacks, some matches, and a candle, all placed on a table. The task is to mount the candle on a wall in such a way that it will burn without dripping wax on the table. The solution requires that the subject empty the box of tacks, tack the empty box to the wall, and place the candle on the box. Duncker found that many subjects could not solve the problem. And it is a difficult task because the box is seen as a container for tacks, not as a support for the candle.

Solution effectiveness also depends on how the objects are verbally labeled by the experimenter. Glucksberg and colleagues (Glucksberg & Weisberg, 1966; Glucksberg and Danks, 1968) found that when the experimenter named the box while instructing the subjects more solutions were obtained. In contrast, when they labeled the tacks "tacks," fewer solutions were obtained. A reasonable interpretation of these results is that when a subject hears the word *box,* the various possible encodings of *box* may be activated and hence a solution is more likely. When they hear the word *tacks* a memory representation of *box* as such is less likely to be activated.

The studies of functional fixedness again attest to the importance of attaining the correct representation of a problem. Unless subjects perceive and represent the pliers as "legs" for the plywood stand, no reasonable solution will occur; similarly, unless subjects perceive and represent the box as a support for the candle, no reasonable solution can occur.

Memory and Problem Solving

The importance of memory can vary in different problem-solving situations. In some cases long-term memory plays a rather limited role, whereas in other cases the ability to draw on information stored in long-term memory is very important. Consider the cryptarithmetic problems discussed earlier. How would memory play a role in solving this class of problems? Certain information, such as the rules of subtraction, must be retrieved from long-term memory. Knowledge of the alphabet and the number system is also assumed. But once a person understands the task, the problem can be solved by application of means-ends analysis. In contrast, in the nine-dot problem presented at the beginning of chapter 11, once the problem is understood a solution can be achieved which depends very little on long-term memory. As a general rule, it is reasonable to assume that, as a problem increases in complexity, more demands on memory will be made.

We noted in chapter 7 on Semantic Memory that people differ in knowledge and that high-knowledge people are better at remembering and comprehending new, related information than are low-knowledge people. As was seen, experts in a given task are better at encoding and remembering new events because of their organized knowledge base. What do these findings suggest for the role of memory in problem solving? One reasonable expectation is that good memory of *relevant* information is related to efficient problem solving, and this expectation has been shown to be valid. A study of chess performance has provided a useful vehicle for examining this question. The role of expertness is obvious in chess, because it takes years of practice to become a master player.

The classic work on the role of memory in chess performance was conducted by DeGroot (1965, 1966). The principal interest was in the difference between expert or master chess players and novices. In order to examine this issue, DeGroot observed the way masters and weaker players performed. Interestingly enough, almost no difference between the master players and the novices was found, except the expected result that master players make better moves. The one exception was that master players can reproduce a chessboard arrangement much more accurately than can novices.

This finding was pursued in a fascinating study by Chase and Simon (1973). In their study subjects were shown a chessboard with various pieces for only five seconds and then required to reproduce the board arrangement. Subjects could not "look back" at the board, but were required to reproduce it from memory. They used three types of subjects in their experiment: master players, very good players, and beginning players. They were given seven trials to reproduce the chessboard. The results are shown in figure 11.2. The figure is a plot of the number of correct reproductions made by each player. It shows that the subjects' memory for the chess pieces is nicely ordered as a function of skill level. Master players show the best recall, very good players are next, and beginning players have the poorest recall.

Does this mean that master chess players have better memories in general? To test this possibility, Chase and Simon showed the players *random* arrangements of pieces on a chessboard, positions that would not normally occur. In this case, reproduction of the positions was the same for both very good and beginning players, and master players were poorest. So it is not the case that master players have better memories in general; they simply are good at encoding and remembering the positions of pieces in chess. Moreover, Chase and Simon argued that the reason master players perform so well is because they can recognize larger groupings of positions (meaningful units) than can poorer players.

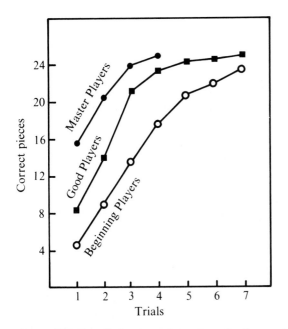

Figure 11.2 Recall of correct chess pieces for three categories of players. (From "The Mind's Eye in Chess" by W. G. Chase and H. A. Simon, in W. G. Chase, Ed., *Visual Information Processing*. New York: Academic Press, 1973.)

Creative Problem Solving

Most of us seem to recognize that there are vast differences in creativity among individuals. If asked to identify highly creative individuals we can easily point to brilliant scientists such as Einstein or renowned artists and musicians such as Rembrandt and Beethoven. But this does not say anything about the creative process itself.

Creative problem solving usually involves the production of original ideas which are practical or relevant to the solution of a problem. Original ideas are uncommon, and frequently it is the juxtaposition of old ideas in a novel way that makes them creative. But having unusual or rare qualities is insufficient for an idea to be called creative. After all, a severely disturbed psychotic person might produce some unusual ideas due to disturbed thought processes. The ideas must also be useful, that is, have some value.

Studies of creative persons have shown that they tend to have a number of distinctive personality characteristics shared in common. As a general rule, persons characterized as creative tend to be highly individualistic and independent, somewhat introverted, low in conformity, intuitive, and self-accepting. They are not necessarily popular and are sometimes self-centered.

Research in creative problem solving has focused on how original and practical ideas are generated. While it is not too difficult to produce original ideas, it is much harder to produce ideas that are both original and practical. Many original ideas are simply not practical, and thus fail to meet the criteria of creativity. There have been attempts to enhance creativity by using originality training. In originality training subjects are given practice and reinforcement for generating unusual ideas. Such practice is effective in increasing the number of original ideas produced; unfortunately, it has no effect on the number of creative ideas produced.

There appears to be a clear relation between age and creativity. Studies show that in most fields creative persons produce their best work at a relatively early age. Usually, the most creative period is between the ages of thirty and forty years; however this age varies with a particular field. Mathematicians and physicists show their greatest creativity between thirty and thirty-five years of age and biologists and psychologists between the ages of thirty and forty years, whereas musicians and painters continue typically to be productive for a longer period of time. Not only do scientists do their best work between the ages of thirty and forty years, but they also are most productive during these years. One way to interpret these age differences is simply to credit it to sheer energy. It seems reasonable that a young person's greater productivity may be related to a high level of energy. And the more productive persons may have a greater likelihood of being more creative simply because they are making more contributions. There is some evidence for this line of reasoning in that in most scientific fields the more distinguished researchers tend to produce more works than their less distinguished colleagues. Another possibility is that senior scientists are more reluctant to publish their work.

Finally, let us consider the relation between creativity and intelligence. It is certainly reasonable to believe that some minimum level of intelligence must be present for creative thinking to occur. While there is a positive correlation between intelligence and creativity, the relation is not a perfect one. In short, creativity is more likely to be observed in more intelligent individuals, but intelligence is not a guarantee of creativity.

Tips on Problem Solving

What can be summarized about problem solving that can be useful in everyday situations? Ellis (1978) identified five rules of thumb which are useful in virtually all problem-solving situations. They include the following: understand the problem, remember the problem, identify alternative hypotheses, acquire coping strategies, and evaluate the final hypothesis.

These rules are reviewed in the following discussion. Additional suggestions are outlined in several texts such as Davis (1973), Wickelgren (1974), and Hayes (1981).

1. *Understand the problem.* Before you can solve a problem, you must first be sure you *understand* it. Perhaps this suggestion appears so obvious as to sound trite. Yet all too frequently the basic difficulty in solving a problem is the failure to have a clear conception of its components. One of the frequent reasons that students do poorly on examinations is that in their haste to answer a question they fail to analyze and reexamine the question itself. An all-too-familiar experience of students is to discover that they have written an answer to a question other than the one asked. Thus, not until you understand a problem can you attempt to solve it effectively. Moreover, once you have clarified a problem, it is good practice to check again to see whether your initial understanding is still correct.

2. *Remember the problem.* Another source of difficulty arises when you *fail to remember* the problem accurately. On occasion students produce incorrect answers on an essay examination because they fail to remember the problem as it is formulated. Somewhere in the course of writing an answer students may veer away from the central issue and deal with irrelevant issues. They may, so to speak, shift in midstream from the main thesis to trivial, secondary, or utterly unrelated topics if they fail to keep the problem in mind. Therefore, periodically recheck your memory of the problem to ensure that you stay with the issue.

3. *Identify alternative hypotheses.* Problem solving requires, of course, that you produce hypotheses. Rather than fixate on one or two hypotheses, *try to identify and classify several hypotheses* that appear reasonable. It is generally advantageous to try the easier or simpler hypotheses first, and if these fail, then to shift to more complex hypotheses. Finally, avoid the premature selection of a particular hypothesis until you have had opportunity to evaluate reasonable alternatives, that is, generate a list of hypotheses.

4. *Acquire coping strategies. Coping strategies* refer to ways of dealing with the difficulty, failure, and frustration encountered in problem situations. Frustration and difficulty are inevitable accompaniments of problem solving. Since frustration cannot in the long run be avoided under all circumstances, a major task is to learn how to *cope* with such difficulty. Blind persistence in using old rules and excessive motivation, particularly in the form of frustration, are seen as barriers to successful problem solving. Therefore, you should attempt to recognize rigidity in yourself and to avoid inflexibility when solving problems. One way of doing this is to cultivate a general plan of using variable modes of attack as the situation demands. The colloquial expression *hang loose* captures much of the meaning of what is required for effective problem solving. Thus, it is important to remain open for new options, alternatives, and approaches.

5. *Evaluate the final hypothesis.* Once you have decided on a final hypothesis, *reevaluate your choice.* Consider the issue of implementing your choice. Even though it may be a good one on rational and logical grounds, is it practical and feasible? In summary, take one final look before you commit yourself to a particular sequence of action.

Two additional tips noted by Moates and Schumacher (1980) are relevant.

6. *Explain the problem to someone.* Talking about the problem to someone else may let you gain a better perspective on the problem.

7. *Put the problem aside.* Incubation appears to work for some persons some of the time, at least according to anecdotal reports. But do not use the waiting period as a way of regularly avoiding problems.

Theoretical Approaches

Current theoretical work in problem solving is dominated by the information-processing approach. This stands in contrast to earlier, traditional approaches stemming from behavioristic or associative theories and Gestalt psychology. In this section these approaches are briefly characterized.

Traditional Approaches

One traditional approach attempted to explain problem solving using principles of stimulus-response (habit) formation derived from studies of conditioning and learning. It is assumed that in any problem situation a learner brings to the task a number of possible habits. These habits are assumed to be readily available in the sense of being already formed at some level of strength. These habit tendencies vary in strength and are arranged in habit-family hierarchy. The stimulus-response associative approach contends that the problem situation is more likely to produce some of these habits than other habits. In problem solving, these habits are run off covertly, and when one is successful the habit is strengthened, whereas the unsuccessful habits are weakened. In general, this approach assumes that problem solving can be explained from principles derived from associative learning.

A different approach to problem solving was outlined by the Gestalt psychologists. How persons solve problems depends on how they perceive and structure their problem environment. The characteristic approach of Gestalt psychologists has been to place subjects in a problem-solving setting and observe the way they go about solving a problem. A typical problem is the *detour* task in which a barrier is placed between subjects and the goal object; the barrier is constructed so as to prevent subjects from directly obtaining the object. The subjects, sometimes children, must detour by going around the barrier to obtain the goal object. Other problem settings have required animals to use two sticks, which are joined so as to form a rake for obtaining food. Descriptions of the behavior of animals solving problems emphasize such features as their observing the objects for a period of time, which is followed by a rapid (insightful) solution of the problem. The Gestalt psychologists contend that this rapid problem-solving activity indicates that subjects are able to reorganize their perception of the problem environment and thus achieve insight into the problem.

A number of experiments have been conducted to test these traditional approaches. Although the data and generalizations resulting from these experiments have been useful, these two approaches have been inadequate as general models of problem-solving activity. They lack the comprehensiveness necessary for a good theory. As an alternative, the information-processing approach, emerging around 1960, now provides the most comprehensive theoretical approach to problem solving. And in some cases, the ideas from the traditional approaches were integrated within the information-processing approach.

Information-Processing Approaches

Information-processing approaches to theorizing about psychological events have received considerable attention since about 1960. Just as there are information-processing approaches to perception, attention, memory, and concept formation, as noted in earlier chapters, there are also information-processing approaches to problem solving.

It is useful at this point to characterize again some of the general features of this approach. Information-processing approaches to psychological events attempt to formulate a flowchart, or sequence of events, using the format of a computer program. A computer program consists of a series of steps or rules that tell a computer what to do. In a similar vein, the basic idea of information processing is to identify the steps involved in a specific psychological activity, list these steps in proper sequence, and then see whether the computer can simulate these activities. To the extent that the computer can simulate the actions of a human being the psychologist may gain some understanding of what must go into a theory designed to explain such actions.

Clearly, of course, a human being is much more than a computer. Basically, all that is implied by information-processing approaches to behavior is that a program which can simulate some psychological process can, in turn, serve as a highly abstract model of the kinds of events that must make up the process. Thus, the theory of a process becomes essentially a statement of the rules of operations, of restrictions placed on the rules, of how the rules combine, and of how much information the program must contain.

Several kinds of programs for problem-solving activities have been developed. An example of an early type is the letter-series completion tasks used by Simon and Kotovsky (1963). These problems contain a series of letters and require that the subject fill in the missing letter. A simple example is as follows:

B D F H _

Here the rule is very simple and can be solved by children seven or eight years old. Another series takes this form:

B T C T D T _

And a more difficult series takes this form:

P X A X O Y B Y N Z _

This type of task can be made even more difficult, so that most college students are unable to solve the problem.

A problem-solving program of this type must contain a number of features. It must be able to recognize and distinguish letters. It must be able to detect regularities in the pattern by looking for repeatable periodicities in the sequence. More generally, it must be programmed to discover whatever regularity is intrinsically built into a particular letter series. Finally, if the program can successfully solve a given class of problems, the psychologist then gains some conception of the kind of rules that must be present in any theory of problem-solving activity.

In discussing a number of experiments on problem solving we have implicitly described some of the general features of the information-processing approach. For example, in the discussion of cryptarithmetic problems, many of the features of the information-processing approach were used. Let us now formalize some of these features.

The general features of information-processing systems were outlined in chapter 1. In addition, as applied to problem solving, these features have been extensively described by Newell and Simon (1972). As a general rule, three characteristics have been noted; these are aspects of the task environment, mental representation of the problem as a problem space, and selection of an appropriate operator.

Task environment refers to the description of the problem as presented to the subject and includes the information, assumptions, and constraints presented as well as the context in which the problem is presented. We saw earlier, for example, that mere verbal labeling an object a "box" can influence the ease of solving the candle problem. Similarly, being told that $D = 5$ in the cryptarithmetic problem points out the reasonable place to begin solving this problem.

Problem space refers to a subject's mental representation of the problem. It is the representation of the problem, as well as the various solutions that may be attempted. Problem spaces are the various ideas or hypotheses that a person might develop about a problem. We have already noted that a critical feature of effective problem solving is the development of effective representation of the problem. The problem space will, of course, change in the course of trying to solve the problem.

Finally, to get from one problem state to another an *operator* must be selected and applied to the problem. An *operator* refers to a sequence of operations that take the problem solver from the initial state to the goal state.

Summary

Chapter 11 outlined some of the major features of and issues in problem solving. The importance of appropriate mental representation of the problem was noted early in the chapter. Problem solving consists of three basic stages which are understanding the problem, generating solutions for the problem, and evaluating the solution. Sometimes incubation is included in this list. Understanding the problem is critical to a good beginning. In generating solutions human beings use a variety of heuristics or rules of thumb. These include the generate-test method, means-ends analysis, and working backward. Evaluating a solution can be easy or difficult, depending on such factors as the complexity of the problem.

We examined several processes in problem solving including persistence of set, functional fixedness, memory and problem solving, and creative problem solving. We also identified several practical rules of problem solving. Finally, we briefly examined two traditional approaches to problem solving and the contemporary information-processing approach. Current theoretical efforts are dominated by the information-processing approach.

Multiple-Choice Items

1. In the discussion of problem solving several stages were described. Which stage was *not* described?
   a. interpreting the problem
   b. associating old ideas
   c. generating hypotheses
   d. testing hypotheses

2. The idea of incubation in problem solving comes from situations in which the problem solver
   a. shows immediate insight
   b. solves the problem in systematic steps
   c. adopts clever strategies
   d. withdraws from the problem for a period and then discovers a solution

3. The water jar problem is designed to study the persistence of set in problem solving. Another way of describing this is
   a. flexibility
   b. accommodation
   c. rigidity
   d. retrieval

4. An important aspect of problem solving is learning how to handle frustration and difficulty. This process was described as acquiring
   a. insight
   b. perceptual reorganization
   c. flexibility
   d. coping strategies

5. A critically important feature of successful problem solving is how the problem is
   a. retrieved
   b. represented
   c. incubated
   d. fixated

6. A rule or procedure which ensures the solution to a problem is called
   a. generate-test method
   b. algorithm
   c. successive approximations
   d. heuristic

True-False Items

1. Persistence of set refers to the fact that human beings may tend to apply old rules or principles when they are no longer appropriate.

2. Information-processing approaches to problem solving attempt to state the rules of operations (or steps) involved in a process.

3. Accurate mental representation is important only in the latter stages of problem solving.

4. Functional fixedness refers to the difficulty in visualizing new ways of using familiar objects.

5. Means-ends analysis refers to a typical algorithm in problem solving.

6. An important aspect of problem solving is being able to identify alternative hypotheses if more than one exists.

Discussion Items

1. Select a particular problem and outline the stages of problem solving you might use.

2. Since persistence of an inappropriate set is an obstacle to problem solving, how might you teach yourself (or someone else) to become more *flexible* in your (or his or her) approach to problems?

3. Give a concrete example describing how you could apply the practical principles of problem solving identified in the text.

4. Speculate on how the levels-of-processing idea in memory might be related to efficient problem solving.

Answers to Multiple-Choice Items

1. (b) Nothing was said about associating old ideas, although this process could occur as a part of the stage of generating hypotheses.

2. (d) Incubation is basically a rest period in which the problem is set aside and you go about other affairs. A solution appears subsequently after you have withdrawn from the task.

3. (c) The persistence of set in water jar problems can be described as a form of rigidity, which is resistance to change or unwillingness to try new approaches or ideas.

4. (d) Learning how to handle frustration is a matter of acquiring appropriate coping skills and strategies.

5. (b) The initial representation of a problem is quite important in determining how readily and effectively a problem will be solved.

6. (b) Algorithms guarantee a solution; heuristics do not.

Answers to True-False Items

1. (True)   The carry-over of old rules, habits, or strategies is called persistence of set.

2. (True)   Information-processing conceptions formulate some kind of sequence of rules, usually in the format of a flowchart showing each step in the process.

3. (False)   Accurate mental representation is important at the earliest stage of problem solving.

4. (True)   The persistence of "seeing" old objects in their typical function is another type of rigidity or persistence of set. In this case it is called functional fixedness.

5. (False)   Means-ends analysis is a typical heuristic.

6. (True)   This is an important part of problem solving, especially if there are disadvantages to some of the alternatives which must be weighed.

Final Thoughts

12

This is an exciting period in which to be introduced to the study of cognitive psychology. Although many issues are yet to be solved, a reasonably clear framework to encompass the findings of cognitive psychology now exists. We have attempted to introduce the topics of memory and cognition in a systematic and organized fashion and to portray some of the excitement of the field without overwhelming you with detail.

This book provides an overview of the basic concepts and processes in memory and cognition. We have been selective rather than encyclopedic and have focused on important features. The topics of memory and cognition will continue to develop and change rapidly during the 1980s, and here the current state of the science is described. This book is thus best viewed as a momentary state-of-the-science report rather than as a final summary.

Our objective has been to present a coherent picture of human memory and cognition within the framework of the information-processing approach. The book was written with the conviction that students can be introduced to these topics by emphasis on basic findings, principles, and theory. These features are portrayed in bold relief and the emphasis is on essential material. Our intent is to provide a broad conceptual framework which will enable you to integrate new information in an orderly fashion. We have used practical examples because we believe they enhance understanding as well as interest.

Using the information-processing approach, we have shown how this system begins with the conversion of environmental stimuli into an internal, mental representation which allows appropriate activities to be carried out. The first stage in this process involves pattern recognition and perceptual registration of information. Information then enters a short-term memory system where it may be rehearsed for further processing, may be briefly rehearsed for maintenance, or may be forgotten. At these stages selective attention plays an important role. When information is selectively processed for long-term memory, it then enters into a relatively permanent memory system. The encoding of information involves both organization and elaboration of individual items, and elaboration can serve to make information more distinctive. The retrieval of information can range from a fairly automatic process to a fairly complex process. Long-term memory involves the development of elaborate semantic networks. The comprehension of information includes integration of information from separate sources and is influenced by inferences and presuppositions. Language is shown to be one of the most distinctively human events. Finally, how these complex cognitive processes influence conceptual and problem-solving activity is described.

What emerges is a vigorous cognitive psychology that examines a wide range of human capabilities. Psychologists are busy exploring the panorama of activities from pattern recognition and attention to memory, language, and problem solving. Moreover, there is an active concern with the applicability of principles in these areas to problems of everyday life. This enterprise is one of continuous development and evolution, and it can be expected to move in new directions, prodded by new research findings and new theories.

Glossary

Algorithm: A solution rule or procedure which ensures a solution.

Associative network models: Models of semantic memory which describe the structure of semantic memory as an interrelation of nodes in a complex network.

Associative strength theory: Theory of the effectiveness of retrieval cues which says that a cue is effective depending on how strongly associated it is with the to-be-remembered item of information.

Attention: Process of focusing selectively on some part of the environment while ignoring other aspects.

Automatic processing: Processing of information that appears to occur without involvement of resources or central capacity requirements.

Backward masking: Process in which previously presented information is erased from sensory memory.

Basic-level category: The level of a category in which it has the clearest perceptual features *and* is most readily distinguished from other categories.

Brown-Peterson paradigm: Famous distractor paradigm for measuring short-term retention.

Capacity model: Model of attention which assumes that attention is the process of allocating resources or capacity to various sensory inputs.

Category size effect: Prediction from semantic memory models that larger categories require more search time than do smaller categories.

Clustering in recall: The tendency of human beings to organize items in free recall so that they are recalled according to conceptual or other categories. Items from a particular category tend to be recalled adjacently.

Coding: Process by which external stimulation is transformed into a representation for purposes of memory.

Cognition: A class of symbolic mental activities such as thinking, reasoning, problem solving, memory search, and so forth.

Cognitive effort: Concept referring to the amount of capacity allocated to a given task. Concept is typically measured in the secondary-task paradigm used in attention.

Constructive processes: The tendency of human beings to construct or reconstruct information in memory, altering the information to make it more consistent with a schema.

Control processes: Term which refers to all regulatory processes in memory models such as attention, search, organization, coding, retrieval, and so forth.

Cue-dependent forgetting: A failure in retrieval due to ineffectiveness of the cue.

Decay theory: Theory of forgetting which says that forgetting is due to an autonomous weakening or decay of the memory trace.

Dichotic listening: Listening to different messages in each of the ears.

Distinctiveness hypothesis: Hypothesis which emphasizes that information is better retained in memory when the memory traces or representations are more distinctive.

Dual-code theory: Theory which says that information stored in memory may be in two forms: verbal codes and imaginal codes.

Elaboration: Process by which information to be remembered is linked or related to information already known.

Encoding: Process by which the to-be-remembered information is transformed into a form suitable for storage in memory.

Encoding specificity theory: Theory which says that a cue is effective only if it was specifically encoded with the to-be-remembered item of information.

Episodic memory: Memory for specific events that happened at a particular time or place.

Feature set theory: Model of semantic memory which emphasizes that semantic memory can be described in terms of bundles or sets of features.

Filter model: Model of attention which assumes that some or all of the information presented to one sensory channel is filtered or blocked.

Forgetting: Process in which failure to access stored information occurs.

Free recall: Task requiring a person to recall items of information in any order.

Generate-test method: A problem-solving strategy in which a possible solution is first generated and then tested to see if it works.

Generation-recognition model of retrieval: Model which involves two stages in retrieval: first, the generation of candidates for retrieval and, second, the decision process in which the candidates are evaluated.

Heuristic: A rule of thumb or approximation which helps in solving a problem but does not ensure its solution.

Interference theory: Theory of forgetting which contends that events are forgotten because other learning interferes with or prevents those events from being remembered.

Levels of processing: Principle which proposes that the depth at which information is processed determines its accessibility in memory.

Memory code: The stored representation of an event in memory.

Mental rotation: The process of rotating mental images so that they are imaged in a new orientation.

Modal model of memory: General or typical memory model which assumes several stages in memory.

Organization: Process by which information to be placed in memory is grouped or rearranged in a new and more optimal manner.

Orienting tasks: Tasks used in human memory experiments which orient the subject to a particular task.

Parallel processing: Model of information processing which assumes that events are processed at the same time.

Partial report technique: Technique used in studies of sensory memory in which subjects produce only part of the information presented.

Pattern recognition: Process in which patterns of sensory signals are translated into psychological experience, that is, the process by which meaning is derived.

Perceptual grouping: Type of organization in which human beings chunk or organize spatially or temporally grouped information into a higher-order or more meaningful structure.

Phonemic restoration: Tendency to perceive speech patterns correctly even when part of the pattern is masked.

Precategorical: Of or relating to information in the sensory register that is assumed to be stored without meaning.

Presupposition: An assumption that is made in order to understand an assertation.

Proactive interference: The forgetting of currently learned material produced by interference from previously learned material.

Propositional code: Abstract representation of both verbal and pictorial materials considered by some theorists to be the language of thought.

Propositional network models: Models of semantic memory which use associative networks and propositions as the basic units stored.

Prototype: The best example of a concept.

Rehearsal, elaborative: The repeating of information aloud or to oneself in the attempt to relate the information to already known events or to other information.

Response competition: Process in forgetting in which different responses made to the same stimuli compete with each other at the time of recall.

Retrieval: Process of accessing information in memory.

Retroactive interference: Process in which an event learned during a retention interval leads to forgetting a previously learned event.

Secondary task technique: Technique for investigating attention in which subjects carry out a primary task but are periodically assessed for attentional involvement by way of a probe signal (the secondary task).

Semantic memory: Understood to be general knowledge of the world.

Sensory register: Memory system designed to store information received by the sensory receptors.

Serial position curve: Finding that in the free recall of serially presented items, items at the beginning and end of a list are best retained and items in the middle of a list are poorly retained.

Serial processing: Model of information processing which assumes that events are processed serially in time.

Shadowing: Procedure in which a listener in an attention study is required to repeat aloud a message presented to one ear.

Spreading-activation model: Model of semantic memory based on associative networks which incorporates the notion of associative distance.

State-dependent memory: Idea that memory may be dependent upon reinstatement of the original state in which information was encoded.

Storage: Refers to the process by which memory representation is held in memory.

Strategy: The cognitive approach used in dealing with a task involving memory, reasoning, problem solving, and so forth.

Subjective organization: Tendency of human beings to organize unrelated items in accord with a self-developed mode of organization.

Teachable Language Comprehender (TLC): The earliest of the major modern models of semantic memory.

Template theory: Class of pattern recognition theories which assume that a literal copy of experience is stored in memory.

Theme: A theme is the central or general topic of a passage.

Unlearning: Loss or weakening of first-list associations during the learning of a second list.

Variability effect in recall: Tendency of human beings to recall material better in a perceptual grouping task when material is variably presented.

Whole report technique: Technique used in studies of sensory information in which subjects are asked to produce all of the to-be-remembered material.

Working memory: An active system of memory where information is assembled and organized prior to recall.

References

Anderson, J. R. *Language, memory, and thought.* Hillsdale, N.J.: Erlbaum, 1976.

Anderson, J. R., & Bower, G. H. *Human associative memory.* Washington, D.C.: Winston, 1973.

Anderson, J. R., & Ross, B. H. Evidence against a semantic-episodic distinction. *Journal of Experimental Psychology: Human Learning and Memory,* 1980, *6,* 441–465.

Atkinson, R. C., & Shiffrin, R. M. Human memory: A proposed system and its control processes. In K. W. Spence & J. T. Spence (Eds.), *The psychology of learning and motivation: Advances in theory and research* (Vol. 2). New York: Academic Press, 1968.

Averbach, E., & Coriell, A. S. Short-term memory in vision. *Bell System Technical Journal,* 1961, *40,* 309–328.

Baddeley, A. D. The influence of acoustic and semantic similarity on long-term memory for word sequences. *Quarterly Journal of Experimental Psychology,* 1966, *18,* 302–309. (a)

Baddeley, A. D. Short-term memory for word sequences as a function of acoustic, semantic, and formal similarity. *Quarterly Journal of Experimental Psychology,* 1966, *18,* 362–365. (b)

Baddeley, A. D., & Hitch, G. Working memory. In G. H. Bower (Ed.), *The psychology of learning and motivation* (Vol. 8). New York: Academic Press, 1974.

Baddeley, A. D., & Warrington, E. K. Amnesia and the distinction between long- and short-term memory. *Journal of Verbal Learning and Verbal Behavior,* 1970, *9,* 176–189.

Baggett, P. Memory for explicit and implicit information in picture stories. *Journal of Verbal Learning and Verbal Behavior,* 1975, *14,* 538–548.

Bartlett, F. C. *Remembering: An experimental and social study.* Cambridge: Cambridge University Press, 1932.

Begg, I. Similarity and contrast in memory for relations. *Memory and Cognition,* 1978, *6,* 509–517.

Bernbach, H. A. Rate of presentation in free recall: A problem for two-stage memory theories. *Journal of Experimental Psychology: Human Learning and Memory*, 1975, *1*, 18–22.

Bourne, L. E., Jr. Learning and utilization of conceptual rules. In B. Kleinmuntz (Ed.), *Concepts and the structure of memory*. New York: Wiley, 1967.

Bourne, L. E., Jr. Knowing and using concepts. *Psychological Review*, 1970, *77*, 546–556.

Bourne, L. E., Jr. An inference model of conceptual rule learning. In R. Solso (Ed.), *Theories in cognitive psychology*. Washington, D.C.: Erlbaum, 1974.

Bourne, L. E., Jr., Dominowski, R. L., & Loftus, E. F. *Cognitive processes*. Englewood Cliffs, N.J.: Prentice-Hall, 1979.

Bourne, L. E., Jr., & Restle, F. A. A mathematical theory of concept identification. *Psychological Review*, 1959, *66*, 278–296.

Bower, G. H. Mood and memory. *American Psychologist*, 1981, *36*, 129–148.

Bower, G. H. Organizational factors in memory. *Cognitive Psychology*, 1970, *1*, 18–46.

Bower, G. H., & Karlin, M. B. Depth of processing pictures of faces and recognition memory. *Journal of Experimental Psychology*, 1974, *103*, 751–757.

Bower, G. H., Monteiro, K. P., & Gilligan, S. G. Emotional mood as a context of learning and recall. *Journal of Verbal Learning and Verbal Behavior*, 1978, *17*, 573–585.

Bower, G. H., & Trabasso, T. Concept identification. In R. C. Atkinson (Ed.), *Studies in mathematical psychology*. Stanford, Calif.: Stanford University Press, 1964.

Bower, G. H., & Winzenz, D. Group structure, coding, and memory for digit series. *Journal of Experimental Psychology Monographs*, 1969, *80*, (2, Pt. 2), 1–17.

Bransford, J. D., Barclay, J. R., & Franks, J. J. Sentence memory: A constructive versus interpretative approach. *Cognitive Psychology*, 1972, *3*, 193–209.

Bransford, J. D., & Franks, J. J. The abstraction of linguistic ideas. *Cognitive Psychology*, 1971, *2*, 331–350.

Bransford, J. D., & Johnson, M. K. Consideration of some problems of comprehension. In W. G. Chase (Ed.), *Visual information processing*. New York: Academic Press, 1973.

Britton, B. K., & Tesser, A. Effects of prior knowledge on use of cognitive capacity in three complex cognitive tasks. *Journal of Verbal Learning and Verbal Behavior*, 1982, *21*, 421–436.

Broadbent, D. E. *Perception and communication.* London: Pergamon Press, 1958.

Brown, J. A. Some tests of the decay theory of immediate memory. *Quarterly Journal of Experimental Psychology,* 1958, *10,* 12–21.

Brown, R. *A first language: The early stages.* Cambridge, Mass.: Harvard University Press, 1973.

Bruner, J. S., Goodnow, J., & Austin, G. A. *A study of thinking.* New York: Wiley, 1956.

Bugelski, B. R., & Alampay, D. A. The role of frequency in developing perceptual sets. *Canadian Journal of Psychology,* 1961, *15,* 205–211.

Chase, W. G., & Simon, H. A. The mind's eye in chess. In W. G. Chase (Ed.), *Visual information processing.* New York: Academic Press, 1973.

Cherry, C. Some experiments on the recognition of speech with one and two ears. *Journal of the Acoustical Society of America,* 1953, *23,* 915–919.

Chiesi, H. L., Spilich, G. J., & Voss, J. F. Acquisition of domain-related information in relation to high- and low-domain knowledge. *Journal of Verbal Learning and Verbal Behavior,* 1979, *18,* 257–273.

Chomsky, N. *Aspects of the theory of syntax.* Cambridge, Mass.: M.I.T. Press, 1965.

Chomsky, N. *Reflections on language.* New York: Pantheon Books, 1975.

Clark, H. H., & Clark, E. V. *Psychology and language.* New York: Harcourt, Brace, & Jovanovich, 1977.

Cohen, J. *Thinking.* Chicago: Rand McNally, 1971.

Cole, R. A. Navigating the slippery stream of speech. *Psychology Today,* 77–87, 1979.

Cole, R. A. *Perception and production of fluent speech.* Hillsdale, N.J.: Erlbaum, 1980.

Collins, A. M., & Loftus, E. F. A spreading activation theory of semantic processing. *Psychological Review,* 1975, *82,* 407–428.

Collins, A. M., & Quillian, M. R. Retrieval time from semantic memory. *Journal of Verbal Learning and Verbal Behavior,* 1969, *8,* 240–247.

Conrad, C. Cognitive economy in semantic memory. *Journal of Experimental Psychology,* 1972, *92,* 149–154.

Cooper, L. A., & Shepard, R. N. Chronometric studies of the rotation of mental images. In W. G. Chase (Ed.), *Visual information processing.* New York: Academic Press, 1973.

Craik, F. I. M., & Jacoby, L. L. Elaboration and distinctiveness in episodic memory. In L. Nilsson (Ed.), *Perspectives on memory research: Essays in honor of Uppsala University's 500th anniversary.* Hillsdale, N.J.: Erlbaum, 1979.

Craik, F. I. M., & Lockhart, R. S. Levels of processing: A framework for memory research. *Journal of Verbal Learning and Verbal Behavior,* 1972, *11,* 671–684.

Craik, F. I. M., & Tulving, E. Depth of processing and the retention of words in episodic memory. *Journal of Experimental Psychology,* 1975, *104,* 268–294.

Daniel, T. C. The nature of the effect of verbal labels on recognition memory for form. *Journal of Experimental Psychology,* 1972, *96,* 152–157.

Darwin, C. T., Turvey, M. T., & Crowder, R. G. An auditory analogue of the Sperling partial report procedure: Evidence for brief auditory storage. *Cognitive Psychology,* 1972, *3,* 255–267.

Davis, G. A. *Psychology of problem solving: Theory and practice.* New York: Basic Books, 1973.

DeCasper, A. J., & Fifer, W. P. Of human bonding: Newborns prefer their mother's voices. *Science,* 1980, *208,* 1174–1175.

DeGroot, A. D. *Thought and choice in chess.* The Hague: Mouton, 1965.

DeGroot, A. D. Perception and memory versus thought. In B. Kleinmuntz (Ed.), *Problem solving.* New York: Wiley, 1966.

Deutsch, J. A., & Deutsch, D. Attention: Some theoretical considerations. *Psychological Review,* 1963, *70,* 80–90.

Dominowski, R. L. Effects of solution familiarity and number of alternatives on problem difficulty. *Journal of Experimental Psychology,* 1972, *95,* 223–225.

Dominowski, R. L. Reasoning. *Inter-American Journal of Psychology,* 1977, *11,* 68–77.

Duncker, K. On problem solving. *Psychological Monographs,* No. 270, *58,* 1945.

Eich, J. E. The cue-dependent nature of state-dependent retention. *Memory and Cognition,* 1980, *8,* 157–173.

Einstein, G. O., & Hunt, R. R. Levels of processing and organization: Additive effects of individual item and relational processing. *Journal of Experimental Psychology: Human Learning and Memory,* 1980, *6,* 588–598.

Ellis, H. C. Transfer of stimulus predifferentiation to shape recognition and identification learning: Role of properties of verbal labels. *Journal of Experimental Psychology,* 1968, *78,* 401–409.

Ellis, H. C. Stimulus encoding processes in human learning and memory. In G. H. Bower (Ed.), *The psychology of learning and motivation* (Vol. 7). New York: Academic Press, 1973.

Ellis, H. C. *Fundamentals of human learning, memory, and cognition.* Dubuque, Iowa: Wm. C. Brown Company, 1978.

Ellis, H. C., Bennett, T. L., Daniel, T. C., & Rickert, E. J. *Psychology of learning and memory.* Monterey, Calif.: Brooks/Cole, 1979.

Ellis, H. C., & Daniel, T. C. Verbal processes in long-term stimulus recognition memory. *Journal of Experimental Psychology, 1971, 90*, 18–26.

Ellis, H. C., Parente, F. J., Grah, C. R., & Spiering, K. Coding strategies, perceptual grouping, and the "variability effect" in free recall. *Memory and Cognition, 1975, 3,* 226–232.

Epstein, M. L., Phillips, W. D., & Johnson, S. J. Recall of related and unrelated word pairs as a function of processing level. *Journal of Experimental Psychology: Human Learning and Memory, 1975, 1,* 149–152.

Eysenck, M. W. Depth, distinctiveness, and elaboration. In L. Cermak & F. I. M. Craik (Eds.), *Levels of processing: An approach to memory.* Hillsdale, N.J.: Erlbaum, 1979.

Gardner, B. T., & Gardner, R. A. Evidence for sentence constituents in the early utterances of child and chimpanzee. *Journal of Experimental Psychology: General, 1975, 104,* 244–267.

Gardner, R. A., & Gardner, B. T. Teaching sign language to a chimpanzee. *Science, 1969, 165,* 664–672.

Gazzaniga, M. S. *The bisected brain.* New York: Appleton-Century-Crofts, 1970.

Gazzaniga, M. S. Consistency and diversity in brain organization. *Annals of the New York Academy of Sciences, 415–423, 299,* 1977.

Glanzer, M., & Cunitz, A. R. Two storage mechanisms in free recall. *Journal of Verbal Learning and Verbal Behavior, 1966, 5,* 351–360.

Glucksberg, S., & Danks, J. Effects of discriminative labels and of nonsense labels upon availability of novel function. *Journal of Verbal Learning and Verbal Behavior, 1968, 7,* 72–76.

Glucksberg, S., & Weisberg, R. W. Verbal behavior and problem solving: Some effects of labeling in a functional fixedness problem. *Journal of Experimental Psychology, 1966, 71,* 659–664.

Greenfield, P. M., & Smith, J. H. *The structure of communication in early language development.* New York: Academic Press, 1976.

Harris, R. J. Comprehension of pragmatic implications in advertising. *Journal of Applied Psychology, 1977, 62,* 603–608.

Hasher, L., & Zacks, R. T. Automatic and effortful processes in memory. *Journal of Experimental Psychology: General,* 1979, *108,* 356–388.

Hayes, J. R. *The complete problem solver.* Philadelphia: Franklin Institute Press, 1981.

Hebb, D. O. The American Revolution. *American Psychologist,* 1960, *15,* 735–745.

Hubel, D. H., & Wiesel, T. N. Receptive fields, binocular interaction, and functional architecture in the cat's visual cortex. *Journal of Physiology,* 1962, *160,* 106–154.

Hunt, E. B. *Concept learning: An information-processing problem.* New York: Wiley, 1962.

Hunt, R. R. How similar are context effects in recognition and recall? *Journal of Experimental Psychology: Human Learning and Memory,* 1975, *1,* 530–537.

Hunt, R. R. List context effects: Inaccessibility or indecision? *Journal of Experimental Psychology: Human Learning and Memory,* 1976, *2,* 423–430.

Hunt, R. R., & Einstein, G. O. Relational and item-specific information in memory. *Journal of Verbal Learning and Verbal Behavior,* 1981, *20,* 497–514.

Hunt, R. R., & Elliott, J. M. The role of nonsemantic information in memory: Orthographic distinctiveness effects upon retention. *Journal of Experimental Psychology: General,* 1980, *109,* 49–74.

Hunt, R. R., Elliott, J. M., & Spence, M. J. Independent effects of process and structure on encoding. *Journal of Experimental Psychology: Human Learning and Memory,* 1979, *5,* 339–347.

Hunt, R. R., & Ellis, H. C. Recognition memory and degree of semantic contextual change. *Journal of Experimental Psychology,* 1974, *103,* 1153–1159.

Hunt, R. R., & Mitchell, D. B. Specificity in nonsemantic orienting tasks and item specific information in memory. *Journal of Experimental Psychology: Human Learning and Memory,* 1978, *4,* 121–135.

Hunt, R. R., & Mitchell, D. B. Independent effects of semantic and nonsemantic distinctiveness. *Journal of Experimental Psychology: Learning, Memory, and Cognition,* 1982, *8,* 81–87.

Jakobson, R., & Halle, M. *Fundamentals of language.* The Hague: Mouton, 1956.

Johnson, M. K., Bransford, J. D., & Solomon, S. Memory for tacit implications of sentences. *Journal of Experimental Psychology,* 1973, *98,* 203–205.

Johnston, W. A., Greenberg, S., Fisher, R., & Martin, D. Divided attention: A vehicle for monitoring memory processes. *Journal of Experimental Psychology,* 1970, *83,* 164–171.

References

Kahneman, D. *Attention and effort.* Englewood Cliffs, N.J.: Prentice-Hall, 1973.

Keenan, J. M., & Moore, R. E. Memory for images of concealed objects: A reexamination of Neisser and Kerr. *Journal of Experimental Psychology: Human Learning and Memory,* 1979, *5,* 374–385.

Keppel, G., & Underwood, B. J. Proactive inhibition in short-term retention of single items. *Journal of Verbal Learning and Verbal Behavior,* 1962, *1,* 153–161.

Kintsch, W. *The representation of meaning in memory.* Hillsdale, N.J.: Erlbaum, 1974.

Kintsch, W., & van Dijk, T. A. Toward a model of text comprehension and production. *Psychological Review,* 1978, *85,* 363–394.

Kosslyn, S. M., Ball, T. M., & Reiser, B. J. Visual images preserve spatial metric information: Evidence from studies of image scanning. *Journal of Experimental Psychology: Human Perception and Performance,* 1978, *4,* 47–60.

Labov, W. The boundaries of words and their meanings. In C. J. N. Bailey & R. W. Shuy (Eds.), *New ways of analyzing variations in English.* Washington, D.C.: Georgetown University Press, 1973.

Lachman, R., Lachman, J. L., & Butterfield, E. C. *Cognitive psychology and information processing.* Hillsdale, N.J.: Erlbaum, 1979.

Leight, K. A., & Ellis, H. C. Emotional mood states, strategies, and state-dependency in memory. *Journal of Verbal Learning and Verbal Behavior,* 1981, *20,* 251–266.

Lettvin, J. Y., Maturana, H. R., McCullock, W. S., & Pitts, W. H. What the frog's eye tells the frog's brain. *Proceedings of the IRE,* 1959, *47,* 1940–1951.

Levine, M. *A cognitive theory of learning: Research on hypothesis testing.* Hillsdale, N.J.: Erlbaum, 1975.

Lewis, C. L., & Anderson, J. R. Interference with real world knowledge. *Cognitive Psychology,* 1976, *8,* 311–335.

Light, L., & Carter-Sobell, L. Effects of changed semantic context on recognition memory. *Journal of Verbal Learning and Verbal Behavior,* 1970, *9,* 1–12.

Loftus, E. F., & Loftus, G. R. On the permanence of stored information in the human brain. *American Psychologist,* 1980, *35,* 409–420.

Loftus, E. F., & Palmer, J. C. Reconstruction of automobile destruction: An example of the interaction between language and memory. *Journal of Verbal Learning and Verbal Behavior,* 1974, *13,* 585–589.

Luchins, A. S. Mechanization in problem solving. *Psychological Monographs,* 1942, *54,* (6, Whole No. 248).

Mandler, G. Organization and memory. In K. W. Spence & J. T. Spence (Eds.), *The psychology of learning and motivation* (Vol. 1). New York: Academic Press, 1967.

Massaro, D. W. *Experimental psychology and information processing.* Chicago: Rand McNally, 1975.

McEwan, N. H., & Yuille, J. C. The effects of training and experience on eyewitness testimony. Paper presented at the meeting of the Canadian Psychological Association, 1981.

McGeoch, J. A. *The psychology of human learning.* New York: McKay, 1942.

McKoon, G., & Ratcliffe, R. Priming in episodic and semantic memory. *Journal of Verbal Learning and Verbal Behavior,* 1979, *18,* 463–480.

Miller, G. A. The magical number seven, plus or minus two: Some limits on our capacity for processing information. *Psychological Review,* 1956, *63,* 81–97.

Miller, G. A., Galanter, E., & Pribram, K. H. *Plans and the structure of behavior.* New York: Holt, 1960.

Milner, B. Memory and the medial temporal regions of the brain. In K. H. Pribram and D. E. Broadbent (Eds.), *Biology of memory.* New York: Academic Press, 1970.

Mitchell, D. B., & Richman, C. L. Confirmed reservations: Mental travel. *Journal of Experimental Psychology: Human Perception and Performance,* 1980, *6,* 58–66.

Moates, D. R., & Schumacher, G. M. *An introduction to cognitive psychology.* Belmont, Calif.: Wadsworth, 1980.

Moray, N. Attention: *Selective processes in vision and hearing.* New York: Academic Press, 1970.

Morris, C. D., Bransford, J. D., & Franks, J. J. Levels of processing versus test-appropriate strategies. *Journal of Verbal Learning and Verbal Behavior,* 1977, *16,* 519–533.

Morrison, F. J., Giordani, B., & Nagy, J. Reading disability: An information processing analysis. *Science,* 1977, *199,* 77–79.

Neisser, U. Visual search. *Scientific American,* 1964, *210,* 94–107.

Neisser, U. *Cognitive psychology.* New York: Appleton-Century-Crofts, 1967.

Neisser, U., & Kerr, N. Spatial and mnemonic properties of visual images. *Cognitive Psychology,* 1973, *5,* 138–150.

Newell, A., & Simon, H. *Human problem solving.* Englewood Cliffs, N.J.: Prentice-Hall, 1972.

Norman, D. A. Toward a theory of memory and attention. *Psychological Review,* 1968, *75,* 522–536.

References

Norman, D. A., & Bobrow, D. G. On data-limited and resource-limited processes. *Cognitive Psychology,* 1975, *7,* 44–64.

Norman, D. A., & Rumelhart, D. E. *Explorations in cognition.* San Francisco: Freeman, 1975.

Paivio, A. Mental imagery in associative learning and memory. *Psychological Review,* 1969, *76,* 241–263.

Paivio, A. *Imagery and verbal processes.* New York: Holt, 1971.

Palmer, S. E. Visual perception and world knowledge: Notes on a model of sensory cognitive interaction. In D. A. Norman, D. E. Rumelhart, & the LNR Research Group, (Eds.), *Explorations in cognition.* San Francisco: Freeman, 1975.

Penfield, W. Consciousness, memory, and man's conditioned reflexes. In K. Pribram (Ed.), *On the biology of learning.* New York: Harcourt, Brace, & World, 1959.

Peterson, L. R., & Peterson, M. J. Short-term retention of individual verbal items. *Journal of Experimental Psychology,* 1959, *58,* 193–198.

Poincaré, H. *The foundations of science.* New York: Science House, 1929.

Pollack, I., & Pickett, J. M. The intelligibility of language from conversations. *Language and Speech,* 1963, *6,* 165–171.

Posner, M. I. *Cognition: An introduction.* Glenview, Ill.: Scott, Foresman, 1973.

Posner, M. I., & Boies, S. J. Components of attention. *Psychological Review,* 1971, *78,* 391–408.

Postman, L., & Underwood, B. J. Critical issues in interference theory. *Memory and Cognition,* 1973, *1,* 19–40.

Premack, D. Language in chimpanzees? *Science,* 1971, *172,* 808–822.

Pylshyn, Z. W. What the mind's eye tells the mind's brain: A critique of mental imagery. *Psychological Bulletin,* 1973, *80,* 1–24.

Quillian, M. R. Semantic memory. In M. Minsky (Ed.), *Semantic information processing.* Cambridge, Mass.: M. I. T. Press, 1968.

Quillian, M. R. The teachable language comprehender: A simulation program and theory of language. *Communications of the Association for Computing Machinery,* 1969, *12,* 459–476.

Rabinowitz, J. C., Mandler, G., & Patterson, K. E. Determinants of recognition and recall: Accessibility and generation. *Journal of Experimental Psychology: General,* 1977, *106,* 302–329.

Reicher, G. M. Perceptual recognition as a function of meaningfulness of stimulus material. *Journal of Experimental Psychology,* 1969, *81,* 275–280.

Reitman, J. S. Mechanisms of forgetting in short-term memory. *Cognitive Psychology,* 1971, *2,* 185–195.

Reitman, J. S. Without surreptitious rehearsal, information in short-term memory decays. *Journal of Verbal Learning and Verbal Behavior,* 1974, *13,* 365–377.

Restle, F. A. The selection of strategies in cue learning. *Psychological Review,* 1962, *69,* 329–343.

Richman, C. L., Mitchell, D. B., & Reznick, J. S. Mental travel: Some reservations. *Journal of Experimental Psychology: Human Perception and Performance,* 1979, *5,* 13–18.

Ricks, D. M. Vocal communication in preverbal normal and autistic children. In N. O'Connor (Ed.), *Language, cognitive deficits, and retardation.* London: Butterworth, 1975.

Rosch, E. Cognitive representations of semantic categories. *Journal of Experimental Psychology: General,* 1975, *104,* 192–233.

Rosch, E. Natural categories. *Cognitive Psychology,* 1973, *4,* 328–350. (a)

Rosch, E. On the internal structure of perceptual and semantic categories. In T. E. Moore (Ed.), *Cognitive development and the acquisition of language.* New York: Academic Press, 1973. (b)

Rosch, E., & Mervis, C. B. Family resemblances: Studies in the internal structure of categories. *Cognitive Psychology,* 1975, *7,* 573–605.

Sachs, J. Recognition memory for syntactic and semantic aspects of connected discourse. *Perception and Psychophysics,* 1967, *2,* 437–442.

Schank, R., & Abelson, R. *Scripts, plans, goals, and understanding.* Hillsdale, N.J.: Erlbaum, 1977.

Searle, J. R. *Speech acts.* Cambridge: Cambridge University Press, 1969.

Searle, J. R. Indirect speech acts. In P. Cole & J. L. Morgan (Eds.), *Syntax and semantics* (Vol. 3), New York: Seminar Press, 1975.

Selfridge, O. G. Pandemonium: A paradigm for learning. In *The mechanization of thought processes.* London: H. M. Stationary Office, 1959.

Shallice, T., & Warrington, E. K. Independent functioning of verbal memory stores: A neuropsychological study. *Quarterly Journal of Experimental Psychology,* 1970, *22,* 261–273.

Sheerer, M. Problem solving. *Scientific American,* 1963, 204(4), 118–128.

Simon, H. A. Information-processing theory of human problem solving. In W. K. Estes (Ed.), *Handbook of learning and cognitive processes,* Hillsdale, N.J.: Erlbaum, 1978.

Simon, H. A., & Kotovsky, K. Human acquisition of concepts for sequential patterns. *Psychological Review,* 1963, *70,* 534–546.

Slobin, D. I. Cognitive prerequisites for the acquisition of grammar. In C. A. Ferguson & D. J. Slobin (Eds.), *Studies of child language development.* New York: Holt, 1973.

Smith, E. E., Shoben, E. J., & Rips, L. J. Structure and process in semantic memory: A featural model for semantic decision. *Psychological Review,* 1974, *81,* 214–241.

Sperling, G. The information available in brief visual presentations. *Psychological Monographs,* 1960, *74* (Whole No. 498).

Spilich, G. J., Vesonder, G. T., Chiesi, H. L., & Voss, J. F. Text processing of domain-related information for individuals with high- and low-domain knowledge. *Journal of Verbal Learning and Verbal Behavior,* 1979, *18,* 275–290.

Standing, L., Conezio, J., & Haber R. N. Perception and memory for pictures: Single trial learning of 2560 visual stimuli. *Psychonomic Science,* 1970, *19,* 73–74.

Stein, B. S. Depth of processing reexamined: The effects of the precision of encoding and test appropriateness. *Journal of Verbal Learning and Verbal Behavior,* 1978, *17,* 165–174.

Sternberg, S. High-speed scanning in human memory. *Science,* 1966, *153,* 652–654.

Sulin, R. A., & Dooling, D. J. Intrusions of a thematic idea in retention of prose. *Journal of Experimental Psychology,* 1974, *103,* 255–262.

Terrace, H. S. How Nim Chimpsky changed my mind. *Psychology Today,* November, 1979.

Terrace, H. S., Pettito, L. A., & Bever, T. G. *Project Nim, Progress Report I.* New York: Columbia University Press, 1976.

Trabasso, T., & Bower, G. H. *Attention in learning.* New York: Wiley, 1968.

Treisman, A. M. Contextual cues in selective listening. *Quarterly Journal of Experimental Psychology.* 1960, *12,* 242–248.

Treisman, A. M. Selective attention in man. *British Medical Bulletin,* 1964, *20,* 12–16.

Treisman, A. M., & Geffen, G. Selective attention: Perception or response? *Quarterly Journal of Experimental Psychology,* 1967, *19,* 1–17.

Tulving, E. Subjective organization in free recall of "unrelated" words. *Psychological Review,* 1962, *69,* 344–354.

Tulving, E. Theoretical issues in free recall. In T. R. Dixon & D. L. Horton (Eds.), *Verbal behavior and general behavior theory.* Englewood Cliffs, N.J.: Prentice-Hall, 1968.

Tulving, E. Episodic and semantic memory. In E. Tulving & W. Donaldson (Eds.), *Organization of memory.* New York: Academic Press, 1972.

Tulving, E. Cue-dependent forgetting. *American Scientist,* 1974, *62,* 74–82.

Tulving, E., & Psotka, J. Retroactive inhibition in free recall: Inaccessibility of information available in the memory store. *Journal of Experimental Psychology,* 1971, *87,* 1–8.

Tulving, E., & Thomson, D. M. Retrieval processes in recognition memory: Effects of associative context. *Journal of Experimental Psychology,* 1971, *87,* 116–124.

Tulving, E., & Thomson, D. M. Encoding specificity and retrieval processes in episodic memory. *Psychological Review,* 1973, *80,* 352–373.

Tyler, S. W., Hertel, P. T., McCallum, M. C., & Ellis, H. C. Cognitive effort and memory. *Journal of Experimental Psychology: Human Learning and Memory,* 1979, *5,* 607–617.

von Wright, J. M. Selection in visual immediate memory. *Quarterly Journal of Experimental Psychology,* 1968, *20,* 62–68.

Warren, R. M., & Obusek, C. J. Speech perception and phonemic restorations. *Perception and Psychophysics,* Vol. 9, No. 3B, 1971.

Warrington, E. K., Logue, V., & Pratt, R. T. C. The anatomical localization of selective impairment of auditory verbal short-term memory. *Neuropsychologia,* 1971, *9,* 377–387.

Whorf, B. L. Science and linguistics. In J. B. Carroll (Ed.), *Language, thought and reality: Selected writings of Benjamin Lee Whorf.* Cambridge, Mass.: M. I. T. Press, 1956.

Wickelgren, W. A. *How to solve problems.* San Francisco: Freeman, 1974.

Winograd, E. Elaboration and distinctiveness in memory for faces. *Journal of Experimental Psychology: Human Learning and Memory,* 1981, *7,* 181–190.

Name Index

Name Index

Subject Index